The Pathway to Peace

Walking Daily with Jesus

Includes 14 Amazing Facts Bible Studies

E.G. White

Roseville, CA

Copyright © 2020 by Amazing Facts International

This book was originally published under the title *Steps to Christ*

Printed in United States of America
All Rights Reserved

Published by Amazing Facts International
P. O. Box 1058
Roseville, CA 95678-8058
800-538-7275

Cover design by Haley Trimmer
Text design by Greg Solie • Altamont Graphics

ISBN 9781580197076

Contents

1. God's Love for Man 5
2. The Sinner's Need of Christ 9
3. Repentance 12
4. Confession 20
5. Consecration 23
6. Faith and Acceptance 26
7. The Test of Discipleship 30
8. Growing Up into Christ 35
9. The Work and the Life 40
10. A Knowledge of God 44
11. The Privilege of Prayer 48
12. What to Do with Doubt 54
13. Rejoicing in the Lord 59

Amazing Facts Topical Study Guides
    Is There Anything Left You Can Trust? 65
    Did God Create the Devil? 72
    Rescue from Above 79
    A Colossal City in Space 85
    Seventeen Keys for a Happy Marriage 91
    Written in Stone 98
    The Lost Day of History 106
    The Ultimate Deliverance 112
    Purity and Power! 121
    Are the Dead Really Dead? 126
    Is the Devil in Charge of Hell? 131
    1,000 Years of Peace 138
    God's Free Health Plan 145
    Is Obedience Legalism? 153

1 God's Love for Man

Nature and revelation alike testify of God's love. Our Father in heaven is the source of life, of wisdom, and of joy. Look at the wonderful and beautiful things of nature. Think of their marvelous adaptation to the needs and happiness, not only of man, but of all living creatures. The sunshine and the rain, that gladden and refresh the earth, the hills and seas and plains, all speak to us of the Creator's love. It is God who supplies the daily needs of all His creatures. In the beautiful words of the psalmist—

"The eyes of all wait upon Thee;
And Thou givest them their meat in due season.
Thou openest Thine hand,
And satisfiest the desire of every living thing."
—Psalm 145:15, 16.

God made man perfectly holy and happy; and the fair earth, as it came from the Creator's hand, bore no blight of decay or shadow of the curse. It is transgression of God's law—the law of love—that has brought woe and death. Yet even amid the suffering that results from sin, God's love is revealed. It is written that God cursed the ground for man's sake (Genesis 3:17). The thorn and the thistle—the difficulties and trials that make his life one of toil and care—were appointed for his good as a part of the training needful in God's plan for his uplifting from the ruin and degradation that sin has wrought. The world, though fallen, is not all sorrow and misery. In nature itself are messages of hope and comfort. There are flowers upon the thistles, and the thorns are covered with roses.

"God is love" is written upon every opening bud, upon every spire of springing grass. The lovely birds making the air vocal with their happy songs, the delicately tinted flowers in their perfection perfuming the air, the lofty trees of the forest with their rich foliage of living green—all testify to the tender, fatherly care of our God and to His desire to make His children happy.

The word of God reveals His character. He Himself has declared His infinite love and pity. When Moses prayed, "Show me Thy glory," the Lord answered, "I will make all My goodness pass before thee" (Exodus 33:18, 19). This is His glory. The Lord passed before Moses, and proclaimed, "The Lord, The Lord God, merciful and gracious, long-suffering, and abundant in goodness and truth, keeping mercy for thousands, forgiving iniquity and transgression and sin" (Exodus 34:6, 7). He is "slow to anger, and of great kindness," "because He delighteth in mercy" (Jonah 4:2; Micah 7:18).

God has bound our hearts to Him by unnumbered tokens in heaven and in earth. Through the things of nature, and the deepest and tenderest earthly ties that human hearts can know, He has sought to reveal Himself to us. Yet these but imperfectly represent His love. Though all these evidences have been given, the enemy of good blinded the minds of men, so that they looked upon God with fear; they thought of Him as severe and unforgiving. Satan led men to conceive of God as a being whose chief attribute is stern justice,—one who is a severe judge, a harsh, exacting creditor. He pictured the Creator as a being who is watching with jealous eye to discern the errors and mistakes of men, that He may visit judgments upon them. It was to remove this dark shadow, by revealing to the world the infinite love of God, that Jesus came to live among men.

The Son of God came from heaven to make manifest the Father. "No man hath seen God at any time; the only begotten Son, which is in the bosom of the Father, He hath declared Him" (John 1:18). "Neither knoweth any man the Father, save the Son, and he to whomsoever the Son will reveal Him" (Matthew 11:27). When one of the disciples made the request, "Show us the Father," Jesus answered, "Have I been so long time with you, and yet hast thou not known Me, Philip? He that hath seen Me hath seen the Father; and how sayest thou then, Show us the Father" (John 14:8, 9)?

In describing His earthly mission, Jesus said, The Lord "hath anointed Me to preach the gospel to the poor; He hath sent Me to heal the brokenhearted, to preach deliverance to the captives, and recovering of sight to the blind, to set at liberty them that are bruised" (Luke 4:18). This was His work. He went about doing good and healing all that were oppressed by Satan. There were whole villages where there was not a moan of sickness in any house, for He had passed through them and healed all their sick. His work gave evidence of His divine anointing. Love, mercy, and compassion were revealed in every act of His life; His heart went out in tender sympathy to the children of men. He took man's nature, that He might reach man's wants. The poorest and humblest were not afraid to approach Him. Even little children were attracted to Him. They loved to climb upon His knees and gaze into the pensive face, benignant with love.

Jesus did not suppress one word of truth, but He uttered it always in love. He exercised the greatest tact and thoughtful, kind attention in His intercourse with the people. He was never rude, never needlessly spoke a severe word, never gave needless pain to a sensitive soul. He did not censure human weakness. He spoke the truth, but always in love. He denounced hypocrisy, unbelief, and iniquity; but tears were in His voice as He uttered His scathing rebukes. He wept over Jerusalem, the city He loved, which refused to receive Him, the way, the truth, and the life. They had rejected Him, the Saviour, but He regarded them with pitying tenderness. His life was one of self-denial and thoughtful care for others. Every soul was precious in His eyes. While He ever bore Himself with divine dignity, He bowed with the tenderest regard to every member of the family of God. In all men He saw fallen souls whom it was His mission to save.

Such is the character of Christ as revealed in His life. This is the character of God. It is from the Father's heart that the streams of divine compassion, manifest in Christ, flow out to the children of men. Jesus, the tender, pitying Saviour, was God "manifest in the flesh" (1 Timothy 3:16).

It was to redeem us that Jesus lived and suffered and died. He became "a Man of Sorrows," that we might be made partakers of everlasting joy. God permitted His beloved Son, full of grace and truth, to come from a world of indescribable glory, to a world marred and blighted with sin, darkened with the shadow of death and the curse. He permitted Him to leave the bosom of His love, the adoration of the angels, to suffer shame, insult, humiliation, hatred, and death. "The chastisement of our peace was upon Him; and with His stripes we are healed" (Isaiah 53:5). Behold Him in the wilderness, in Gethsemane, upon the cross! The spotless Son of God took upon Himself the burden of sin. He who had been one with God, felt in His soul the awful separation that sin makes between God and man. This wrung from His lips the anguished cry, "My God, My God, why hast Thou forsaken Me" (Matthew 27:46)? It was the burden of sin, the sense of its terrible enormity, of its separation of the soul from God—it was this that broke the heart of the Son of God.

But this great sacrifice was not made in order to create in the Father's heart a love for man, not to make Him willing to save. No, no! "God so loved the world, that He gave His only-begotten Son" (John 3:16). The Father loves us, not because of the great propitiation, but He provided the propitiation because He loves us. Christ was the medium through which He could pour out His infinite love upon a fallen world. "God was in Christ, reconciling the world unto Himself" (2 Corinthians 5:19). God suffered with His Son. In the agony of Gethsemane, the death of Calvary, the heart of Infinite Love paid the price of our redemption.

Jesus said, "Therefore doth My Father love Me, because I lay down My life, that I might take it again" (John 10:17). That is, "My Father has so loved you that He even loves Me more for giving My life to redeem you. In becoming your Substitute and Surety, by surrendering My life, by taking your liabilities, your transgressions, I am endeared to My Father; for by My sacrifice, God can be just, and yet the Justifier of him who believeth in Jesus."

None but the Son of God could accomplish our redemption; for only He who was in the bosom of the Father could declare Him. Only He who knew the height and depth of the love of God could make it manifest. Nothing less than the infinite sacrifice made by Christ in behalf of fallen man could express the Father's love to lost humanity.

"God so loved the world, that He gave His only-begotten Son." He gave Him not only to live among men, to bear their sins, and die their sacrifice. He gave Him to the fallen race. Christ was to identify Himself with the interests and needs of humanity. He who was one with God has linked Himself with the children of men by ties that are never to be broken. Jesus is "not ashamed to call them brethren" (Hebrews 2:11); He is our Sacrifice, our Advocate, our Brother, bearing our human form before the Father's throne, and through eternal ages one with the race He has redeemed—the Son of man. And all this that man might be uplifted from the ruin and degradation of sin that he might reflect the love of God and share the joy of holiness.

The price paid for our redemption, the infinite sacrifice of our heavenly Father in giving His Son to die for us, should give us exalted conceptions of what we may become through Christ. As the inspired apostle John beheld the height, the depth, the breadth of the Father's love toward the perishing race, he was filled with adoration and reverence; and, failing to find suitable language in which to express the greatness and tenderness of this love, he called upon the world to behold it. "Behold, what manner of love the Father hath bestowed upon us, that we should be called the sons of God" (1 John 3:1). What a value this places upon man! Through transgression the sons of man become subjects of Satan. Through faith in the atoning sacrifice of Christ the sons of Adam may become the sons of God. By assuming human nature, Christ elevates humanity. Fallen men are placed where, through connection with Christ, they may indeed become worthy of the name "sons of God."

Such love is without a parallel. Children of the heavenly King! Precious promise! Theme for the most profound meditation! The matchless love of God for a world that did not love Him! The thought has a subduing power upon the soul and brings the mind into captivity to the will of God. The more we study the divine character in the light of the cross, the more we see mercy, tenderness, and forgiveness blended with equity and justice, and the more clearly we discern innumerable evidences of a love that is infinite and a tender pity surpassing a mother's yearning sympathy for her wayward child.

2 The Sinner's Need of Christ

Man was originally endowed with noble powers and a well-balanced mind. He was perfect in his being, and in harmony with God. His thoughts were pure, his aims holy. But through disobedience, his powers were perverted, and selfishness took the place of love. His nature became so weakened through transgression that it was impossible for him, in his own strength, to resist the power of evil. He was made captive by Satan, and would have remained so forever had not God specially interposed. It was the tempter's purpose to thwart the divine plan in man's creation, and fill the earth with woe and desolation. And he would point to all this evil as the result of God's work in creating man.

In his sinless state, man held joyful communion with Him "in whom are hid all the treasures of wisdom and knowledge" (Colossians 2:3). But after his sin, he could no longer find joy in holiness, and he sought to hide from the presence of God. Such is still the condition of the unrenewed heart. It is not in harmony with God, and finds no joy in communion with Him. The sinner could not be happy in God's presence; he would shrink from the companionship of holy beings. Could he be permitted to enter heaven, it would have no joy for him. The spirit of unselfish love that reigns there—every heart responding to the heart of Infinite Love—would touch no answering chord in his soul. His thoughts, his interests, his motives, would be alien to those that actuate the sinless dwellers there. He would be a discordant note in the melody of heaven. Heaven would be to him a place of torture; he would long to be hidden from Him who is its light, and the center of its joy. It is no arbitrary decree on the part of God that excludes the wicked from heaven; they are shut out by their own unfitness for its companionship. The glory of God would be to them a consuming fire. They would welcome destruction, that they might be hidden from the face of Him who died to redeem them.

It is impossible for us, of ourselves, to escape from the pit of sin in which we are sunken. Our hearts are evil, and we cannot change them. "Who can bring a clean thing out of an unclean? not one." "The carnal mind is enmity against God: for it is not subject to the law of God, neither indeed can be" (Job 14:4; Romans 8:7). Education, culture, the exercise of the will, human effort, all have their proper sphere, but here they are powerless. They may produce an outward correctness of behavior, but they cannot change the heart; they cannot purify the springs of life. There must be a power working from within, a new life from above, before men can be changed from sin to holiness. That power is Christ. His grace alone can quicken the lifeless faculties of the soul, and attract it to God, to holiness.

The Saviour said, "Except a man be born from above," unless he shall receive a new heart, new desires, purposes, and motives, leading to a new life, "he cannot see the kingdom of God" (John 3:3, margin). The idea that it is necessary only to develop the good that exists in man by nature, is a fatal deception. "The natural man receiveth not the things of the Spirit of God: for they are foolishness unto him: neither can he know them, because they are spiritually discerned." "Marvel not that I said unto thee, Ye must be born again" (1 Corinthians 2:14; John 3:7). Of Christ it is written, "In Him was life; and the life was the light of men"—the only "name under heaven given among men, whereby we must be saved" (John 1:4; Acts 4:12).

It is not enough to perceive the loving-kindness of God, to see the benevolence, the fatherly tenderness, of His character. It is not enough to discern the wisdom and justice of His law, to see that it is founded upon the eternal principle of love. Paul the apostle saw all this when he exclaimed, "I consent unto the law that it is good." "The law is holy, and the commandment holy, and just, and good." But he added, in the bitterness of his soul-anguish and despair, "I am carnal, sold under sin" (Romans 7:16, 12, 14). He longed for the purity, the righteousness, to which in himself he was powerless to attain, and cried out, "O wretched man that I am! who shall deliver me from this body of death" (Romans 7:24, margin)? Such is the cry that has gone up from burdened hearts in all lands and in all ages. To all, there is but one answer, "Behold the Lamb of God, which taketh away the sin of the world" (John 1:29).

Many are the figures by which the Spirit of God has sought to illustrate this truth, and make it plain to souls that long to be freed from the burden of guilt. When, after his sin in deceiving Esau, Jacob fled from his father's home, he was weighed down with a sense of guilt. Lonely and outcast as he was, separated from all that had made life dear, the one thought that above all others pressed upon his soul, was the fear that his sin had cut him off from God, that he was forsaken of Heaven. In sadness he lay down to rest on the bare earth, around him only the lonely hills, and above, the heavens bright with stars. As he slept, a strange light broke upon his vision; and lo, from the plain on which he lay, vast shadowy stairs seemed to lead upward to the very gates of heaven, and upon them angels of God were passing up and down; while from the glory above, the divine voice was heard in a message of comfort and hope. Thus was made known to Jacob that which met the need and longing of his soul—a Saviour. With joy and gratitude he saw revealed a way by which he, a sinner, could be restored to communion with God. The mystic ladder of his dream represented Jesus, the only medium of communication between God and man.

This is the same figure to which Christ referred in His conversation with Nathanael, when He said, "Ye shall see heaven open, and the angels of God ascending and descending upon the Son of man" (John 1:51). In the apostasy, man alienated himself from God; earth was cut off from heaven. Across the gulf that lay between, there could be no communion. But through Christ, earth is again linked with heaven. With His own merits, Christ has bridged the gulf which sin had made, so that the ministering angels can hold communion with man. Christ connects fallen man in his weakness and helplessness with the Source of infinite power.

But in vain are men's dreams of progress, in vain all efforts for the uplifting of humanity, if they neglect the one Source of hope and help for the fallen race. "Every good gift and every perfect gift" (James 1:17) is from God. There is no true excellence of character apart from Him. And the only way to God is Christ. He says, "I am the way, the truth, and the life: no man cometh unto the Father, but by Me" (John 14:6).

The heart of God yearns over His earthly children with a love stronger than death. In giving up His Son, He has poured out to us all heaven in one gift. The Saviour's life and death and intercession, the ministry of angels, the pleading of the Spirit, the Father working above and through all, the unceasing interest of heavenly beings,—all are enlisted in behalf of man's redemption.

Oh, let us contemplate the amazing sacrifice that has been made for us! Let us try to appreciate the labor and energy that Heaven is expending to reclaim the lost, and bring them back to the Father's house. Motives stronger, and agencies more powerful, could never be brought into operation; the exceeding rewards for right-doing, the enjoyment of heaven, the society of the angels, the communion and love of God and His Son, the elevation and extension of all our powers throughout eternal ages—are these not mighty incentives and encouragements to urge us to give the heart's loving service to our Creator and Redeemer?

And, on the other hand, the judgments of God pronounced against sin, the inevitable retribution, the degradation of our character, and the final destruction, are presented in God's word to warn us against the service of Satan.

Shall we not regard the mercy of God? What more could He do? Let us place ourselves in right relation to Him who has loved us with amazing love. Let us avail ourselves of the means provided for us that we may be transformed into His likeness, and be restored to fellowship with the ministering angels, to harmony and communion with the Father and the Son.

3 Repentance

How shall a man be just with God? How shall the sinner be made righteous? It is only through Christ that we can be brought into harmony with God, with holiness; but how are we to come to Christ? Many are asking the same question as did the multitude on the Day of Pentecost, when, convicted of sin, they cried out, "What shall we do?" The first word of Peter's answer was, "Repent" (Acts 2:37, 38). At another time, shortly after, he said, "Repent, ... and be converted, that your sins may be blotted out" (Acts 3:19).

Repentance includes sorrow for sin and a turning away from it. We shall not renounce sin unless we see its sinfulness; until we turn away from it in heart, there will be no real change in the life.

There are many who fail to understand the true nature of repentance. Multitudes sorrow that they have sinned and even make an outward reformation because they fear that their wrongdoing will bring suffering upon themselves. But this is not repentance in the Bible sense. They lament the suffering rather than the sin. Such was the grief of Esau when he saw that the birthright was lost to him forever. Balaam, terrified by the angel standing in his pathway with drawn sword, acknowledged his guilt lest he should lose his life; but there was no genuine repentance for sin, no conversion of purpose, no abhorrence of evil. Judas Iscariot, after betraying his Lord, exclaimed, "I have sinned in that I have betrayed the innocent blood" (Matthew 27:4).

The confession was forced from his guilty soul by an awful sense of condemnation and a fearful looking for of judgment. The consequences that were to result to him filled him with terror, but there was no deep, heartbreaking grief in his soul, that he had betrayed the spotless Son of God and denied the Holy One of Israel. Pharaoh, when suffering under the judgments of God, acknowledged his sin in order to escape further punishment, but returned to his defiance of Heaven as soon as the plagues were stayed. These all lamented the results of sin, but did not sorrow for the sin itself.

But when the heart yields to the influence of the Spirit of God, the conscience will be quickened, and the sinner will discern something of the depth and sacredness of God's holy law, the foundation of His government in heaven and on earth. The "Light, which lighteth every man that cometh into the world," illumines the secret chambers of the soul, and the hidden things of darkness are made manifest (John 1:9). Conviction takes hold upon the mind and heart. The sinner has a sense of the righteousness of Jehovah and feels the terror of appearing, in his own guilt and uncleanness, before the Searcher of hearts. He sees the love of God, the beauty of holiness, the joy of purity; he longs to be cleansed and to be restored to communion with Heaven.

The prayer of David after his fall, illustrates the nature of true sorrow for sin. His repentance was sincere and deep. There was no effort to palliate his guilt; no desire to escape the judgment threatened, inspired his prayer. David saw the enormity of his transgression; he saw the defilement of his soul; he loathed his sin. It was not for pardon only that he prayed, but for purity of heart. He longed for the joy of holiness—to be restored to harmony and communion with God. This was the language of his soul:

> "Blessed is he whose transgression is forgiven,
>   whose sin is covered.
> Blessed is the man unto whom the Lord
>   imputeth not iniquity,
> And in whose spirit there is no guile."
>
> —Psalm 32:1, 2

> "Have mercy upon me, O God, according to
>   Thy loving-kindness:
> According unto the multitude of Thy tender
>   mercies blot out my transgressions. ...
> For I acknowledge my transgressions: and my
>   sin is ever before me. ...
> Purge me with hyssop, and I shall be clean:
>   wash me, and I shall be whiter than snow. ...
> Create in me a clean heart, O God;
>   And renew a right spirit within me.
> Cast me not away from Thy presence;
>   And take not Thy Holy Spirit from me.
> Restore unto me the joy of Thy salvation;
>   And uphold me with Thy free spirit. ...
> Deliver me from bloodguiltiness, O God, Thou
>   God of my salvation:
> And my tongue shall sing aloud of Thy
>   righteousness."
>
> —Psalm 51:1-14.

A repentance such as this, is beyond the reach of our own power to accomplish; it is obtained only from Christ, who ascended up on high and has given gifts unto men.

Just here is a point on which many may err, and hence they fail of receiving the help that Christ desires to give them. They think that they cannot come to Christ unless they first repent, and that repentance prepares for the forgiveness of their sins. It is true that repentance does precede the forgiveness of sins; for it is only the broken and contrite heart that will feel the need of a Saviour. But must the sinner wait till he has repented before he can come to Jesus? Is repentance to be made an obstacle between the sinner and the Saviour?

The Bible does not teach that the sinner must repent before he can heed the invitation of Christ, "Come unto Me, all ye that labor and are heavy-laden, and I will give you rest" (Matthew 11:28). It is the virtue that goes forth from Christ, that leads to genuine repentance. Peter made the matter clear in his statement to the Israelites when he said, "Him hath God exalted with His right hand to be a Prince and a Saviour, for to give repentance to Israel, and forgiveness of sins" (Acts 5:31). We can no more repent without the Spirit of Christ to awaken the conscience than we can be pardoned without Christ.

Christ is the source of every right impulse. He is the only one that can implant in the heart enmity against sin. Every desire for truth and purity, every conviction of our own sinfulness, is an evidence that His Spirit is moving upon our hearts.

Jesus has said, "I, if I be lifted up from the earth, will draw all men unto Me" (John 12:32). Christ must be revealed to the sinner as the Saviour dying for the sins of the world; and as we behold the Lamb of God upon the cross of Calvary, the mystery of redemption begins to unfold to our minds and the goodness of God leads us to repentance. In dying for sinners, Christ manifested a love that is incomprehensible; and as the sinner beholds this love, it softens the heart, impresses the mind, and inspires contrition in the soul.

It is true that men sometimes become ashamed of their sinful ways, and give up some of their evil habits, before they are conscious that they are being drawn to Christ. But whenever they make an effort to reform, from a sincere desire to do right, it is the power of Christ that is drawing them. An influence of which they are unconscious works upon the soul, and the conscience is quickened, and the outward life is amended. And as Christ draws them to look upon His cross, to behold Him whom their sins have pierced, the commandment comes home to the conscience. The wickedness of their life, the deep-seated sin of the soul, is revealed to them. They begin to comprehend something of the righteousness of Christ, and exclaim, "What is sin, that it should require such a sacrifice for the redemption of its victim? Was all this love, all this suffering, all this humiliation, demanded, that we might not perish, but have everlasting life?"

The sinner may resist this love, may refuse to be drawn to Christ; but if he does not resist he will be drawn to Jesus; a knowledge of the plan of salvation will lead him to the foot of the cross in repentance for his sins, which have caused the sufferings of God's dear Son.

The same divine mind that is working upon the things of nature is speaking to the hearts of men and creating an inexpressible craving for something they have not. The things of the world cannot satisfy their longing. The Spirit of God is pleading with them to seek for those things that alone can give peace and rest—the grace of Christ, the joy of holiness. Through influences seen and unseen, our Saviour is constantly at work to attract the minds of men from the unsatisfying pleasures of sin to the infinite blessings that may be theirs in Him. To all these souls, who are vainly seeking to drink from the broken cisterns of this world, the divine message is addressed, "Let him that is athirst come. And whosoever will, let him take the water of life freely" (Revelation 22:17).

You who in heart long for something better than this world can give, recognize this longing as the voice of God to your soul. Ask Him to give you repentance, to reveal Christ to you in His infinite love, in His perfect purity. In the Saviour's life the principles of God's law—love to God and man—were perfectly exemplified. Benevolence, unselfish love, was the life of His soul. It is as we behold Him, as the light from our Saviour falls upon us, that we see the sinfulness of our own hearts.

We may have flattered ourselves, as did Nicodemus, that our life has been upright, that our moral character is correct, and think that we need not humble the heart before God, like the common sinner: but when the light from Christ shines into our souls, we shall see how impure we are; we shall discern the selfishness of motive, the enmity against God, that has defiled every act of life. Then we shall know that our own righteousness is indeed as filthy rags, and that the blood of Christ alone can cleanse us from the defilement of sin, and renew our hearts in His own likeness.

One ray of the glory of God, one gleam of the purity of Christ, penetrating the soul, makes every spot of defilement painfully distinct, and lays bare the deformity and defects of the human character. It makes apparent the unhallowed desires, the infidelity of the heart, the impurity of the lips. The sinner's acts of disloyalty in making void the law of God, are exposed to his sight, and his spirit is stricken and afflicted under the searching influence of the Spirit of God. He loathes himself as he views the pure, spotless character of Christ.

When the prophet Daniel beheld the glory surrounding the heavenly messenger that was sent unto him, he was overwhelmed with a sense of his own weakness and imperfection. Describing the effect of the wonderful scene, he says, "There remained no strength in me: for my comeliness was turned in me into corruption, and I retained no strength" (Daniel 10:8). The soul thus touched will hate its selfishness, abhor its self-love, and will seek, through Christ's righteousness, for the purity of heart that is in harmony with the law of God and the character of Christ.

Paul says that as "touching the righteousness which is in the law"—as far as outward acts were concerned—he was "blameless" (Philippians 3:6); but when the spiritual character of the law was discerned, he saw himself a sinner. Judged by the letter of the law as men apply it to the outward life, he had abstained from sin; but when he looked into the depths of its holy precepts, and saw himself as God saw him, he bowed in humiliation and confessed his guilt. He says, "I was alive without the law once: but when the commandment came, sin revived, and I died" (Romans 7:9). When he saw the spiritual nature of the law, sin appeared in its true hideousness, and his self-esteem was gone.

God does not regard all sins as of equal magnitude; there are degrees of guilt in His estimation, as well as in that of man; but however trifling this or that wrong act may seem in the eyes of men, no sin is small in the sight of God. Man's judgment is partial, imperfect; but God estimates all things as they really are. The drunkard is despised and is told that his sin will exclude him from heaven; while pride, selfishness, and covetousness too often go unrebuked. But these are sins that are especially offensive to God; for they are contrary to the benevolence of His character, to that unselfish love which is the very atmosphere of the unfallen universe. He who falls into some of the grosser sins may feel a sense of his shame and poverty and his need of the grace of Christ; but pride feels no need, and so it closes the heart against Christ and the infinite blessings He came to give.

The poor publican who prayed, "God be merciful to me a sinner" (Luke 18:13), regarded himself as a very wicked man, and others looked upon him in the same light; but he felt his need, and with his burden of guilt and shame he came before God, asking for His mercy. His heart was open for the Spirit of God to do its gracious work and set him free from the power of sin. The Pharisee's boastful, self-righteous prayer showed that his heart was closed against the influence of the Holy Spirit. Because of his distance from God, he had no sense of his own defilement, in contrast with the perfection of the divine holiness. He felt no need, and he received nothing.

If you see your sinfulness, do not wait to make yourself better. How many there are who think they are not good enough to come to Christ. Do you expect to become better through your own efforts? "Can the Ethiopian change his skin, or the leopard his spots? then may ye also do good, that are accustomed to do evil" (Jeremiah 13:23). There is help for us only in God. We must not wait for stronger persuasions, for better opportunities, or for holier tempers. We can do nothing of ourselves. We must come to Christ just as we are.

But let none deceive themselves with the thought that God, in His great love and mercy, will yet save even the rejecters of His grace. The exceeding sinfulness of sin can be estimated only in the light of the cross. When men urge that God is too good to cast off the sinner, let them look to Calvary. It was because there was no other way in which man could be saved, because without this sacrifice it was impossible for the human race to escape from the defiling power of sin, and be restored to communion with holy beings,—impossible for them again to become partakers of spiritual life,—it was because of this that Christ took upon Himself the guilt of the disobedient and suffered in the sinner's stead. The love and suffering and death of the Son of God all testify to the terrible enormity of sin and declare that there is no escape from its power, no hope of the higher life, but through the submission of the soul to Christ.

The impenitent sometimes excuse themselves by saying of professed Christians, "I am as good as they are. They are no more self-denying, sober, or circumspect in their conduct than I am. They love pleasure and self-indulgence as well as I do." Thus they make the faults of others an excuse for their own neglect of duty. But the sins and defects of others do not excuse anyone, for the

Repentance

Lord has not given us an erring human pattern. The spotless Son of God has been given as our example, and those who complain of the wrong course of professed Christians are the ones who should show better lives and nobler examples. If they have so high a conception of what a Christian should be, is not their own sin so much the greater? They know what is right, and yet refuse to do it.

Beware of procrastination. Do not put off the work of forsaking your sins and seeking purity of heart through Jesus. Here is where thousands upon thousands have erred to their eternal loss. I will not here dwell upon the shortness and uncertainty of life; but there is a terrible danger—a danger not sufficiently understood—in delaying to yield to the pleading voice of God's Holy Spirit, in choosing to live in sin; for such this delay really is. Sin, however small it may be esteemed, can be indulged in only at the peril of infinite loss. What we do not overcome, will overcome us and work out our destruction.

Adam and Eve persuaded themselves that in so small a matter as eating of the forbidden fruit there could not result such terrible consequences as God had declared. But this small matter was the transgression of God's immutable and holy law, and it separated man from God and opened the floodgates of death and untold woe upon our world. Age after age there has gone up from our earth a continual cry of mourning, and the whole creation groaneth and travaileth together in pain as a consequence of man's disobedience. Heaven itself has felt the effects of his rebellion against God. Calvary stands as a memorial of the amazing sacrifice required to atone for the transgression of the divine law. Let us not regard sin as a trivial thing.

Every act of transgression, every neglect or rejection of the grace of Christ, is reacting upon yourself; it is hardening the heart, depraving the will, benumbing the understanding, and not only making you less inclined to yield, but less capable of yielding, to the tender pleading of God's Holy Spirit.

Many are quieting a troubled conscience with the thought that they can change a course of evil when they choose; that they can trifle with the invitations of mercy, and yet be again and again impressed. They think that after doing despite to the Spirit of grace, after casting their influence on the side of Satan, in a moment of terrible extremity they can change their course. But this is not so easily done. The experience, the education, of a lifetime, has so thoroughly molded the character that few then desire to receive the image of Jesus.

Even one wrong trait of character, one sinful desire, persistently cherished, will eventually neutralize all the power of the gospel. Every sinful indulgence strengthens the soul's aversion to God. The man who manifests an infidel hardihood, or a stolid indifference to divine truth, is but reaping the harvest of that which he has himself sown. In all the Bible there is not a more fearful warning against trifling with evil than the words of the wise man that the sinner "shall be holden with the cords of his sins" (Proverbs 5:22).

Christ is ready to set us free from sin, but He does not force the will; and if by persistent transgression the will itself is wholly bent on evil, and we do not *desire* to be set free, if we *will* not accept His grace, what more can He do? We have destroyed ourselves by our determined rejection of His love. "Behold, now is the accepted time; behold, now is the day of salvation." "Today if ye will hear His voice, harden not your hearts" (2 Corinthians 6:2; Hebrews 3:7, 8).

"Man looketh on the outward appearance, but the Lord looketh on the heart"—the human heart, with its conflicting emotions of joy and sorrow; the wandering, wayward heart, which is the abode of so much impurity and deceit (1 Samuel 16:7). He knows its motives, its very intents and purposes. Go to Him with your soul all stained as it is. Like the psalmist, throw its chambers open to the all-seeing eye, exclaiming, "Search me, O God, and know my heart: try me, and know my thoughts: and see if there be any wicked way in me, and lead me in the way everlasting" (Psalm 139: 23, 24).

Many accept an intellectual religion, a form of godliness, when the heart is not cleansed. Let it be your prayer, "Create in me a clean heart, O God; and renew a right spirit within me" (Psalm 51:10). Deal truly with your own soul. Be as earnest, as persistent, as you would be if your mortal life were at stake. This is a matter to be settled between God and your own soul, settled for eternity. A supposed hope, and nothing more, will prove your ruin.

Study God's word prayerfully. That word presents before you, in the law of God and the life of Christ, the great principles of holiness, without which "no man shall see the Lord" (Hebrews 12:14). It convinces of sin; it plainly reveals the way of salvation. Give heed to it as the voice of God speaking to your soul.

As you see the enormity of sin, as you see yourself as you really are, do not give up to despair. It was sinners that Christ came to save. We have not to reconcile God to us, but—O wondrous love!—God in Christ is "reconciling the world unto Himself" (2 Corinthians 5:19). He is wooing by His tender love the hearts of His erring children. No earthly parent could be as patient with the faults and mistakes of his children, as is God with those He seeks to save. No one could plead more tenderly with the transgressor. No human lips ever poured out more tender entreaties to the wanderer than does He. All His promises, His warnings, are but the breathing of unutterable love.

When Satan comes to tell you that you are a great sinner, look up to your Redeemer and talk of His merits. That which will help you is to look to His light. Acknowledge your sin, but tell the enemy that "Christ Jesus came into the world to save sinners" and that you may be saved by His matchless love (1 Timothy 1:15). Jesus asked Simon a question in regard to two debtors. One owed his lord a small sum, and the other owed him a very large sum; but he forgave them both, and Christ asked Simon which debtor would love his lord most. Simon answered, "He to whom he forgave most" (Luke 7:43). We have been great sinners, but Christ died that we might be forgiven. The merits of His sacrifice are sufficient to present to the Father in our behalf. Those to whom He has forgiven most will love Him most, and will stand nearest to His throne to praise Him for His great love and infinite sacrifice. It is when we most fully comprehend the love of God that we best realize the sinfulness of sin. When we see the length of the chain that was let down for us, when we understand something of the infinite sacrifice that Christ has made in our behalf, the heart is melted with tenderness and contrition.

4 Confession

"He that covereth his sins shall not prosper: but whoso confesseth and forsaketh them shall have mercy" (Proverbs 28:13).

The conditions of obtaining mercy of God are simple and just and reasonable. The Lord does not require us to do some grievous thing in order that we may have the forgiveness of sin. We need not make long and wearisome pilgrimages, or perform painful penances, to commend our souls to the God of heaven or to expiate our transgression; but he that confesseth and forsaketh his sin shall have mercy.

The apostle says, "Confess your faults one to another, and pray one for another, that ye may be healed" (James 5:16). Confess your sins to God, who only can forgive them, and your faults to one another. If you have given offense to your friend or neighbor, you are to acknowledge your wrong, and it is his duty freely to forgive you. Then you are to seek the forgiveness of God, because the brother you have wounded is the property of God, and in injuring him you sinned against his Creator and Redeemer. The case is brought before the only true Mediator, our great High Priest, who "was in all points tempted like as we are, yet without sin," and who is "touched with the feeling of our infirmities," and is able to cleanse from every stain of iniquity (Hebrews 4:15).

Those who have not humbled their souls before God in acknowledging their guilt, have not yet fulfilled the first condition of acceptance. If we have not experienced that repentance which is not to be repented of, and have not with true humiliation of soul and brokenness of spirit confessed our sins, abhorring our iniquity, we have never truly sought for the forgiveness of sin; and if we have never sought, we have never found the peace of God. The only reason why we do not have remission of sins that are past is that we are not willing to humble our hearts and comply with the conditions of the word of truth. Explicit instruction is given concerning this matter. Confession of sin, whether public or private, should be heartfelt and freely expressed. It is not to be urged from the sinner. It is not to be made in a flippant and careless way, or forced from those who have no realizing sense of the abhorrent character of sin. The confession that is the outpouring of the inmost soul finds its way to the God of infinite pity. The psalmist says, "The Lord is nigh unto them that are of a broken heart; and saveth such as be of a contrite spirit" (Psalm 34:18).

True confession is always of a specific character, and acknowledges particular sins. They may be of such a nature as to be brought before God only; they may be wrongs that should be confessed to individuals who have suffered injury through them; or they may be of a public character, and should then be as publicly confessed. But all confession should be definite and to the point, acknowledging the very sins of which you are guilty.

Confession

In the days of Samuel the Israelites wandered from God. They were suffering the consequences of sin; for they had lost their faith in God, lost their discernment of His power and wisdom to rule the nation, lost their confidence in His ability to defend and vindicate His cause. They turned from the great Ruler of the universe and desired to be governed as were the nations around them. Before they found peace they made this definite confession: "We have added unto all our sins this evil, to ask us a king" (1 Samuel 12:19). The very sin of which they were convicted had to be confessed. Their ingratitude oppressed their souls and severed them from God.

Confession will not be acceptable to God without sincere repentance and reformation. There must be decided changes in the life; everything offensive to God must be put away. This will be the result of genuine sorrow for sin. The work that we have to do on our part is plainly set before us: "Wash you, make you clean; put away the evil of your doings from before Mine eyes; cease to do evil; learn to do well; seek judgment, relieve the oppressed, judge the fatherless, plead for the widow" (Isaiah 1:16, 17). "If the wicked restore the pledge, give again that he had robbed, walk in the statutes of life, without committing iniquity; he shall surely live, he shall not die" (Ezekiel 33:15). Paul says, speaking of the work of repentance: "Ye sorrowed after a godly sort, what carefulness it wrought in you, yea, what clearing of yourselves, yea, what indignation, yea, what fear, yea, what vehement desire, yea, what zeal, yea, what revenge! In all things ye have approved yourselves to be clear in this matter" (2 Corinthians 7:11).

When sin has deadened the moral perceptions, the wrongdoer does not discern the defects of his character nor realize the enormity of the evil he has committed; and unless he yields to the convicting power of the Holy Spirit he remains in partial blindness to his sin. His confessions are not sincere and in earnest. To every acknowledgment of his guilt he adds an apology in excuse of his course, declaring that if it had not been for certain circumstances he would not have done this or that for which he is reproved.

After Adam and Eve had eaten of the forbidden fruit, they were filled with a sense of shame and terror. At first their only thought was how to excuse their sin and escape the dreaded sentence of death. When the Lord inquired concerning their sin, Adam replied, laying the guilt partly upon God and partly upon his companion: "The woman whom Thou gavest to be with me, she gave me of the tree, and I did eat." The woman put the blame upon the serpent, saying, "The serpent beguiled me, and I did eat" (Genesis 3: 12, 13). Why did You make the serpent? Why did You suffer him to come into Eden? These were the questions implied in her excuse for her sin, thus charging God with the responsibility of their fall. The spirit of self-justification originated in the father of lies and has been exhibited by all the sons and daughters of Adam. Confessions of this order are not inspired by the divine Spirit and will not be acceptable to God. True repentance will lead a man to bear his guilt himself and acknowledge it without deception or hypocrisy. Like the poor publican, not lifting up so much as his eyes unto heaven, he will cry, "God be merciful to me a sinner," and those who do acknowledge their guilt will be justified, for Jesus will plead His blood in behalf of the repentant soul.

The examples in God's word of genuine repentance and humiliation reveal a spirit of confession in which there is no excuse for sin or attempt at self-justification. Paul did not seek to shield himself; he paints his sin in its darkest hue, not attempting to lessen his guilt. He says, "Many of the saints did I shut up in prison, having received authority from the chief priests; and when they were put to death, I gave my voice against them. And I punished them oft in every synagogue, and compelled them to blaspheme; and being exceedingly mad against them, I persecuted them even unto strange cities" (Acts 26: 10, 11). He does not hesitate to declare that "Christ Jesus came into the world to save sinners; of whom I am chief" (1 Timothy 1:15).

The humble and broken heart, subdued by genuine repentance, will appreciate something of the love of God and the cost of Calvary; and as a son confesses to a loving father, so will the truly penitent bring all his sins before God. And it is written, "If we confess our sins, He is faithful and just to forgive us our sins, and to cleanse us from all unrighteousness" (1 John 1:9).

5 Consecration

God's promise is, "Ye shall seek Me, and find Me, when ye shall search for Me with all your heart" (Jeremiah 29:13).

The whole heart must be yielded to God, or the change can never be wrought in us by which we are to be restored to His likeness. By nature we are alienated from God. The Holy Spirit describes our condition in such words as these: "Dead in trespasses and sins;" "the whole head is sick, and the whole heart faint;" "no soundness in it." We are held fast in the snare of Satan, "taken captive by him at his will" (Ephesians 2:1; Isaiah 1:5, 6; 2 Timothy 2:26). God desires to heal us, to set us free. But since this requires an entire transformation, a renewing of our whole nature, we must yield ourselves wholly to Him.

The warfare against self is the greatest battle that was ever fought. The yielding of self, surrendering all to the will of God, requires a struggle; but the soul must submit to God before it can be renewed in holiness.

The government of God is not, as Satan would make it appear, founded upon a blind submission, an unreasoning control. It appeals to the intellect and the conscience. "Come now, and let us reason together" is the Creator's invitation to the beings He has made (Isaiah 1:18). God does not force the will of His creatures. He cannot accept an homage that is not willingly and intelligently given. A mere forced submission would prevent all real development of mind or character; it would make man a mere automaton. Such is not the purpose of the Creator. He desires that man, the crowning work of His creative power, shall reach the highest possible development. He sets before us the height of blessing to which He desires to bring us through His grace. He invites us to give ourselves to Him, that He may work His will in us. It remains for us to choose whether we will be set free from the bondage of sin, to share the glorious liberty of the sons of God.

In giving ourselves to God, we must necessarily give up all that would separate us from Him. Hence the Saviour says, "Whosoever he be of you that forsaketh not all that he hath, he cannot be My disciple" (Luke 14:33). Whatever shall draw away the heart from God must be given up. Mammon is the idol of many. The love of money, the desire for wealth, is the golden chain that binds them to Satan. Reputation and worldly honor are worshiped by another class. The life of selfish ease and freedom from responsibility is the idol of others. But these slavish bands must be broken. We cannot be half the Lord's and half the world's. We are not God's children unless we are such entirely.

There are those who profess to serve God, while they rely upon their own efforts to obey His law, to form a right character, and secure salvation. Their hearts are not moved by any deep sense of the love of Christ, but they seek to perform the duties of the Christian life as that which God requires of them in order to gain heaven. Such religion is worth nothing. When Christ dwells in the heart, the soul will be so filled with His love, with the joy of communion with Him, that it will cleave to Him; and in the contemplation of Him, self will be forgotten. Love to Christ will be the spring of action. Those who feel the constraining love of God, do not ask how little may be given to meet the requirements of God; they do not ask for the lowest standard, but aim at perfect conformity to the will of their Redeemer. With earnest desire they yield all and manifest an interest proportionate to the value of the object which they seek. A profession of Christ without this deep love is mere talk, dry formality, and heavy drudgery.

Do you feel that it is too great a sacrifice to yield all to Christ? Ask yourself the question, "What has Christ given for me?" The Son of God gave all—life and love and suffering—for our redemption. And can it be that we, the unworthy objects of so great love, will withhold our hearts from Him? Every moment of our lives we have been partakers of the blessings of His grace, and for this very reason we cannot fully realize the depths of ignorance and misery from which we have been saved. Can we look upon Him whom our sins have pierced, and yet be willing to do despite to all His love and sacrifice? In view of the infinite humiliation of the Lord of glory, shall we murmur because we can enter into life only through conflict and self-abasement?

The inquiry of many a proud heart is, "Why need I go in penitence and humiliation before I can have the assurance of my acceptance with God?" I point you to Christ. He was sinless, and, more than this, He was the Prince of heaven; but in man's behalf He became sin for the race. "He was numbered with the transgressors; and He bare the sin of many, and made intercession for the transgressors" (Isaiah 53:12).

But what do we give up, when we give all? A sin-polluted heart, for Jesus to purify, to cleanse by His own blood, and to save by His matchless love. And yet men think it hard to give up all! I am ashamed to hear it spoken of, ashamed to write it.

God does not require us to give up anything that it is for our best interest to retain. In all that He does, He has the well-being of His children in view. Would that all who have not chosen Christ might realize that He has something vastly better to offer them than they are seeking for themselves. Man is doing the greatest injury and injustice to his own soul when he thinks and acts contrary to the will of God. No real joy can be found in the path forbidden by Him who knows what is best and who plans for the good of His creatures. The path of transgression is the path of misery and destruction.

It is a mistake to entertain the thought that God is pleased to see His children suffer. All heaven is interested in the happiness of man. Our heavenly Father does not close the avenues of joy to any of His creatures. The divine requirements call upon us to shun those indulgences that would bring suffering and disappointment, that would close to us the door of happiness and heaven. The world's Redeemer accepts men as they are, with all their wants, imperfections, and weaknesses; and He will not only cleanse from sin and grant redemption through His blood, but will satisfy the heart-longing of all who consent to wear His yoke, to bear His burden. It is His purpose to impart peace and rest to all who come to Him for the bread of life. He requires us to perform only those duties that will lead our steps to heights of bliss to which the disobedient can never attain. The true, joyous life of the soul is to have Christ formed within, the hope of glory.

Many are inquiring, "*How* am I to make the surrender of myself to God?" You desire to give yourself to Him, but you are weak in moral power, in slavery to doubt, and controlled by the habits of your life of sin. Your promises and resolutions are like ropes of sand. You cannot control your thoughts, your impulses, your affections. The knowledge of your broken promises and forfeited pledges weakens your confidence in your own sincerity, and causes you to feel that God cannot accept you; but you need not despair. What you need to understand is the true force of the will. This is the governing power in the nature of man, the power of decision, or of choice. Everything depends on the right action of the will. The power of choice God has given to men; it is theirs to exercise. You cannot change your heart, you cannot of yourself give to God its affections; but you can *choose* to serve Him. You can give Him your will; He will then work in you to will and to do according to His good pleasure. Thus your whole nature will be brought under the control of the Spirit of Christ; your affections will be centered upon Him, your thoughts will be in harmony with Him.

Desires for goodness and holiness are right as far as they go; but if you stop here, they will avail nothing. Many will be lost while hoping and desiring to be Christians. They do not come to the point of yielding the will to God. They do not now *choose* to be Christians.

Through the right exercise of the will, an entire change may be made in your life. By yielding up your will to Christ, you ally yourself with the power that is above all principalities and powers. You will have strength from above to hold you steadfast, and thus through constant surrender to God you will be enabled to live the new life, even the life of faith.

6 Faith and Acceptance

As your conscience has been quickened by the Holy Spirit, you have seen something of the evil of sin, of its power, its guilt, its woe; and you look upon it with abhorrence. You feel that sin has separated you from God, that you are in bondage to the power of evil. The more you struggle to escape, the more you realize your helplessness. Your motives are impure; your heart is unclean. You see that your life has been filled with selfishness and sin. You long to be forgiven, to be cleansed, to be set free. Harmony with God, likeness to Him—what can you do to obtain it?

It is peace that you need—Heaven's forgiveness and peace and love in the soul. Money cannot buy it, intellect cannot procure it, wisdom cannot attain to it; you can never hope, by your own efforts, to secure it. But God offers it to you as a gift, "without money and without price" (Isaiah 55:1). It is yours if you will but reach out your hand and grasp it. The Lord says, "Though your sins be as scarlet, they shall be as white as snow; though they be red like crimson, they shall be as wool" (Isaiah 1:18). "A new heart also will I give you, and a new spirit will I put within you" (Ezekiel 36:26).

You have confessed your sins, and in heart put them away. You have resolved to give yourself to God. Now go to Him, and ask that He will wash away your sins and give you a new heart. Then believe that He does this *because* He *has promised*. This is the lesson which Jesus taught while He was on earth, that the gift which God promises us, we must believe we do receive, and it is ours. Jesus healed the people of their diseases when they had faith in His power; He helped them in the things which they could see, thus inspiring them with confidence in Him concerning things which they could not see—leading them to believe in His power to forgive sins. This He plainly stated in the healing of the man sick with palsy: *"That ye may know that the Son of man hath power on earth to forgive sins,* (then saith He to the sick of the palsy,) *Arise, take up thy bed, and go unto thine house"* (Matthew 9:6). So also John the evangelist says, speaking of the miracles of Christ, "These are written, that ye might believe that Jesus is the Christ, the Son of God; and that believing ye might have life through His name" (John 20:31).

From the simple Bible account of how Jesus healed the sick, we may learn something about how to believe in Him for the forgiveness of sins. Let us turn to the story of the paralytic at Bethesda. The poor sufferer was helpless; he had not used his limbs for thirty-eight years. Yet Jesus bade him, "Rise, take up thy bed, and walk." The sick man might have said, "Lord, if Thou wilt make me whole, I will obey Thy word." But, no, he believed Christ's word, believed that he was made whole, and he made the effort at once; he *willed* to walk, and he did walk. He acted on the word of Christ, and God gave the power. He was made whole.

In like manner you are a sinner. You cannot atone for your past sins; you cannot change your heart and make yourself holy. But God promises to do all

Faith and Acceptance

this for you through Christ. You *believe* that promise. You confess your sins and give yourself to God. You *will* to serve Him. Just as surely as you do this, God will fulfill His word to you. If you believe the promise,—believe that you are forgiven and cleansed,—God supplies the fact; you are made whole, just as Christ gave the paralytic power to walk when the man believed that he was healed. It *is* so if you believe it.

Do not wait to *feel* that you are made whole, but say, "I believe it; it *is* so, not because I feel it, but because God has promised."

Jesus says, "What things soever ye desire, when ye pray, believe that ye receive them, and ye shall have them" (Mark 11:24). There is a condition to this promise—that we pray according to the will of God. But it is the will of God to cleanse us from sin, to make us His children, and to enable us to live a holy life. So we may ask for these blessings, and believe that we receive them, and thank God that we *have* received them. It is our privilege to go to Jesus and be cleansed, and to stand before the law without shame or remorse. "There is therefore now no condemnation to them which are in Christ Jesus, who walk not after the flesh, but after the Spirit" (Romans 8:1).

Henceforth you are not your own; you are bought with a price. "Ye were not redeemed with corruptible things, as silver and gold; … but with the precious blood of Christ, as of a lamb without blemish and without spot" (1 Peter 1:18, 19). Through this simple act of believing God, the Holy Spirit has begotten a new life in your heart. You are as a child born into the family of God, and He loves you as He loves His Son.

Now that you have given yourself to Jesus, do not draw back, do not take yourself away from Him, but day by day say, "I am Christ's; I have given myself to Him;" and ask Him to give you His Spirit and keep you by His grace. As it is by giving yourself to God, and believing Him, that you become His child, so you are to live in Him. The apostle says, "As ye have therefore received Christ Jesus the Lord, so walk ye in Him" (Colossians 2:6).

Some seem to feel that they must be on probation, and must prove to the Lord that they are reformed, before they can claim His blessing. But they may claim the blessing of God even now. They must have His grace, the Spirit of Christ, to help their infirmities, or they cannot resist evil. Jesus loves to have us come to Him just as we are, sinful, helpless, dependent. We may come with all our weakness, our folly, our sinfulness, and fall at His feet in penitence. It is His glory to encircle us in the arms of His love and to bind up our wounds, to cleanse us from all impurity.

Here is where thousands fail; they do not believe that Jesus pardons them personally, individually. They do not take God at His word. It is the privilege of all who comply with the conditions to know for themselves that pardon is freely extended for every sin. Put away the suspicion that God's promises are not meant for you. They are for every repentant transgressor. Strength and grace have been provided through Christ to be brought by ministering angels to every believing soul. None are so sinful that they cannot find strength, purity, and righteousness in Jesus, who died for them. He is waiting to strip them of their garments stained and polluted with sin, and to put upon them the white robes of righteousness; He bids them live and not die.

God does not deal with us as finite men deal with one another. His thoughts are thoughts of mercy, love, and tenderest compassion. He says, "Let the wicked forsake his way, and the unrighteous man his thoughts: and let him return unto the Lord, and He will have mercy upon him; and to our God, for He will abundantly pardon." "I have blotted out, as a thick cloud, thy transgressions, and, as a cloud, thy sins" (Isaiah 55:7; 44:22).

"I have no pleasure in the death of him that dieth, saith the Lord God: wherefore turn yourselves, and live ye" (Ezekiel 18:32). Satan is ready to steal away the blessed assurances of God. He desires to take every glimmer of hope and every ray of light from the soul; but you must not permit him to do this. Do not give ear to the tempter, but say, "Jesus has died that I might live. He loves me, and wills not that I should perish. I have a compassionate heavenly Father; and although I have abused His love, though the blessings He has given me have been squandered, I will arise, and go to my Father, and say, 'I have sinned against heaven, and before Thee, and am no more worthy to be called Thy son: make me as one of Thy hired servants.'" The parable tells you how the wanderer will be received: *"When he was yet a great way off,* his father saw him, and had compassion, and ran, and fell on his neck, and kissed him" (Luke 15:18-20).

But even this parable, tender and touching as it is, comes short of expressing the infinite compassion of the heavenly Father. The Lord declares by His prophet, "I have loved thee with an everlasting love: *therefore with loving-kindness have I drawn thee*" (Jeremiah 31:3). While the sinner is yet far from the Father's house, wasting his substance in a strange country, the Father's heart is yearning over him; and every longing awakened in the soul to return to God is but the tender pleading of His Spirit, wooing, entreating, drawing the wanderer to his Father's heart of love.

With the rich promises of the Bible before you, can you give place to doubt? Can you believe that when the poor sinner longs to return, longs to forsake his sins, the Lord sternly withholds him from coming to His feet in repentance? Away with such thoughts! Nothing can hurt your own soul more than to entertain such a conception of our heavenly Father. He hates sin, but He loves the sinner, and He gave Himself in the person of Christ, that all who would might be saved and have eternal blessedness in the kingdom of glory. What stronger or more tender language could have been employed than He has chosen in which to express His love toward us? He declares, "Can a woman forget her sucking child, that she should not have compassion on the son of her womb? yea, they may forget, yet will I not forget thee" (Isaiah 49:15).

Look up, you that are doubting and trembling; for Jesus lives to make intercession for us. Thank God for the gift of His dear Son and pray that He may not have died for you in vain. The Spirit invites you today. Come with your whole heart to Jesus, and you may claim His blessing.

As you read the promises, remember they are the expression of unutterable love and pity. The great heart of Infinite Love is drawn toward the sinner with boundless compassion. "We have redemption through His blood, the forgiveness of sins" (Ephesians 1:7). Yes, only believe that God is your helper. He wants to restore His moral image in man. As you draw near to Him with confession and repentance, He will draw near to you with mercy and forgiveness.

7 The Test of Discipleship

If any man be in Christ, he is a new creature: old things are passed away; behold, all things are become new" (2 Corinthians 5:17).

A person may not be able to tell the exact time or place, or trace all the chain of circumstances in the process of conversion; but this does not prove him to be unconverted. Christ said to Nicodemus, "The wind bloweth where it listeth, and thou hearest the sound thereof, but canst not tell whence it cometh, and whither it goeth: so is everyone that is born of the Spirit" (John 3:8). Like the wind, which is invisible, yet the effects of which are plainly seen and felt, is the Spirit of God in its work upon the human heart. That regenerating power, which no human eye can see, begets a new life in the soul; it creates a new being in the image of God. While the work of the Spirit is silent and imperceptible, its effects are manifest. If the heart has been renewed by the Spirit of God, the life will bear witness to the fact. While we cannot do anything to change our hearts or to bring ourselves into harmony with God; while we must not trust at all to ourselves or our good works, our lives will reveal whether the grace of God is dwelling within us. A change will be seen in the character, the habits, the pursuits. The contrast will be clear and decided between what they have been and what they are. The character is revealed, not by occasional good deeds and occasional misdeeds, but by the tendency of the habitual words and acts.

It is true that there may be an outward correctness of deportment without the renewing power of Christ. The love of influence and the desire for the esteem of others may produce a well-ordered life. Self-respect may lead us to avoid the appearance of evil. A selfish heart may perform generous actions. By what means, then, shall we determine whose side we are on?

Who has the heart? With whom are our thoughts? Of whom do we love to converse? Who has our warmest affections and our best energies? If we are Christ's, our thoughts are with Him, and our sweetest thoughts are of Him. All we have and are is consecrated to Him. We long to bear His image, breathe His spirit, do His will, and please Him in all things.

Those who become new creatures in Christ Jesus will bring forth the fruits of the Spirit, "love, joy, peace, long-suffering, gentleness, goodness, faith, meekness, temperance" (Galatians 5:22, 23). They will no longer fashion themselves according to the former lusts, but by the faith of the Son of God they will follow in His steps, reflect His character, and purify themselves even as He is pure. The things they once hated they now love, and the things they once loved they hate. The proud and self-assertive become meek and lowly in heart. The vain and supercilious become serious and unobtrusive. The drunken become sober, and the profligate pure. The vain customs and fashions of the world are laid aside. Christians will seek not the "outward adorning," but "the hidden man of the heart, in that which is not corruptible, even the ornament of a meek and quiet spirit" (1 Peter 3:3, 4).

There is no evidence of genuine repentance unless it works reformation. If he restore the pledge, give again that he had robbed, confess his sins, and love God and his fellow men, the sinner may be sure that he has passed from death unto life.

When, as erring, sinful beings, we come to Christ and become partakers of His pardoning grace, love springs up in the heart. Every burden is light, for the yoke that Christ imposes is easy. Duty becomes a delight, and sacrifice a pleasure. The path that before seemed shrouded in darkness, becomes bright with beams from the Sun of Righteousness.

The loveliness of the character of Christ will be seen in His followers. It was His delight to do the will of God. Love to God, zeal for His glory, was the controlling power in our Saviour's life. Love beautified and ennobled all His actions. Love is of God. The unconsecrated heart cannot originate or produce it. It is found only in the heart where Jesus reigns. "We love, because He first loved us" (1 John 4:19 R.V.). In the heart renewed by divine grace, love is the principle of action. It modifies the character, governs the impulses, controls the passions, subdues enmity, and ennobles the affections. This love, cherished in the soul, sweetens the life and sheds a refining influence on all around.

There are two errors against which the children of God—particularly those who have just come to trust in His grace—especially need to guard. The first, already dwelt upon, is that of looking to their own works, trusting to anything they can do, to bring themselves into harmony with God. He who is trying to become holy by his own works in keeping the law, is attempting an impossibility. All that man can do without Christ is polluted with selfishness and sin. It is the grace of Christ alone, through faith, that can make us holy.

The opposite and no less dangerous error is that belief in Christ releases men from keeping the law of God; that since by faith alone we become partakers of the grace of Christ, our works have nothing to do with our redemption.

But notice here that obedience is not a mere outward compliance, but the service of love. The law of God is an expression of His very nature; it is an embodiment of the great principle of love, and hence is the foundation of His government in heaven and earth. If our hearts are renewed in the likeness of God, if the divine love is implanted in the soul, will not the law of God be carried out in the life? When the principle of love is implanted in the heart, when man is renewed after the image of Him that created him, the new-covenant promise is fulfilled, "I will put My laws into their hearts, and in their minds will I write them" (Hebrews 10:16). And if the law is written in the heart, will it not shape the life? Obedience—the service and allegiance of love—is the true sign of discipleship. Thus the Scripture says, "This is the love of God, that we keep His commandments." "He that saith, I know Him, and keepeth not His commandments, is a liar, and the truth is not in him" (1 John 5:3; 2:4).

Instead of releasing man from obedience, it is faith, and faith only, that makes us partakers of the grace of Christ, which enables us to render obedience.

We do not earn salvation by our obedience; for salvation is the free gift of God, to be received by faith. But obedience is the fruit of faith. "Ye know that He was manifested to take away our sins; and in Him is no sin. Whosoever abideth in Him sinneth not: whosoever sinneth hath not seen Him, neither known Him" (1 John 3:5, 6). Here is the true test. If we abide in Christ, if the love of God dwells in us, our feelings, our thoughts, our purposes, our actions, will be in harmony with the will of God as expressed in the precepts of His holy law. "Little children, let no man deceive you: he that doeth righteousness is righteous, even as He is righteous" (1 John 3:7). Righteousness is defined by the standard of God's holy law, as expressed in the ten precepts given on Sinai.

That so-called faith in Christ which professes to release men from the obligation of obedience to God, is not faith, but presumption. "By grace are ye saved through faith." But "faith, if it hath not works, is dead" (Ephesians 2:8; James 2:17). Jesus said of Himself before He came to earth, "I delight to do Thy will, O My God: yea, Thy law is within My heart" (Psalm 40:8). And just before He ascended again to heaven He declared, "I have kept My Father's commandments, and abide in His love" (John 15:10). The Scripture says, "Hereby we do know that we know Him, if we keep His commandments. ... He that saith he abideth in Him ought himself also so to walk even as He walked" (1 John 2:3-6). "Because Christ also suffered for us, leaving us an example, that ye should follow His steps" (1 Peter 2:21).

The condition of eternal life is now just what it always has been,—just what it was in Paradise before the fall of our first parents,—perfect obedience to the law of God, perfect righteousness. If eternal life were granted on any condition short of this, then the happiness of the whole universe would be imperiled. The way would be open for sin, with all its train of woe and misery, to be immortalized.

It was possible for Adam, before the fall, to form a righteous character by obedience to God's law. But he failed to do this, and because of his sin our natures are fallen and we cannot make ourselves righteous. Since we are sinful, unholy, we cannot perfectly obey the holy law. We have no righteousness of our own with which to meet the claims of the law of God. But Christ has made a way of escape for us. He lived on earth amid trials and temptations such as we have to meet. He lived a sinless life. He died for us, and now He offers to take our sins and give us His righteousness. If you give yourself to Him, and accept Him as your Saviour, then, sinful as your life may have been, for His sake you are accounted righteous. Christ's character stands in place of your character, and you are accepted before God just as if you had not sinned.

More than this, Christ changes the heart. He abides in your heart by faith. You are to maintain this connection with Christ by faith and the continual surrender of your will to Him; and so long as you do this, He will work in you to will and to do according to His good pleasure. So you may say, "The life which I now live in the flesh I live by the faith of the Son of God, who loved me, and gave Himself for me" (Galatians 2:20). So Jesus said to His disciples, "It is not ye that speak, but the Spirit of your Father which speaketh in you" (Matthew 10:20). Then with Christ working in you, you will manifest the same spirit and do the same good works—works of righteousness, obedience.

So we have nothing in ourselves of which to boast. We have no ground for self-exaltation. Our only ground of hope is in the righteousness of Christ imputed to us, and in that wrought by His Spirit working in and through us.

When we speak of faith, there is a distinction that should be borne in mind. There is a kind of belief that is wholly distinct from faith. The existence and power of God, the truth of His word, are facts that even Satan and his hosts cannot at heart deny. The Bible says that "the devils also believe, and tremble;" but this is not faith (James 2:19). Where there is not only a belief in God's word, but a submission of the will to Him; where the heart is yielded to Him, the affections fixed upon Him, there is faith—faith that works by love and purifies the soul. Through this faith the heart is renewed in the image of God. And the heart that in its unrenewed state is not subject to the law of God, neither indeed can be, now delights in its holy precepts, exclaiming with the psalmist, "O how love I Thy law! it is my meditation all the day" (Psalm 119:97). And the righteousness of the law is fulfilled in us, "who walk not after the flesh, but after the Spirit" (Romans 8:1).

There are those who have known the pardoning love of Christ and who really desire to be children of God, yet they realize that their character is imperfect, their life faulty, and they are ready to doubt whether their hearts have been renewed by the Holy Spirit. To such I would say, Do not draw back in despair. We shall often have to bow down and weep at the feet of Jesus because of our shortcomings and mistakes, but we are not to be discouraged. Even if we are overcome by the enemy, we are not cast off, not forsaken and rejected of God. No; Christ is at the right hand of God, who also maketh intercession for us. Said the beloved John, "These things write I unto you, that ye sin not. And if any man sin, we have an advocate with the Father, Jesus Christ the righteous" (1 John 2:1). And do not forget the words of Christ, "The Father Himself loveth you" (John 16:27). He desires to restore you to Himself, to see His own purity and holiness reflected in you. And if you will but yield yourself to Him, He that hath begun a good work in you will carry it forward to the day of Jesus Christ. Pray more fervently; believe more fully. As we come to distrust our own power, let us trust the power of our Redeemer, and we shall praise Him who is the health of our countenance.

The closer you come to Jesus, the more faulty you will appear in your own eyes; for your vision will be clearer, and your imperfections will be seen in broad and distinct contrast to His perfect nature. This is evidence that Satan's delusions have lost their power; that the vivifying influence of the Spirit of God is arousing you.

No deep-seated love for Jesus can dwell in the heart that does not realize its own sinfulness. The soul that is transformed by the grace of Christ will admire His divine character; but if we do not see our own moral deformity, it is unmistakable evidence that we have not had a view of the beauty and excellence of Christ.

The less we see to esteem in ourselves, the more we shall see to esteem in the infinite purity and loveliness of our Saviour. A view of our sinfulness drives us to Him who can pardon; and when the soul, realizing its helplessness, reaches out after Christ, He will reveal Himself in power. The more our sense of need drives us to Him and to the word of God, the more exalted views we shall have of His character, and the more fully we shall reflect His image.

8 Growing Up into Christ

The change of heart by which we become children of God is in the Bible spoken of as birth. Again, it is compared to the germination of the good seed sown by the husbandman. In like manner those who are just converted to Christ are, "as new-born babes," to "grow up" to the stature of men and women in Christ Jesus (1 Peter 2:2; Ephesians 4:15). Or like the good seed sown in the field, they are to grow up and bring forth fruit. Isaiah says that they shall "be called trees of righteousness, the planting of the Lord, that He might be glorified" (Isaiah 61:3). So from natural life, illustrations are drawn, to help us better to understand the mysterious truths of spiritual life.

Not all the wisdom and skill of man can produce life in the smallest object in nature. It is only through the life which God Himself has imparted, that either plant or animal can live. So it is only through the life from God that spiritual life is begotten in the hearts of men. Unless a man is "born from above," he cannot become a partaker of the life which Christ came to give (John 3:3, margin).

As with life, so it is with growth. It is God who brings the bud to bloom and the flower to fruit. It is by His power that the seed develops, "first the blade, then the ear, after that the full corn in the ear" (Mark 4:28). And the prophet Hosea says of Israel, that "he shall grow as the lily." "They shall revive as the corn, and grow as the vine" (Hosea 14:5, 7). And Jesus bids us "consider the lilies how they grow" (Luke 12:27). The plants and flowers grow not by their own care or anxiety or effort, but by receiving that which God has furnished to minister to their life. The child cannot, by any anxiety or power of its own, add to its stature. No more can you, by anxiety or effort of yourself, secure spiritual growth. The plant, the child, grows by receiving from its surroundings that which ministers to its life—air, sunshine, and food. What these gifts of nature are to animal and plant, such is Christ to those who trust in Him. He is their "everlasting light," "a sun and shield" (Isaiah 60:19; Psalm 84:11). He shall be as "the dew unto Israel." "He shall come down like rain upon the mown grass" (Hosea 14:5; Psalm 72:6). He is the living water, "the Bread of God ... which cometh down from heaven, and giveth life unto the world" (John 6:33).

In the matchless gift of His Son, God has encircled the whole world with an atmosphere of grace as real as the air which circulates around the globe. All who choose to breathe this life-giving atmosphere will live and grow up to the stature of men and women in Christ Jesus.

As the flower turns to the sun, that the bright beams may aid in perfecting its beauty and symmetry, so should we turn to the Sun of Righteousness, that heaven's light may shine upon us, that our character may be developed into the likeness of Christ.

Jesus teaches the same thing when He says, "Abide in Me, and I in you. As the branch cannot bear fruit of itself, except it abide in the vine; no more can ye, except ye abide in Me. ... Without Me ye can do nothing" (John 15:4, 5). You are just as dependent upon Christ, in order to live a holy life, as is the branch upon the parent stock for growth and fruitfulness. Apart from Him you have no life. You have no power to resist temptation or to grow in grace and holiness. Abiding in Him, you may flourish. Drawing your life from Him, you will not wither nor be fruitless. You will be like a tree planted by the rivers of water.

Many have an idea that they must do some part of the work alone. They have trusted in Christ for the forgiveness of sin, but now they seek by their own efforts to live aright. But every such effort must fail. Jesus says, "Without Me ye can do nothing." Our growth in grace, our joy, our usefulness,—all depend upon our union with Christ. It is by communion with Him, daily, hourly,—by abiding in Him,—that we are to grow in grace. He is not only the Author, but the Finisher of our faith. It is Christ first and last and always. He is to be with us, not only at the beginning and the end of our course, but at every step of the way. David says, "I have set the Lord always before me: because He is at my right hand, I shall not be moved" (Psalm 16:8).

Do you ask, "How am I to abide in Christ?" In the same way as you received Him at first. "As ye have therefore received Christ Jesus the Lord, so walk ye in Him." "The just shall live by faith" (Colossians 2:6; Hebrews 10:38). You gave yourself to God, to be His wholly, to serve and obey Him, and you took Christ as your Saviour. You could not yourself atone for your sins or change your heart; but having given yourself to God, you believe that He for Christ's sake did all this for you. By *faith* you became Christ's, and by faith you are to grow up in Him—by giving and taking. You are to *give* all,—your heart, your will, your service,—give yourself to Him to obey all His requirements; and you must *take* all,—Christ, the fullness of all blessing, to abide in your heart, to be your strength, your righteousness, your everlasting helper,—to give you power to obey.

Consecrate yourself to God in the morning; make this your very first work. Let your prayer be, "Take me, O Lord, as wholly Thine. I lay all my plans at Thy feet. Use me today in Thy service. Abide with me, and let all my work be wrought in Thee." This is a daily matter. Each morning consecrate yourself to God for that day. Surrender all your plans to Him, to be carried out or given up as His providence shall indicate. Thus day by day you may be giving your life into the hands of God, and thus your life will be molded more and more after the life of Christ.

A life in Christ is a life of restfulness. There may be no ecstasy of feeling, but there should be an abiding, peaceful trust. Your hope is not in yourself; it is in Christ. Your weakness is united to His strength, your ignorance to His wisdom, your frailty to His enduring might. So you are not to look to yourself, not to let the mind dwell upon self, but look to Christ. Let the mind dwell upon His love, upon the beauty, the perfection, of His character. Christ in His self-denial, Christ in His humiliation, Christ in His purity and holiness, Christ in His matchless love—this is the subject for the soul's contemplation. It is by loving Him, copying Him, depending wholly upon Him, that you are to be transformed into His likeness.

Jesus says, "Abide in Me." These words convey the idea of rest, stability, confidence. Again He invites, "Come unto Me, ... and I will give you rest" (Matthew 11:28). The words of the psalmist express the same thought: "Rest in the Lord, and wait patiently for Him." And Isaiah gives the assurance, "In quietness and in confidence shall be your strength" (Psalm 37:7; Isaiah 30:15). This rest is not found in inactivity; for in the Saviour's invitation the promise of rest is united with the call to labor: "Take My yoke upon you: ... and ye shall find rest" (Matthew 11:29). The heart that rests most fully upon Christ will be most earnest and active in labor for Him.

When the mind dwells upon self, it is turned away from Christ, the source of strength and life. Hence it is Satan's constant effort to keep the attention diverted from the Saviour and thus prevent the union and communion of the soul with Christ. The pleasures of the world, life's cares and perplexities and sorrows, the faults of others, or your own faults and imperfections—to any or all of these he will seek to divert the mind. Do not be misled by his devices. Many who are really conscientious, and who desire to live for God, he too often leads to dwell upon their own faults and weaknesses, and thus by separating them from Christ he hopes to gain the victory. We should not make self the center and indulge anxiety and fear as to whether we shall be saved. All this turns the soul away from the Source of our strength. Commit the keeping of your soul to God, and trust in Him. Talk and think of Jesus. Let self be lost in Him. Put away all doubt; dismiss your fears. Say with the apostle Paul, "I live; yet not I, but Christ liveth in me: and the life which I now live in the flesh I live by the faith of the Son of God, who loved me, and gave Himself for me" (Galatians 2:20). Rest in God. He is able to keep that which you have committed to Him. If you will leave yourself in His hands, He will bring you off more than conqueror through Him that has loved you.

When Christ took human nature upon Him, He bound humanity to Himself by a tie of love that can never be broken by any power save the choice of man himself. Satan will constantly present allurements to induce us to break this tie—to choose to separate ourselves from Christ. Here is where we need to watch, to strive, to pray, that nothing may entice us to *choose* another master; for we are always free to do this. But let us keep our eyes fixed upon Christ, and He will preserve us. Looking unto Jesus, we are safe. Nothing can pluck us out of His hand. In constantly beholding Him, we "are changed into the same image from glory to glory, even as by the Spirit of the Lord" (2 Corinthians 3:18).

It was thus that the early disciples gained their likeness to the dear Saviour. When those disciples heard the words of Jesus, they felt their need of Him. They sought, they found, they followed Him. They were with Him in the house, at the table, in the closet, in the field. They were with Him as pupils with a teacher, daily receiving from His lips lessons of holy truth. They looked to Him, as servants to their master, to learn their duty. Those disciples were men "subject to like passions as we are" (James 5:17). They had the same battle with sin to fight. They needed the same grace, in order to live a holy life.

Even John, the beloved disciple, the one who most fully reflected the likeness of the Saviour, did not naturally possess that loveliness of character. He was not only self-assertive and ambitious for honor, but impetuous, and resentful under injuries. But as the character of the Divine One was manifested to him, he saw his own deficiency and was humbled by the knowledge. The strength and patience, the power and tenderness, the majesty and meekness, that he beheld in the daily life of the Son of God, filled his soul with admiration and love. Day by day his heart was drawn out toward Christ, until he lost sight of self in love for his Master. His resentful, ambitious temper was yielded to the molding power of Christ. The regenerating influence of the Holy Spirit renewed his heart. The power of the love of Christ wrought a transformation of character. This is the sure result of union with Jesus. When Christ abides in the heart, the whole nature is transformed. Christ's Spirit, His love, softens the heart, subdues the soul, and raises the thoughts and desires toward God and heaven.

When Christ ascended to heaven, the sense of His presence was still with His followers. It was a personal presence, full of love and light. Jesus, the Saviour, who had walked and talked and prayed with them, who had spoken hope and comfort to their hearts, had, while the message of peace was still upon His lips, been taken up from them into heaven, and the tones of His voice had come back to them, as the cloud of angels received Him—"Lo, I am with you alway, even unto the end of the world" (Matthew 28:20). He had ascended to heaven in the form of humanity. They knew that He was before the throne of God, their Friend and Saviour still; that His sympathies were unchanged; that He was still identified with suffering humanity. He was presenting before God the merits of His own precious blood, showing His wounded hands and feet, in remembrance of the price He had paid for His redeemed. They knew that He had ascended to heaven to prepare places for them, and that He would come again and take them to Himself.

As they met together after the ascension they were eager to present their requests to the Father in the name of Jesus. In solemn awe they bowed in prayer, repeating the assurance, "Whatsoever ye shall ask the Father in My name, He will give it you. Hitherto have ye asked nothing in My name: ask, and ye shall receive, that your joy may be full" (John 16:23, 24). They extended the hand of faith higher and higher with the mighty argument, "It is Christ that died, yea rather, that is risen again, who is even at the right hand of God, who also maketh intercession for us" (Romans 8:34). And Pentecost brought them the presence of the Comforter, of whom Christ had said, He "shall be in you." And He had further said, "It is expedient for you that I go away: for if I go not away, the Comforter will not come unto you; but if I depart, I will send Him unto you"

(John 14:17; 16:7). Henceforth through the Spirit, Christ was to abide continually in the hearts of His children. Their union with Him was closer than when He was personally with them. The light, and love, and power of the indwelling Christ shone out through them, so that men, beholding, "marveled; and they took knowledge of them, that they had been with Jesus" (Acts 4:13).

All that Christ was to the disciples, He desires to be to His children today; for in that last prayer, with the little band of disciples gathered about Him, He said, "Neither pray I for these alone, but for them also which shall believe on Me through their word" (John 17:20).

Jesus prayed for us, and He asked that we might be one with Him, even as He is one with the Father. What a union is this! The Saviour has said of Himself, "The Son can do nothing of Himself;" "the Father that dwelleth in Me, He doeth the works" (John 5:19; 14:10). Then if Christ is dwelling in our hearts, He will work in us "both to will and to do of His good pleasure" Philippians 2:13. We shall work as He worked; we shall manifest the same spirit. And thus, loving Him and abiding in Him, we shall "grow up into Him in all things, which is the head, even Christ" (Ephesians 4:15).

9 The Work and the Life

God is the source of life and light and joy to the universe. Like rays of light from the sun, like the streams of water bursting from a living spring, blessings flow out from Him to all His creatures. And wherever the life of God is in the hearts of men, it will flow out to others in love and blessing.

Our Saviour's joy was in the uplifting and redemption of fallen men. For this He counted not His life dear unto Himself, but endured the cross, despising the shame. So angels are ever engaged in working for the happiness of others. This is their joy. That which selfish hearts would regard as humiliating service, ministering to those who are wretched and in every way inferior in character and rank, is the work of sinless angels. The spirit of Christ's self-sacrificing love is the spirit that pervades heaven and is the very essence of its bliss. This is the spirit that Christ's followers will possess, the work that they will do.

When the love of Christ is enshrined in the heart, like sweet fragrance it cannot be hidden. Its holy influence will be felt by all with whom we come in contact. The spirit of Christ in the heart is like a spring in the desert, flowing to refresh all and making those who are ready to perish, eager to drink of the water of life.

Love to Jesus will be manifested in a desire to work as He worked for the blessing and uplifting of humanity. It will lead to love, tenderness, and sympathy toward all the creatures of our heavenly Father's care.

The Saviour's life on earth was not a life of ease and devotion to Himself, but He toiled with persistent, earnest, untiring effort for the salvation of lost mankind. From the manger to Calvary He followed the path of self-denial and sought not to be released from arduous tasks, painful travels and exhausting care and labor. He said, "The Son of man came not to be ministered unto, but to minister, and to give His life a ransom for many" (Matthew 20:28). This was the one great object of His life. Everything else was secondary and subservient. It was His meat and drink to do the will of God and to finish His work. Self and self-interest had no part in His labor.

So those who are the partakers of the grace of Christ will be ready to make any sacrifice, that others for whom He died may share the heavenly gift. They will do all they can to make the world better for their stay in it. This spirit is the sure outgrowth of a soul truly converted. No sooner does one come to Christ than there is born in his heart a desire to make known to others what a precious friend he has found in Jesus; the saving and sanctifying truth cannot be shut up in his heart. If we are clothed with the righteousness of Christ and are filled with the joy of His indwelling Spirit, we shall not be able to hold our peace. If we have tasted and seen that the Lord is good we shall have something to tell. Like Philip when he found the Saviour, we shall invite others into His presence. We shall seek to present to them the attractions of Christ and the unseen realities of the world to come. There will be an intensity of desire to follow in the path that Jesus trod. There will be an earnest longing that those around us may "behold the Lamb of God, which taketh away the sin of the world" (John 1:29).

And the effort to bless others will react in blessings upon ourselves. This was the purpose of God in giving us a part to act in the plan of redemption. He has granted men the privilege of becoming partakers of the divine nature and, in their turn, of diffusing blessings to their fellow men. This is the highest honor, the greatest joy, that it is possible for God to bestow upon men. Those who thus become participants in labors of love are brought nearest to their Creator.

God might have committed the message of the gospel, and all the work of loving ministry, to the heavenly angels. He might have employed other means for accomplishing His purpose. But in His infinite love He chose to make us co-workers with Himself, with Christ and the angels, that we might share the blessing, the joy, the spiritual uplifting, which results from this unselfish ministry.

We are brought into sympathy with Christ through the fellowship of His sufferings. Every act of self-sacrifice for the good of others strengthens the spirit of beneficence in the giver's heart, allying him more closely to the Redeemer of the world, who "was rich, yet for your sakes ... became poor, that ye through His poverty might be rich" (2 Corinthians 8:9). And it is only as we thus fulfill the divine purpose in our creation that life can be a blessing to us.

If you will go to work as Christ designs that His disciples shall, and win souls for Him, you will feel the need of a deeper experience and a greater knowledge in divine things, and will hunger and thirst after righteousness. You will plead with God, and your faith will be strengthened, and your soul will drink deeper drafts at the well of salvation. Encountering opposition and trials will drive you to the Bible and prayer. You will grow in grace and the knowledge of Christ, and will develop a rich experience.

The spirit of unselfish labor for others gives depth, stability, and Christlike loveliness to the character, and brings peace and happiness to its possessor. The aspirations are elevated. There is no room for sloth or selfishness. Those who thus exercise the Christian graces will grow and will become strong to work for God. They will have clear spiritual perceptions, a steady, growing faith, and an increased power in prayer. The Spirit of God, moving upon their spirit, calls forth the sacred harmonies of the soul in answer to the divine touch. Those who thus devote themselves to unselfish effort for the good of others are most surely working out their own salvation.

The only way to grow in grace is to be disinterestedly doing the very work which Christ has enjoined upon us—to engage, to the extent of our ability, in helping and blessing those who need the help we can give them. Strength comes by exercise; activity is the very condition of life. Those who endeavor to maintain Christian life by passively accepting the blessings that come through the means of grace, and doing nothing for Christ, are simply trying to live by eating without working. And in the spiritual as in the natural world, this always results in degeneration and decay. A man who would refuse to exercise his limbs would soon lose all power to use them. Thus the Christian who will not exercise his God-given powers not only fails to grow up into Christ, but he loses the strength that he already had.

The church of Christ is God's appointed agency for the salvation of men. Its mission is to carry the gospel to the world. And the obligation rests upon all Christians. Everyone, to the extent of his talent and opportunity, is to fulfill the Saviour's commission. The love of Christ, revealed to us, makes us debtors to all who know Him not. God has given us light, not for ourselves alone, but to shed upon them.

If the followers of Christ were awake to duty, there would be thousands where there is one today proclaiming the gospel in heathen lands. And all who could not personally engage in the work, would yet sustain it with their means, their sympathy, and their prayers. And there would be far more earnest labor for souls in Christian countries.

We need not go to heathen lands, or even leave the narrow circle of the home, if it is there that our duty lies, in order to work for Christ. We can do this in the home circle, in the church, among those with whom we associate, and with whom we do business.

The greater part of our Saviour's life on earth was spent in patient toil in the carpenter's shop at Nazareth. Ministering angels attended the Lord of life as He walked side by side with peasants and laborers, unrecognized and unhonored. He was as faithfully fulfilling His mission while working at His humble trade as when He healed the sick or walked upon the storm-tossed waves of Galilee. So in the humblest duties and lowliest positions of life, we may walk and work with Jesus.

The apostle says, "Let every man, wherein he is called, therein abide with God" (1 Corinthians 7:24). The businessman may conduct his business in a way that will glorify his Master because of his fidelity. If he is a true follower of Christ he will carry his religion into everything that is done and reveal to men the spirit of Christ. The mechanic may be a diligent and faithful representative of Him who toiled in the lowly walks of life among the hills of Galilee. Everyone who names the name of Christ should so work that others, by seeing his good works, may be led to glorify their Creator and Redeemer.

Many have excused themselves from rendering their gifts to the service of Christ because others were possessed of superior endowments and advantages. The opinion has prevailed that only those who are especially talented are required to consecrate their abilities to the service of God. It has come to be understood by many that talents are given to only a certain favored class to the exclusion of others who of course are not called upon to share in the toils or the rewards. But it is not so represented in the parable. When the master of the house called his servants, he gave to every man *his* work.

With a loving spirit we may perform life's humblest duties "as to the Lord" (Colossians 3:23). If the love of God is in the heart, it will be manifested in the life. The sweet savor of Christ will surround us, and our influence will elevate and bless.

You are not to wait for great occasions or to expect extraordinary abilities before you go to work for God. You need not have a thought of what the world will think of you. If your daily life is a testimony to the purity and sincerity of your faith, and others are convinced that you desire to benefit them, your efforts will not be wholly lost.

The humblest and poorest of the disciples of Jesus can be a blessing to others. They may not realize that they are doing any special good, but by their unconscious influence they may start waves of blessing that will widen and deepen, and the blessed results they may never know until the day of final reward. They do not feel or know that they are doing anything great. They are not required to weary themselves with anxiety about success. They have only to go forward quietly, doing faithfully the work that God's providence assigns, and their life will not be in vain. Their own souls will be growing more and more into the likeness of Christ; they are workers together with God in this life and are thus fitting for the higher work and the unshadowed joy of the life to come.

10 A Knowledge of God

Many are the ways in which God is seeking to make Himself known to us and bring us into communion with Him. Nature speaks to our senses without ceasing. The open heart will be impressed with the love and glory of God as revealed through the works of His hands. The listening ear can hear and understand the communications of God through the things of nature. The green fields, the lofty trees, the buds and flowers, the passing cloud, the falling rain, the babbling brook, the glories of the heavens, speak to our hearts, and invite us to become acquainted with Him who made them all.

Our Saviour bound up His precious lessons with the things of nature. The trees, the birds, the flowers of the valleys, the hills, the lakes, and the beautiful heavens, as well as the incidents and surroundings of daily life, were all linked with the words of truth, that His lessons might thus be often recalled to mind, even amid the busy cares of man's life of toil.

God would have His children appreciate His works and delight in the simple, quiet beauty with which He has adorned our earthly home. He is a lover of the beautiful, and above all that is outwardly attractive He loves beauty of character; He would have us cultivate purity and simplicity, the quiet graces of the flowers.

If we will but listen, God's created works will teach us precious lessons of obedience and trust. From the stars that in their trackless courses through space follow from age to age their appointed path, down to the minutest atom, the things of nature obey the Creator's will. And God cares for everything and sustains everything that He has created. He who upholds the unnumbered worlds throughout immensity, at the same time cares for the wants of the little brown sparrow that sings its humble song without fear. When men go forth to their daily toil, as when they engage in prayer; when they lie down at night, and when they rise in the morning; when the rich man feasts in his palace, or when the poor man gathers his children about the scanty board, each is tenderly watched by the heavenly Father. No tears are shed that God does not notice. There is no smile that He does not mark.

If we would but fully believe this, all undue anxieties would be dismissed. Our lives would not be so filled with disappointment as now; for everything, whether great or small, would be left in the hands of God, who is not perplexed by the multiplicity of cares, or overwhelmed by their weight. We should then enjoy a rest of soul to which many have long been strangers.

As your senses delight in the attractive loveliness of the earth, think of the world that is to come, that shall never know the blight of sin and death; where the face of nature will no more wear the shadow of the curse. Let your imagination picture the home of the saved, and remember that it will be more glorious than your brightest imagination can portray. In the varied gifts of God in nature we see but the faintest gleaming of His glory. It is written, "Eye hath not seen, nor ear heard, neither have entered into the heart of man, the things which God hath prepared for them that love Him" (1 Corinthians 2:9).

The poet and the naturalist have many things to say about nature, but it is the Christian who enjoys the beauty of the earth with the highest appreciation, because he recognizes his Father's handiwork and perceives His love in flower and shrub and tree. No one can fully appreciate the significance of hill and vale, river and sea, who does not look upon them as an expression of God's love to man.

God speaks to us through His providential workings and through the influence of His Spirit upon the heart. In our circumstances and surroundings, in the changes daily taking place around us, we may find precious lessons if our hearts are but open to discern them. The psalmist, tracing the work of God's providence, says, "The earth is full of the goodness of the Lord." "Whoso is wise, and will observe these things, even they shall understand the loving-kindness of the Lord" (Psalm 33:5; 107:43).

God speaks to us in His word. Here we have in clearer lines the revelation of His character, of His dealings with men, and the great work of redemption. Here is open before us the history of patriarchs and prophets and other holy men of old. They were men "subject to like passions as we are" (James 5:17). We see how they struggled through discouragements like our own, how they fell under temptation as we have done, and yet took heart again and conquered through the grace of God; and, beholding, we are encouraged in our striving after righteousness. As we read of the precious experiences granted them, of the light and love and blessing it was theirs to enjoy, and of the work they wrought through the grace given them, the spirit that inspired them kindles a flame of holy emulation in our hearts and a desire to be like them in character—like them to walk with God.

Jesus said of the Old Testament Scriptures,—and how much more is it true of the New,—"They are they which testify of Me," the Redeemer, Him in whom our hopes of eternal life are centered (John 5:39). Yes, the whole Bible tells of Christ. From the first record of creation—for "without Him was not anything made that was made"—to the closing promise, "Behold, I come quickly," we are reading of His works and listening to His voice (John 1:3; Revelation 22:12). If you would become acquainted with the Saviour, study the Holy Scriptures.

Fill the whole heart with the words of God. They are the living water, quenching your burning thirst. They are the living bread from heaven. Jesus declares, "Except ye eat the flesh of the Son of man, and drink His blood, ye have no life in you." And He explains Himself by saying, "The words that I speak unto you, they are spirit, and they are life" (John 6:53, 63). Our bodies are built up from what we eat and drink; and as in the natural economy, so in the spiritual economy: it is what we meditate upon that will give tone and strength to our spiritual nature.

The theme of redemption is one that the angels desire to look into; it will be the science and the song of the redeemed throughout the ceaseless ages of eternity. Is it not worthy of careful thought and study now? The infinite mercy and love of Jesus, the sacrifice made in our behalf, call for the most serious and solemn reflection. We should dwell upon the character of our dear Redeemer and Intercessor. We should meditate upon the mission of Him who came to save His people from their sins. As we thus contemplate heavenly themes, our faith and love will grow stronger, and our prayers will be more and more acceptable to God, because they will be more and more mixed with faith and love. They will be intelligent and fervent. There will be more constant confidence in Jesus, and a daily, living experience in His power to save to the uttermost all that come unto God by Him.

As we meditate upon the perfections of the Saviour, we shall desire to be wholly transformed and renewed in the image of His purity. There will be a hungering and thirsting of soul to become like Him whom we adore. The more our thoughts are upon Christ, the more we shall speak of Him to others and represent Him to the world.

The Bible was not written for the scholar alone; on the contrary, it was designed for the common people. The great truths necessary for salvation are made as clear as noonday; and none will mistake and lose their way except those who follow their own judgment instead of the plainly revealed will of God.

We should not take the testimony of any man as to what the Scriptures teach, but should study the words of God for ourselves. If we allow others to do our thinking, we shall have crippled energies and contracted abilities. The noble powers of the mind may be so dwarfed by lack of exercise on themes worthy of their concentration as to lose their ability to grasp the deep meaning of the word of God. The mind will enlarge if it is employed in tracing out the relation of the subjects of the Bible, comparing scripture with scripture and spiritual things with spiritual.

There is nothing more calculated to strengthen the intellect than the study of the Scriptures. No other book is so potent to elevate the thoughts, to give vigor to the faculties, as the broad, ennobling truths of the Bible. If God's word were studied as it should be, men would have a breadth of mind, a nobility of character, and a stability of purpose rarely seen in these times.

But there is but little benefit derived from a hasty reading of the Scriptures. One may read the whole Bible through and yet fail to see its beauty or comprehend its deep and hidden meaning. One passage studied until its significance is clear to the mind and its relation to the plan of salvation is evident, is of more value than the perusal of many chapters with no definite purpose in view and no positive instruction gained. Keep your Bible with you. As you have opportunity, read it; fix the texts in your memory. Even while you are walking the streets you may read a passage and meditate upon it, thus fixing it in the mind.

We cannot obtain wisdom without earnest attention and prayerful study. Some portions of Scripture are indeed too plain to be misunderstood, but there are others whose meaning does not lie on the surface to be seen at a glance. Scripture must be compared with scripture. There must be careful research and prayerful reflection. And such study will be richly repaid. As the miner discovers veins of precious metal concealed beneath the surface of the earth, so will he who perseveringly searches the word of God as for hid treasure find truths of the greatest value, which are concealed from the view of the careless seeker. The words of inspiration, pondered in the heart, will be as streams flowing from the fountain of life.

Never should the Bible be studied without prayer. Before opening its pages we should ask for the enlightenment of the Holy Spirit, and it will be given. When Nathanael came to Jesus, the Saviour exclaimed, "Behold an Israelite indeed, in whom is no guile!" Nathanael said, "Whence knowest Thou me?" Jesus answered, "Before that Philip called thee, when thou wast under the fig tree, I saw thee" (John 1:47, 48). And Jesus will see us also in the secret places of prayer if we will seek Him for light that we may know what is truth. Angels from the world of light will be with those who in humility of heart seek for divine guidance.

The Holy Spirit exalts and glorifies the Saviour. It is His office to present Christ, the purity of His righteousness, and the great salvation that we have through Him. Jesus says, "He shall receive of Mine, and shall show it unto you" (John 16:14). The Spirit of truth is the only effectual teacher of divine truth. How must God esteem the human race, since He gave His Son to die for them and appoints His Spirit to be man's teacher and continual guide!

11 The Privilege of Prayer

Through nature and revelation, through His providence, and by the influence of His Spirit, God speaks to us. But these are not enough; we need also to pour out our hearts to Him. In order to have spiritual life and energy, we must have actual intercourse with our heavenly Father. Our minds may be drawn out toward Him; we may meditate upon His works, His mercies, His blessings; but this is not, in the fullest sense, communing with Him. In order to commune with God, we must have something to say to Him concerning our actual life.

Prayer is the opening of the heart to God as to a friend. Not that it is necessary in order to make known to God what we are, but in order to enable us to receive Him. Prayer does not bring God down to us, but brings us up to Him.

When Jesus was upon the earth, He taught His disciples how to pray. He directed them to present their daily needs before God, and to cast all their care upon Him. And the assurance He gave them that their petitions should be heard, is assurance also to us.

Jesus Himself, while He dwelt among men, was often in prayer. Our Saviour identified Himself with our needs and weakness, in that He became a suppliant, a petitioner, seeking from His Father fresh supplies of strength, that He might come forth braced for duty and trial. He is our example in all things. He is a brother in our infirmities, "in all points tempted like as we are;" but as the sinless one His nature recoiled from evil; He endured struggles and torture of soul in a world of sin. His humanity made prayer a necessity and a privilege. He found comfort and joy in communion with His Father. And if the Saviour of men, the Son of God, felt the need of prayer, how much more should feeble, sinful mortals feel the necessity of fervent, constant prayer.

Our heavenly Father waits to bestow upon us the fullness of His blessing. It is our privilege to drink largely at the fountain of boundless love. What a wonder it is that we pray so little! God is ready and willing to hear the sincere prayer of the humblest of His children, and yet there is much manifest reluctance on our part to make known our wants to God. What can the angels of heaven think of poor helpless human beings, who are subject to temptation, when God's heart of infinite love yearns toward them, ready to give them more than they can ask or think, and yet they pray so little and have so little faith? The angels love to bow before God; they love to be near Him. They regard communion with God as their highest joy; and yet the children of earth, who need so much the help that God only can give, seem satisfied to walk without the light of His Spirit, the companionship of His presence.

The darkness of the evil one encloses those who neglect to pray. The whispered temptations of the enemy entice them to sin; and it is all because they do not make use of the privileges that God has given them in the divine

The Privilege of Prayer

appointment of prayer. Why should the sons and daughters of God be reluctant to pray, when prayer is the key in the hand of faith to unlock heaven's storehouse, where are treasured the boundless resources of Omnipotence? Without unceasing prayer and diligent watching we are in danger of growing careless and of deviating from the right path. The adversary seeks continually to obstruct the way to the mercy seat, that we may not by earnest supplication and faith obtain grace and power to resist temptation.

There are certain conditions upon which we may expect that God will hear and answer our prayers. One of the first of these is that we feel our need of help from Him. He has promised, "I will pour water upon him that is thirsty, and floods upon the dry ground" (Isaiah 44:3). Those who hunger and thirst after righteousness, who long after God, may be sure that they will be filled. The heart must be open to the Spirit's influence, or God's blessing cannot be received.

Our great need is itself an argument and pleads most eloquently in our behalf. But the Lord is to be sought unto to do these things for us. He says, "Ask, and it shall be given you." And "He that spared not His own Son, but delivered Him up for us all, how shall He not with Him also freely give us all things?" (Matthew 7:7; Romans 8:32).

If we regard iniquity in our hearts, if we cling to any known sin, the Lord will not hear us; but the prayer of the penitent, contrite soul is always accepted. When all known wrongs are righted, we may believe that God will answer our petitions. Our own merit will never commend us to the favor of God; it is the worthiness of Jesus that will save us, His blood that will cleanse us; yet we have a work to do in complying with the conditions of acceptance.

Another element of prevailing prayer is faith. "He that cometh to God must believe that He is, and that He is a rewarder of them that diligently seek Him" (Hebrews 11:6). Jesus said to His disciples, "What things soever ye desire, when ye pray, believe that ye receive them, and ye shall have them" (Mark 11:24). Do we take Him at His word?

The assurance is broad and unlimited, and He is faithful who has promised. When we do not receive the very things we asked for, at the time we ask, we are still to believe that the Lord hears and that He will answer our prayers. We are so erring and short-sighted that we sometimes ask for things that would not be a blessing to us, and our heavenly Father in love answers our prayers by giving us that which will be for our highest good—that which we ourselves would desire if with vision divinely enlightened we could see all things as they really are. When our prayers seem not to be answered, we are to cling to the promise; for the time of answering will surely come, and we shall receive the blessing we need most. But to claim that prayer will always be answered in the very way and for the particular thing that we desire, is presumption. God is too wise to err, and too good to withhold any good thing from them that walk uprightly. Then do not fear to trust Him, even though you do not see the immediate answer to your prayers. Rely upon His sure promise, "Ask, and it shall be given you."

If we take counsel with our doubts and fears, or try to solve everything that we cannot see clearly, before we have faith, perplexities will only increase and deepen. But if we come to God, feeling helpless and dependent, as we really are, and in humble, trusting faith make known our wants to Him whose knowledge is infinite, who sees everything in creation, and who governs everything by His will and word, He can and will attend to our cry, and will let light shine into our hearts. Through sincere prayer we are brought into connection with the mind of the Infinite. We may have no remarkable evidence at the time that the face of our Redeemer is bending over us in compassion and love, but this is even so. We may not feel His visible touch, but His hand is upon us in love and pitying tenderness.

When we come to ask mercy and blessing from God we should have a spirit of love and forgiveness in our own hearts. How can we pray, "Forgive us our debts, *as* we forgive our debtors," and yet indulge an unforgiving spirit (Matthew 6:12)? If we expect our own prayers to be heard we must forgive others in the same manner and to the same extent as we hope to be forgiven.

Perseverance in prayer has been made a condition of receiving. We must pray always if we would grow in faith and experience. We are to be "instant in prayer," to "continue in prayer, and watch in the same with thanksgiving" (Romans 12:12; Colossians 4:2). Peter exhorts believers to be "sober, and watch unto prayer" (1 Peter 4:7). Paul directs, "In everything by prayer and supplication with thanksgiving let your requests be made known unto God" (Philippians 4:6). "But ye, beloved," says Jude, "praying in the Holy Ghost, keep yourselves in the love of God" (Jude 20, 21). Unceasing prayer is the unbroken union of the soul with God, so that life from God flows into our life; and from our life, purity and holiness flow back to God.

There is necessity for diligence in prayer; let nothing hinder you. Make every effort to keep open the communion between Jesus and your own soul. Seek every opportunity to go where prayer is wont to be made. Those who are really seeking for communion with God will be seen in the prayer meeting, faithful to do their duty and earnest and anxious to reap all the benefits they can gain. They will improve every opportunity of placing themselves where they can receive the rays of light from heaven.

We should pray in the family circle, and above all we must not neglect secret prayer, for this is the life of the soul. It is impossible for the soul to flourish while prayer is neglected. Family or public prayer alone is not sufficient. In solitude let the soul be laid open to the inspecting eye of God. Secret prayer is to be heard only by the prayer-hearing God. No curious ear is to receive the burden of such petitions. In secret prayer the soul is free from surrounding influences, free from excitement. Calmly, yet fervently, will it reach out after God. Sweet and abiding will be the influence emanating from Him who seeth in secret, whose ear is open to hear the prayer arising from the heart. By calm, simple faith the soul holds communion with God and gathers to itself rays of divine light to strengthen and sustain it in the conflict with Satan. God is our tower of strength.

Pray in your closet, and as you go about your daily labor let your heart be often uplifted to God. It was thus that Enoch walked with God. These silent prayers rise like precious incense before the throne of grace. Satan cannot overcome him whose heart is thus stayed upon God.

There is no time or place in which it is inappropriate to offer up a petition to God. There is nothing that can prevent us from lifting up our hearts in the spirit of earnest prayer. In the crowds of the street, in the midst of a business engagement, we may send up a petition to God and plead for divine guidance, as did Nehemiah when he made his request before King Artaxerxes. A closet of communion may be found wherever we are. We should have the door of the heart open continually and our invitation going up that Jesus may come and abide as a heavenly guest in the soul.

Although there may be a tainted, corrupted atmosphere around us, we need not breathe its miasma, but may live in the pure air of heaven. We may close every door to impure imaginings and unholy thoughts by lifting the soul into the presence of God through sincere prayer. Those whose hearts are open to receive the support and blessing of God will walk in a holier atmosphere than that of earth and will have constant communion with heaven.

We need to have more distinct views of Jesus and a fuller comprehension of the value of eternal realities. The beauty of holiness is to fill the hearts of God's children; and that this may be accomplished, we should seek for divine disclosures of heavenly things.

Let the soul be drawn out and upward, that God may grant us a breath of the heavenly atmosphere. We may keep so near to God that in every unexpected trial our thoughts will turn to Him as naturally as the flower turns to the sun.

Keep your wants, your joys, your sorrows, your cares, and your fears before God. You cannot burden Him; you cannot weary Him. He who numbers the hairs of your head is not indifferent to the wants of His children. "The Lord is very pitiful, and of tender mercy" (James 5:11). His heart of love is touched by our sorrows and even by our utterances of them. Take to Him everything that perplexes the mind. Nothing is too great for Him to bear, for He holds up worlds, He rules over all the affairs of the universe. Nothing that in any way concerns our peace is too small for Him to notice. There is no chapter in our experience too dark for Him to read; there is no perplexity too difficult for Him to unravel. No calamity can befall the least of His children, no anxiety harass the soul, no joy cheer, no sincere prayer escape the lips, of which our heavenly Father is unobservant, or in which He takes no immediate interest. "He healeth the broken in heart, and bindeth up their wounds" (Psalm 147:3). The relations between God and each soul are as distinct and full as though there were not another soul upon the earth to share His watchcare, not another soul for whom He gave His beloved Son.

Jesus said, "Ye shall ask in My name: and I say not unto you, that I will pray the Father for you: for the Father Himself loveth you." "I have chosen you: ... that whatsoever ye shall ask of the Father in My name, He may give it you" (John 16:26, 27; 15:16). But to pray in the name of Jesus is something more than a mere mention of that name at the beginning and the ending of a prayer. It is to pray in the mind and spirit of Jesus, while we believe His promises, rely upon His grace, and work His works.

God does not mean that any of us should become hermits or monks and retire from the world in order to devote ourselves to acts of worship. The life must be like Christ's life—between the mountain and the multitude. He who does nothing but pray will soon cease to pray, or his prayers will become a formal routine. When men take themselves out of social life, away from the sphere of Christian duty and cross bearing; when they cease to work earnestly for the Master, who worked earnestly for them, they lose the subject matter of prayer and have no incentive to devotion. Their prayers become personal and selfish. They cannot pray in regard to the wants of humanity or the upbuilding of Christ's kingdom, pleading for strength wherewith to work.

We sustain a loss when we neglect the privilege of associating together to strengthen and encourage one another in the service of God. The truths of His word lose their vividness and importance in our minds. Our hearts cease to be enlightened and aroused by their sanctifying influence, and we decline in spirituality. In our association as Christians we lose much by lack of sympathy with one another. He who shuts himself up to himself is not filling the position that God designed he should. The proper cultivation of the social elements in our nature brings us into sympathy with others and is a means of development and strength to us in the service of God.

If Christians would associate together, speaking to each other of the love of God and of the precious truths of redemption, their own hearts would be refreshed and they would refresh one another. We may be daily learning more of our heavenly Father, gaining a fresh experience of His grace; then we shall desire to speak of His love; and as we do this, our own hearts will be warmed and encouraged. If we thought and talked more of Jesus, and less of self, we should have far more of His presence.

If we would but think of God as often as we have evidence of His care for us we should keep Him ever in our thoughts and should delight to talk of Him and to praise Him. We talk of temporal things because we have an interest in them. We talk of our friends because we love them; our joys and our sorrows are bound up with them. Yet we have infinitely greater reason to love God than to love our earthly friends; it should be the most natural thing in the world to make Him first in all our thoughts, to talk of His goodness and tell of His power. The rich gifts He has bestowed upon us were not intended to absorb our thoughts and love so much that we should have nothing to give to God; they are constantly to remind us of Him and to bind us in bonds of love and gratitude to our heavenly Benefactor. We dwell too near the lowlands of earth. Let us raise our eyes to the open door of the sanctuary above, where the light of the glory of God shines in the face of Christ, who "is able also to save them to the uttermost that come unto God by Him" (Hebrews 7:25).

We need to praise God more "for His goodness, and for His wonderful works to the children of men" (Psalm 107:8). Our devotional exercises should not consist wholly in asking and receiving. Let us not be always thinking of our wants and never of the benefits we receive. We do not pray any too much, but we are too sparing of giving thanks. We are the constant recipients of God's mercies, and yet how little gratitude we express, how little we praise Him for what He has done for us.

Anciently the Lord bade Israel, when they met together for His service, "Ye shall eat before the Lord your God, and ye shall rejoice in all that ye put your hand unto, ye and your households, wherein the Lord thy God hath blessed thee" (Deuteronomy 12:7). That which is done for the glory of God should be done with cheerfulness, with songs of praise and thanksgiving, not with sadness and gloom.

Our God is a tender, merciful Father. His service should not be looked upon as a heart-saddening, distressing exercise. It should be a pleasure to worship the Lord and to take part in His work. God would not have His children, for whom so great salvation has been provided, act as if He were a hard, exacting taskmaster. He is their best friend; and when they worship Him, He expects to be with them, to bless and comfort them, filling their hearts with joy and love. The Lord desires His children to take comfort in His service and to find more pleasure than hardship in His work. He desires that those who come to worship Him shall carry away with them precious thoughts of His care and love, that they may be cheered in all the employments of daily life, that they may have grace to deal honestly and faithfully in all things.

We must gather about the cross. Christ and Him crucified should be the theme of contemplation, of conversation, and of our most joyful emotion. We should keep in our thoughts every blessing we receive from God, and when we realize His great love we should be willing to trust everything to the hand that was nailed to the cross for us.

The soul may ascend nearer heaven on the wings of praise. God is worshiped with song and music in the courts above, and as we express our gratitude we are approximating to the worship of the heavenly hosts. "Whoso offereth praise glorifieth" God (Psalm 50:23). Let us with reverent joy come before our Creator, with "thanksgiving, and the voice of melody" (Isaiah 51:3).

12 What to Do with Doubt

Many, especially those who are young in the Christian life, are at times troubled with the suggestions of skepticism. There are in the Bible many things which they cannot explain, or even understand, and Satan employs these to shake their faith in the Scriptures as a revelation from God. They ask, "How shall I know the right way? If the Bible is indeed the word of God, how can I be freed from these doubts and perplexities?"

God never asks us to believe, without giving sufficient evidence upon which to base our faith. His existence, His character, the truthfulness of His word, are all established by testimony that appeals to our reason; and this testimony is abundant. Yet God has never removed the possibility of doubt. Our faith must rest upon evidence, not demonstration. Those who wish to doubt will have opportunity; while those who really desire to know the truth will find plenty of evidence on which to rest their faith.

It is impossible for finite minds fully to comprehend the character or the works of the Infinite One. To the keenest intellect, the most highly educated mind, that holy Being must ever remain clothed in mystery. "Canst thou by searching find out God? canst thou find out the Almighty unto perfection? It is as high as heaven; what canst thou do? deeper than hell; what canst thou know" (Job 11:7, 8)?

The apostle Paul exclaims, "O the depth of the riches both of the wisdom and knowledge of God! how unsearchable are His judgments, and His ways past finding out" (Romans 11:33)! But though "clouds and darkness are round about Him," "righteousness and judgment are the foundation of His throne" (Psalm 97:2 R.V.). We can so far comprehend His dealings with us, and the motives by which He is actuated, that we may discern boundless love and mercy united to infinite power. We can understand as much of His purposes as it is for our good to know; and beyond this we must still trust the hand that is omnipotent, the heart that is full of love.

The word of God, like the character of its divine Author, presents mysteries that can never be fully comprehended by finite beings. The entrance of sin into the world, the incarnation of Christ, regeneration, the resurrection, and many other subjects presented in the Bible, are mysteries too deep for the human mind to explain, or even fully to comprehend. But we have no reason to doubt God's word because we cannot understand the mysteries of His providence. In the natural world we are constantly surrounded with mysteries that we cannot fathom. The very humblest forms of life present a problem that the wisest of philosophers is powerless to explain. Everywhere are wonders beyond our ken. Should we then be surprised to find that in the spiritual world also there are mysteries that we cannot fathom? The difficulty lies solely in the weakness and narrowness of the human mind. God has given us in the Scriptures sufficient evidence of their divine character, and we are not to doubt His word because we cannot understand all the mysteries of His providence.

The apostle Peter says that there are in Scripture "things hard to be understood, which they that are unlearned and unstable wrest ... unto their own destruction" (2 Peter 3:16). The difficulties of Scripture have been urged by skeptics as an argument against the Bible; but so far from this, they constitute a strong evidence of its divine inspiration. If it contained no account of God but that which we could easily comprehend; if His greatness and majesty could be grasped by finite minds, then the Bible would not bear the unmistakable credentials of divine authority. The very grandeur and mystery of the themes presented should inspire faith in it as the word of God.

The Bible unfolds truth with a simplicity and a perfect adaptation to the needs and longings of the human heart, that has astonished and charmed the most highly cultivated minds, while it enables the humblest and uncultured to discern the way of salvation. And yet these simply stated truths lay hold upon subjects so elevated, so far-reaching, so infinitely beyond the power of human comprehension, that we can accept them only because God has declared them. Thus the plan of redemption is laid open to us, so that every soul may see the steps he is to take in repentance toward God and faith toward our Lord Jesus Christ, in order to be saved in God's appointed way; yet beneath these truths, so easily understood, lie mysteries that are the hiding of His glory—mysteries that overpower the mind in its research, yet inspire the sincere seeker for truth with reverence and faith. The more he searches the Bible, the deeper is his conviction that it is the word of the living God, and human reason bows before the majesty of divine revelation.

To acknowledge that we cannot fully comprehend the great truths of the Bible is only to admit that the finite mind is inadequate to grasp the infinite; that man, with his limited, human knowledge, cannot understand the purposes of Omniscience.

Because they cannot fathom all its mysteries, the skeptic and the infidel reject God's word; and not all who profess to believe the Bible are free from danger on this point. The apostle says, "Take heed, brethren, lest there be in any of you an evil heart of unbelief, in departing from the living God" (Hebrews 3:12). It is right to study closely the teachings of the Bible and to search into "the deep things of God" so far as they are revealed in Scripture (1 Corinthians 2:10). While "the secret things belong unto the Lord our God," "those things which are revealed belong unto us" (Deuteronomy 29:29). But it is Satan's work to pervert the investigative powers of the mind. A certain pride is mingled with the consideration of Bible truth, so that men feel impatient and defeated if they cannot explain every portion of Scripture to their satisfaction. It is too humiliating to them to acknowledge that they do not understand the inspired words. They are unwilling to wait patiently until God shall see fit to reveal the truth to them. They feel that their unaided human wisdom is sufficient to enable them to comprehend the Scripture, and failing to do this, they virtually deny its authority. It is true that many theories and doctrines popularly supposed to be derived from the Bible have no foundation in its teaching, and indeed are contrary to the whole tenor of inspiration. These things have been a cause of doubt and perplexity to many minds. They are not, however, chargeable to God's word, but to man's perversion of it.

If it were possible for created beings to attain to a full understanding of God and His works, then, having reached this point, there would be for them no further discovery of truth, no growth in knowledge, no further development of mind or heart. God would no longer be supreme; and man, having reached the limit of knowledge and attainment, would cease to advance. Let us thank God that it is not so. God is infinite; in Him are "all the treasures of wisdom and knowledge" (Colossians 2:3). And to all eternity men may be ever searching, ever learning, and yet never exhaust the treasures of His wisdom, His goodness, and His power.

God intends that even in this life the truths of His word shall be ever unfolding to His people. There is only one way in which this knowledge can be obtained. We can attain to an understanding of God's word only through the illumination of that Spirit by which the word was given. "The things of God knoweth no man, but the Spirit of God;" "for the Spirit searcheth all things, yea, the deep things of God" (1 Corinthians 2:11, 10). And the Saviour's promise to His followers was, "When He, the Spirit of truth, is come, He will guide you into all truth. ... For He shall receive of Mine, and shall show it unto you" (John 16:13, 14).

God desires man to exercise his reasoning powers; and the study of the Bible will strengthen and elevate the mind as no other study can. Yet we are to beware of deifying reason, which is subject to the weakness and infirmity of humanity. If we would not have the Scriptures clouded to our understanding, so that the plainest truths shall not be comprehended, we must have the simplicity and faith of a little child, ready to learn, and beseeching the aid of the Holy Spirit. A sense of the power and wisdom of God, and of our inability to comprehend His greatness, should inspire us with humility, and we should open His word, as we would enter His presence, with holy awe. When we come to the Bible, reason must acknowledge an authority superior to itself, and heart and intellect must bow to the great I AM.

There are many things apparently difficult or obscure, which God will make plain and simple to those who thus seek an understanding of them. But without the guidance of the Holy Spirit we shall be continually liable to wrest the Scriptures or to misinterpret them. There is much reading of the Bible that is without profit and in many cases a positive injury. When the word of God is opened without reverence and without prayer; when the thoughts and affections are not fixed upon God, or in harmony with His will, the mind is clouded with doubts; and in the very study of the Bible, skepticism strengthens. The enemy takes control of the thoughts, and he suggests interpretations that are not correct. Whenever men are not in word and deed seeking to be in harmony with God, then, however learned they may be, they are liable to err in their understanding of Scripture, and it is not safe to trust to their explanations. Those who look to the Scriptures to find discrepancies, have not spiritual in-sight. With distorted vision they will see many causes for doubt and unbelief in things that are really plain and simple.

Disguise it as they may, the real cause of doubt and skepticism, in most cases, is the love of sin. The teachings and restrictions of God's word are not welcome to the proud, sin-loving heart, and those who are unwilling to obey its requirements are ready to doubt its authority. In order to arrive at truth, we must have a sincere desire to know the truth and a willingness of heart to obey it. And all who come in this spirit to the study of the Bible will find abundant evidence that it is God's word, and they may gain an understanding of its truths that will make them wise unto salvation.

Christ has said, "If any man willeth to do His will, he shall know of the teaching" (John 7:17 R.V.). Instead of questioning and caviling concerning that which you do not understand, give heed to the light that already shines upon you, and you will receive greater light. By the grace of Christ, perform every duty that has been made plain to your understanding, and you will be enabled to understand and perform those of which you are now in doubt.

There is an evidence that is open to all,—the most highly educated, and the most illiterate,—the evidence of experience. God invites us to prove for ourselves the reality of His word, the truth of His promises. He bids us "taste and see that the Lord is good" (Psalm 34:8). Instead of depending upon the word of another, we are to taste for ourselves. He declares, "Ask, and ye shall receive" (John 16:24). His promises will be fulfilled. They have never failed; they never can fail. And as we draw near to Jesus, and rejoice in the fullness of His love, our doubt and darkness will disappear in the light of His presence.

The apostle Paul says that God "hath delivered us from the power of darkness, and hath translated us into the kingdom of His dear Son" (Colossians 1:13). And everyone who has passed from death unto life is able to "set to his seal that God is true" (John 3:33). He can testify, "I needed help, and I found it in Jesus. Every want was supplied, the hunger of my soul was satisfied; and now the Bible is to me the revelation of Jesus Christ. Do you ask why I believe in Jesus? Because He is to me a divine Saviour. Why do I believe the Bible? Because I have found it to be the voice of God to my soul." We may have the witness in ourselves that the Bible is true, that Christ is the Son of God. We know that we are not following cunningly devised fables.

Peter exhorts his brethren to "grow in grace, and in the knowledge of our Lord and Saviour Jesus Christ" (2 Peter 3:18). When the people of God are growing in grace, they will be constantly obtaining a clearer understanding of His word. They will discern new light and beauty in its sacred truths. This has been true in the history of the church in all ages, and thus it will continue to the end. "The path of the righteous is as the light of dawn, that shineth more and more unto the perfect day" (Proverbs 4:18 R.V., margin).

By faith we may look to the hereafter and grasp the pledge of God for a growth of intellect, the human faculties uniting with the divine, and every power of the soul being brought into direct contact with the Source of light. We may rejoice that all which has perplexed us in the providences of God will then be made plain, things hard to be understood will then find an explanation; and where our finite minds discovered only confusion and broken purposes, we shall see the most perfect and beautiful harmony. "Now we see through a glass, darkly; but then face to face: now I know in part; but then shall I know even as also I am known" (1 Corinthians 13:12).

13 Rejoicing in the Lord

The children of God are called to be representatives of Christ, showing forth the goodness and mercy of the Lord. As Jesus has revealed to us the true character of the Father, so we are to reveal Christ to a world that does not know His tender, pitying love. "As Thou hast sent Me into the world," said Jesus, "even so have I also sent them into the world." "I in them, and Thou in Me; ... that the world may know that Thou hast sent Me" (John 17: 18, 23). The apostle Paul says to the disciples of Jesus, "Ye are manifestly declared to be the epistle of Christ," "known and read of all men" (2 Corinthians 3:3, 2). In every one of His children, Jesus sends a letter to the world. If you are Christ's follower, He sends in you a letter to the family, the village, the street, where you live. Jesus, dwelling in you, desires to speak to the hearts of those who are not acquainted with Him. Perhaps they do not read the Bible, or do not hear the voice that speaks to them in its pages; they do not see the love of God through His works. But if you are a true representative of Jesus, it may be that through you they will be led to understand something of His goodness and be won to love and serve Him.

Christians are set as light bearers on the way to heaven. They are to reflect to the world the light shining upon them from Christ. Their life and character should be such that through them others will get a right conception of Christ and of His service.

If we do represent Christ, we shall make His service appear attractive, as it really is. Christians who gather up gloom and sadness to their souls, and murmur and complain, are giving to others a false representation of God and the Christian life. They give the impression that God is not pleased to have His children happy, and in this they bear false witness against our heavenly Father.

Satan is exultant when he can lead the children of God into unbelief and despondency. He delights to see us mistrusting God, doubting His willingness and power to save us. He loves to have us feel that the Lord will do us harm by His providences. It is the work of Satan to represent the Lord as lacking in compassion and pity. He misstates the truth in regard to Him. He fills the imagination with false ideas concerning God; and instead of dwelling upon the truth in regard to our heavenly Father, we too often fix our minds upon the misrepresentations of Satan and dishonor God by distrusting Him and murmuring against Him. Satan ever seeks to make the religious life one of gloom. He desires it to appear toilsome and difficult; and when the Christian presents in his own life this view of religion, he is, through his unbelief, seconding the falsehood of Satan.

Many, walking along the path of life, dwell upon their mistakes and failures and disappointments, and their hearts are filled with grief and discouragement. While I was in Europe, a sister who had been doing this, and who was in deep distress, wrote to me, asking for some word of encouragement. The night after I had read her letter I dreamed that I was in a garden, and one who seemed to be the owner of the garden was conducting me through its paths. I was gathering the flowers and enjoying their fragrance, when this sister, who had been walking by my side, called my attention to some unsightly briers that were impeding her way. There she was mourning and grieving. She was not walking in the pathway, following the guide, but was walking among the briers and thorns. "Oh," she mourned, "is it not a pity that this beautiful garden is spoiled with thorns?" Then the guide said, "Let the thorns alone, for they will only wound you. Gather the roses, the lilies, and the pinks."

Have there not been some bright spots in your experience? Have you not had some precious seasons when your heart throbbed with joy in response to the Spirit of God? When you look back into the chapters of your life experience do you not find some pleasant pages? Are not God's promises, like the fragrant flowers, growing beside your path on every hand? Will you not let their beauty and sweetness fill your heart with joy?

The briers and thorns will only wound and grieve you; and if you gather only these things, and present them to others, are you not, besides slighting the goodness of God yourself, preventing those around you from walking in the path of life?

It is not wise to gather together all the unpleasant recollections of a past life,—its iniquities and disappointments,—to talk over them and mourn over them until we are overwhelmed with discouragement. A discouraged soul is filled with darkness, shutting out the light of God from his own soul and casting a shadow upon the pathway of others.

Thank God for the bright pictures which He has presented to us. Let us group together the blessed assurances of His love, that we may look upon them continually: The Son of God leaving His Father's throne, clothing His divinity with humanity, that He might rescue man from the power of Satan; His triumph in our behalf, opening heaven to men, revealing to human vision the presence chamber where the Deity unveils His glory; the fallen race uplifted from the pit of ruin into which sin had plunged it, and brought again into connection with the infinite God, and having endured the divine test through faith in our Redeemer, clothed in the righteousness of Christ, and exalted to His throne—these are the pictures which God would have us contemplate.

When we seem to doubt God's love and distrust His promises we dishonor Him and grieve His Holy Spirit. How would a mother feel if her children were constantly complaining of her, just as though she did not mean them well, when her whole life's effort had been to forward their interests and to give them comfort? Suppose they should doubt her love; it would break her heart. How would any parent feel to be thus treated by his children? And how can our heavenly Father regard us when we distrust His love, which has led Him to give His only-begotten Son that we might have life? The apostle writes, "He that spared not His own Son, but delivered Him up for us all, how shall He not with Him also freely give us all things" (Romans 8:32)? And yet how many, by their actions, if not in word, are saying, "The Lord does not mean this for me. Perhaps He loves others, but He does not love me."

All this is harming your own soul; for every word of doubt you utter is inviting Satan's temptations; it is strengthening in you the tendency to doubt, and it is grieving from you the ministering angels. When Satan tempts you, breathe not a word of doubt or darkness. If you choose to open the door to his suggestions, your mind will be filled with distrust and rebellious questioning. If you talk out your feelings, every doubt you express not only reacts upon yourself, but it is a seed that will germinate and bear fruit in the life of others, and it may be impossible to counteract the influence of your words. You yourself may be able to recover from the season of temptation and from the snare of Satan, but others who have been swayed by your influence may not be able to escape from the unbelief you have suggested. How important that we speak only those things that will give spiritual strength and life!

Angels are listening to hear what kind of report you are bearing to the world about your heavenly Master. Let your conversation be of Him who liveth to make intercession for you before the Father. When you take the hand of a friend, let praise to God be on your lips and in your heart. This will attract his thoughts to Jesus.

All have trials; griefs hard to bear, temptations hard to resist. Do not tell your troubles to your fellow mortals, but carry everything to God in prayer. Make it a rule never to utter one word of doubt or discouragement. You can do much to brighten the life of others and strengthen their efforts, by words of hope and holy cheer.

There is many a brave soul sorely pressed by temptation, almost ready to faint in the conflict with self and with the powers of evil. Do not discourage such a one in his hard struggle. Cheer him with brave, hopeful words that shall urge him on his way. Thus the light of Christ may shine from you. "None of us liveth to himself" (Romans 14:7). By our unconscious influence others may be encouraged and strengthened, or they may be discouraged, and repelled from Christ and the truth.

There are many who have an erroneous idea of the life and character of Christ. They think that He was devoid of warmth and sunniness, that He was stern, severe, and joyless. In many cases the whole religious experience is colored by these gloomy views.

It is often said that Jesus wept, but that He was never known to smile. Our Saviour was indeed a Man of Sorrows, and acquainted with grief, for He opened His heart to all the woes of men. But though His life was self-denying and shadowed with pain and care, His spirit was not crushed. His countenance did not wear an expression of grief and repining, but ever one of peaceful serenity. His heart was a wellspring of life, and wherever He went He carried rest and peace, joy and gladness.

Our Saviour was deeply serious and intensely in earnest, but never gloomy or morose. The life of those who imitate Him will be full of earnest purpose;

they will have a deep sense of personal responsibility. Levity will be repressed; there will be no boisterous merriment, no rude jesting; but the religion of Jesus gives peace like a river. It does not quench the light of joy; it does not restrain cheerfulness nor cloud the sunny, smiling face. Christ came not to be ministered unto but to minister; and when His love reigns in the heart, we shall follow His example.

If we keep uppermost in our minds the unkind and unjust acts of others we shall find it impossible to love them as Christ has loved us; but if our thoughts dwell upon the wondrous love and pity of Christ for us, the same spirit will flow out to others. We should love and respect one another, notwithstanding the faults and imperfections that we cannot help seeing. Humility and self-distrust should be cultivated, and a patient tenderness with the faults of others. This will kill out all narrowing selfishness and make us large-hearted and generous.

The psalmist says, "Trust in the Lord, and do good; so shalt thou dwell in the land, and verily thou shalt be fed" (Psalm 37:3). "Trust in the Lord." Each day has its burdens, its cares and perplexities; and when we meet how ready we are to talk of our difficulties and trials. So many borrowed troubles intrude, so many fears are indulged, such a weight of anxiety is expressed, that one might suppose we had no pitying, loving Saviour ready to hear all our requests and to be to us a present help in every time of need.

Some are always fearing, and borrowing trouble. Every day they are surrounded with the tokens of God's love; every day they are enjoying the bounties of His providence; but they overlook these present blessings. Their minds are continually dwelling upon something disagreeable which they fear may come; or some difficulty may really exist which, though small, blinds their eyes to the many things that demand gratitude. The difficulties they encounter, instead of driving them to God, the only source of their help, separate them from Him because they awaken unrest and repining.

Do we well to be thus unbelieving? Why should we be ungrateful and distrustful? Jesus is our friend; all heaven is interested in our welfare. We should not allow the perplexities and worries of everyday life to fret the mind and cloud the brow. If we do we shall always have something to vex and annoy. We should not indulge a solicitude that only frets and wears us, but does not help us to bear trials.

You may be perplexed in business; your prospects may grow darker and darker, and you may be threatened with loss; but do not become discouraged; cast your care upon God, and remain calm and cheerful. Pray for wisdom to manage your affairs with discretion, and thus prevent loss and disaster. Do all you can on your part to bring about favorable results. Jesus has promised His aid, but not apart from our effort. When, relying upon our Helper, you have done all you can, accept the result cheerfully.

It is not the will of God that His people should be weighed down with care. But our Lord does not deceive us. He does not say to us, "Do not fear; there are no dangers in your path." He knows there are trials and dangers, and He deals with us plainly. He does not propose to take His people out of a world of sin and evil, but He points them to a never-failing refuge. His prayer for His disciples was, "I pray not that Thou shouldest take them out of the world, but that Thou shouldest keep them from the evil." "In the world," He says, "ye shall have tribulation: but be of good cheer; I have overcome the world" (John 17:15, 16:33).

In His Sermon on the Mount, Christ taught His disciples precious lessons in regard to the necessity of trusting in God. These lessons were designed to encourage the children of God through all ages, and they have come down to our time full of instruction and comfort. The Saviour pointed His followers to the birds of the air as they warbled their carols of praise, unencumbered with thoughts of care, for "they sow not, neither do they reap." And yet the great Father provides for their needs. The Saviour asks, "Are ye not much better than they?" Matthew 6:26. The great Provider for man and beast opens His hand and supplies all His creatures. The birds of the air are not beneath His notice. He does not drop the food into their bills, but He makes provision for their needs. They must gather the grains He has scattered for them. They must prepare the material for their little nests. They must feed their young. They go forth singing to their labor, for "your heavenly Father feedeth them." And "are ye not much better than they?" Are not you, as intelligent, spiritual worshipers, of more value than the birds of the air? Will not the Author of our being, the Preserver of our life, the One who formed us in His own divine image, provide for our necessities if we but trust in Him?

Christ pointed His disciples to the flowers of the field, growing in rich profusion and glowing in the simple beauty which the heavenly Father had given them, as an expression of His love to man. He said, "Consider the lilies of the field, how they grow." The beauty and simplicity of these natural flowers far outrival the splendor of Solomon. The most gorgeous attire produced by the skill of art cannot bear comparison with the natural grace and radiant beauty of the flowers of God's creation. Jesus asks, "If God so clothe the grass of the field, which today is, and tomorrow is cast into the oven, shall He not much more clothe you, O ye of little faith" (Matthew 6:28, 30). If God, the divine Artist, gives to the simple flowers that perish in a day their delicate and varied colors, how much greater care will He have for those who are created in His own image? This lesson of Christ's is a rebuke to the anxious thought, the perplexity and doubt, of the faithless heart.

The Lord would have all His sons and daughters happy, peaceful, and obedient. Jesus says, "My peace I give unto you: not as the world giveth, give I unto you. Let not your heart be troubled, neither let it be afraid." "These things have I spoken unto you, that My joy might remain in you, and that your joy might be full" (John 14:27; 15:11).

Happiness that is sought from selfish motives, outside of the path of duty, is ill-balanced, fitful, and transitory; it passes away, and the soul is filled with loneliness and sorrow; but there is joy and satisfaction in the service of God; the Christian is not left to walk in uncertain paths; he is not left to vain regrets and disappointments. If we do not have the pleasures of this life we may still be joyful in looking to the life beyond.

But even here Christians may have the joy of communion with Christ; they may have the light of His love, the perpetual comfort of His presence. Every step in life may bring us closer to Jesus, may give us a deeper experience of His love, and may bring us one step nearer to the blessed home of peace. Then let us not cast away our confidence, but have firm assurance, firmer than ever before. "Hitherto hath the Lord helped us," and He will help us to the end (1 Samuel 7:12). Let us look to the monumental pillars, reminders of what the Lord has done to comfort us and to save us from the hand of the destroyer. Let us keep fresh in our memory all the tender mercies that God has shown us,—the tears He has wiped away, the pains He has soothed, the anxieties removed, the fears dispelled, the wants supplied, the blessings bestowed,—thus strengthening ourselves for all that is before us through the remainder of our pilgrimage.

We cannot but look forward to new perplexities in the coming conflict, but we may look on what is past as well as on what is to come, and say, "Hitherto hath the Lord helped us." "As thy days, so shall thy strength be" (Deuteronomy 33:25). The trial will not exceed the strength that shall be given us to bear it. Then let us take up our work just where we find it, believing that whatever may come, strength proportionate to the trial will be given.

And by and by the gates of heaven will be thrown open to admit God's children, and from the lips of the King of glory the benediction will fall on their ears like richest music, "Come, ye blessed of My Father, inherit the kingdom prepared for you from the foundation of the world" (Matthew 25:34).

Then the redeemed will be welcomed to the home that Jesus is preparing for them. There their companions will not be the vile of earth, liars, idolaters, the impure, and unbelieving; but they will associate with those who have overcome Satan and through divine grace have formed perfect characters. Every sinful tendency, every imperfection, that afflicts them here has been removed by the blood of Christ, and the excellence and brightness of His glory, far exceeding the brightness of the sun, is imparted to them. And the moral beauty, the perfection of His character, shines through them, in worth far exceeding this outward splendor. They are without fault before the great white throne, sharing the dignity and the privileges of the angels.

In view of the glorious inheritance that may be his, "what shall a man give in exchange for his soul" (Matthew 16:26)? He may be poor, yet he possesses in himself a wealth and dignity that the world could never bestow. The soul redeemed and cleansed from sin, with all its noble powers dedicated to the service of God, is of surpassing worth; and there is joy in heaven in the presence of God and the holy angels over one soul redeemed, a joy that is expressed in songs of holy triumph.

1   Is There Anything Left You Can Trust?

In these morally challenged times—when billions are embezzled through corporate fraud; when trusted, spiritual leaders prove false; when lying in politics seems to be the norm; when those you depend on the most often hurt you the deepest—is there anything left you can trust? Yes! You can fully trust the Bible! Why? Just take a look at the evidence ...

1. What does the Bible claim about itself?

The Bible says, "All Scripture is given by inspiration of God" (2 Timothy 3:16). "Prophecy never came by the will of man, but holy men of God spoke as they were moved by the Holy Spirit" (2 Peter 1:21). "The Scripture cannot be broken" (John 10:35).

Answer: It claims to be inspired. It was written by men who were guided by the Holy Spirit. It cannot be broken or proved untrue.

2. How did Jesus demonstrate His confidence and belief in Scripture?

Jesus said, "It is written: 'Man shall not live by bread alone'" ... "It is written again, 'You shall not tempt the Lord your God'" ... "For it is written, 'You shall worship the Lord your God, and Him only you shall serve'" (Matthew 4:4, 7, 10). "Sanctify them by Your truth. Your word is truth" (John 17:17).

Answer: Jesus quoted Scripture when meeting the temptations of Satan. He also stated that the Word is truth (John 17:17). Jesus often quoted Scripture as authority for the truth He was teaching.

3. Do Bible prophecies confirm inspiration?

The Bible says, "I am the Lord ... new things I declare; before they spring forth I tell you of them" (Isaiah 42:8, 9). "I am God ... Declaring the end from the beginning, and from ancient times things that are not yet done" (Isaiah 46:9, 10).

Answer: Bible predictions of things to happen in the future confirm the inspiration of Scripture as they come to pass. Notice the following examples of fulfilled Bible prophecies:

- A. Four world empires to arise: Babylon, Medo-Persia, Greece, and Rome (Daniel chapters 2, 7, 8).
- B. Cyrus to be the warrior to capture Babylon (Isaiah 45:1-3).
- C. After Babylon's destruction, it would never be inhabited again (Isaiah 13:19, 20; Jeremiah 51:37).
- D. Egypt would never again have a commanding position among the nations (Ezekiel 29:14, 15; 30:12, 13).
- E. Earth-shaking calamities and fear toward the time of the end (Luke 21:25, 26).
- F. Moral degeneracy and decline of spirituality in the last days (2 Timothy 3:1-5).

4. Can we expect scientific statements made in the Bible to be accurate?

The Bible says, "The entirety of Your word is truth" (Psalm 119:160). "The Spirit ... will guide you into all truth" (John 16:13).

Answer: Yes, the Bible is true. The Holy Spirit, who guided the Bible writers, always speaks the truth. Here are a few Bible statements that have been confirmed by science:

A. "He hangs the earth on nothing" (Job 26:7). This scientific fact is from Job, the Bible's oldest book.

B. "He ... sits above the circle of the earth" (Isaiah 40:22). The Bible said the earth is round centuries before man found out.

C. "To establish a weight for the wind" (Job 28:25). Long before scientists knew, God said air has weight.

D. "In Him [Jesus] all things consist" (Colossians 1:17). The word "consist" here literally means "hold together" or "cohere." Many Bible translations put it "hold together." This is the answer to the nuclear physicists' worrisome question about the atom. The real mystery of the atom does not involve its benumbing mega-power, but rather, "Why doesn't the atom fly apart?" Scientific knowledge says it should, but it doesn't. Some scientists are wondering what puzzling power, completely unknown to them, is holding it together. The Bible says that mysterious power is the Creator, God Himself.

5. Are biblical health principles tuned to the twenty-first century mind?

Answer:

A. Cover body waste with dirt (Deuteronomy 23:12, 13). The Bible provision of Moses' day that body waste would be buried outside the camp was thousands of years ahead of its time. When human waste is not properly buried, diseases can be quickly spread to untold thousands through the water supply or not washing one's hands. This Bible fact continues to save millions of lives.

B. "Nor let us commit sexual immorality" (1 Corinthians 10:8). The words "sexual immorality" denote all kinds of immoral sexual conduct (see Leviticus 18 for a comprehensive list). When the clear counsel of the Bible is followed people have little or no problems with sexually transmitted diseases such as Syphilis, Gonorrhea or AIDS. Additionally the temptation to abort unwanted pregnancy would be essentially non-existent.

C. Leave alcoholic beverages alone (Proverbs 23:29-32). If this extremely effective Bible solution were implemented, just think what it would mean:
 1. Millions of alcoholics becoming sober, respectable citizens.
 2. Millions of families reunited.
 3. Millions of broken homes mended.
 4. Multiplied thousands of lives saved by sober driving.

5. Thousands of government, business, and professional leaders making clear-minded decisions.
6. Billions of dollars available for humanitarian use.

Note: *God not only tells us how to succeed with joy amid today's harrowing problems, but He also gives us the miraculous power to do it (1 Corinthians 15:57; Philippians 4:13; Romans 1:16). Bible health principles are relevant and desperately needed, but few are listening. (For more on health, see Study Guide 13.)*

6. Are the historical statements of the Bible accurate?

The Bible says, "I, the Lord, speak righteousness, I declare things that are right" (Isaiah 45:19).

Answer: Yes, Bible historical statements are accurate. What God says in His book is true. Sometimes, temporarily, evidence may not be found to substantiate certain historical facts from the Bible, but in time the evidence surfaces. Note the following:

A. For years skeptics said the Bible was unreliable because it mentions the Hittite nation (Deuteronomy 7:1) and cities like Nineveh (Jonah 1:1, 2) and Sodom (Genesis 19:1), which they denied ever existed. But now modern archaeology has confirmed that all three did, indeed, exist.

B. Critics also said that Bible-mentioned kings Belshazzar (Daniel 5:1) and Sargon (Isaiah 20:1) never existed. Once again, it has now been confirmed they did exist.

C. Skeptics also said the Bible record of Moses was not reliable because it mentions writing (Exodus 24:4) and wheeled vehicles (Exodus 14:25), neither of which they said existed at the time. They, of course, know better today.

D. At one time the 39 kings of ancient Israel and Judah who reigned during the divided kingdom were authenticated only from the Bible record, so critics charged fabrication. But then archaeologists found cuneiform records that mentioned many of these kings and, once again, the Bible record was proved accurate. Critics have repeatedly been proved wrong as new discoveries confirm biblical people, places, and events. It will always be so.

7. One of the greatest miracles of the Bible is its unity. Please ponder the following amazing facts:

A. The 66 books of the Bible were written:
  1. On three continents.
  2. In three languages.
  3. By about 40 different people (kings, shepherds, theologians, an army general, fishermen, priests, and a physician).
  4. Over a period of about 1,500 years.
  5. On the most controversial subjects.
  6. By people who, in most cases, had never met.

7. By writers whose educations and backgrounds varied greatly.
  B. Yet, though it seems totally inconceivable,
   1. The 66 books maintain harmony with each other.
   2. Often new concepts on a subject are expressed, but these concepts do not undermine what other Bible writers say on the same subject.
  C. Talk about astounding! Ask people who have viewed an identical event to each give a report of what happened. They will differ widely and will virtually always contradict each other in some way. Yet the Bible, penned by 40 writers over a 1,500-year period, reads as if authored by one great mind. And, indeed, it was: "Holy men of God spoke as they were moved by the Holy Spirit" (2 Peter 1:21). The Holy Spirit "moved" them all. He is the real Bible Author. The four Gospels do sometimes differ in the way they report the same event, but they complement each other.

8. What evidence of Bible inspiration is found in the lives of people?

The Bible says, "Therefore, if anyone is in Christ, he is a new creation; old things have passed away; behold, all things have become new" (2 Corinthians 5:17).

Answer: The changed lives of those who follow Jesus and obey Scripture constitute the most heartwarming proof of Bible inspiration. The drunkard becomes sober; the immoral, pure; the addicted, free; the profane, reverent; the fearful, courageous; and the rude, kind.

An American skeptic was visiting an island whose natives were originally cannibals. When he spotted an old man reading the Bible, he ridiculed him for reading a book "full of myths which had already been exposed." The native smiled at him and said, "My friend, be grateful we do believe this book. Otherwise, we would be serving you for dinner." The Bible really does change people, and this amazing fact confirms its inspiration.

9. What evidence for Bible inspiration emerges when we compare Old Testament prophecies of the coming Messiah with New Testament happenings in the life of Jesus?

The Bible says, "And beginning at Moses and all the Prophets, He [Jesus] expounded to them in all the Scriptures the things concerning Himself" (Luke 24:27). "For he [Apollos] vigorously refuted the Jews publicly, showing from the Scriptures that Jesus is the Christ" (Acts 18:28).

Answer: The Old Testament predictions of the Messiah to come were so specific and so clearly fulfilled by Jesus of Nazareth that both Jesus and Apollos used these prophecies to prove to the Jews that Jesus was, indeed, the Messiah. There are more than 125 of these prophecies. Let's review just 10 of them:

Prophecy	Old Testament Scripture	New Testament Fulfillment
1. Born in Bethlehem	Micah 5:2	Matthew 2:1-6
2. Born of a virgin	Isaiah 7:14	Matthew 1:18-23

3. Of David's lineage	Jeremiah 23:5	Revelation 22:16
4. Betrayal by a friend	Psalm 41:9	John 13:18, 19, 26
5. Sold for 30 silver coins	Zechariah 11:12	Matthew 26:14-16
6. Crucified	Zechariah 12:10	John 19:16-18, 37
7. Lots cast for His clothes	Psalm 22:18	Matthew 27:35
8. No bones broken	Psalm 34:20; Exodus 12:46	John 19:31-36
9. Buried in rich man's tomb	Isaiah 53:9	Matthew 27:57-60
10. Year, day, hour of His death	Daniel 9:26, 27; Exodus 12:6	Matthew 27:45-50

Dr. Peter Stoner, former chairman of the departments of mathematics, astronomy, and engineering at Pasadena College (California), worked with 600 students for several years applying the "principle of probability" to the prophecies of the Messiah's coming. They chose just eight from the many available and finally decided the chances of all eight being fulfilled in one man in a lifetime is one in 1,000,000,000,000,000,000,000,000,000,000,000. What would the odds be on the more than 125 prophecies of the Messiah? It couldn't just happen!

10. What great advantage does a person have who accepts the Bible as God's inspired word?

The Bible says, "I understand more than the ancients, because I keep Your precepts" (Psalm 119:100). "You ... make me wiser than my enemies" (Psalm 119:98). "For as the heavens are higher than the earth, so are ... My thoughts [higher] than your thoughts" (Isaiah 55:9).

Answer: A person who accepts the Word of God will soon know the answers to many complex challenges that secular scholars may never figure out. For example, the Bible teaches:

A. God created the earth and all living organisms in six literal, 24-hour days (Exodus 20:11; Psalm 33:6, 9).
B. A worldwide flood destroyed every living thing except the sea life and what was inside Noah's ark (Genesis chapters 6, 7, 8).
C. The different languages of the world began at the Tower of Babel (Genesis 11:1-9).

God, who has always existed and knows everything, shares the above three truths with us, recognizing that we could never figure them out on our own. We know only "in part" now (1 Corinthians 13:9). And God's knowledge is "past finding out" (Romans 11:33). According to the chronology of the Bible, the earth's age is thousands of years, not millions. This confounds evolutionists, but it shouldn't. The Bible indicates that God created Adam and Eve as full grown. The couple was only one day old on their second day of life, but they were mature. Couldn't He have done the same thing with the earth? Of course! Man's measuring instruments cannot allow for apparent age. In such cases, they are not trustworthy. Believe the Bible, and you will always be ahead of the speculation of secular scholars and the worldly-wise.

11. What recent happenings have brought the power and appeal of the Bible into sharp focus?

Answer: The increasing number of natural disasters and the rise of worldwide terrorism are signs predicted by the Bible. The Bible predicted that at the end of time, "On the earth distress of nations, with perplexity, the sea and the waves roaring" (Luke 21:25). The Asian tsunami of December 26, 2004, is just one example. Over 250,000 people were reported dead or missing in what was one of the deadliest natural disasters of modern history. A year later, Hurricane Katrina ripped through New Orleans. The hurricanes and water disasters since then remind us of the prophetic power of Jesus' words that there would be "waves roaring."

The Bible also predicted that "nation would rise against nation and kingdom against kingdom" (Matthew 24:7). After the devastating attack on the twin towers on 9/11, people have realized that no nation on earth is secure against those who wish to harm it. The ongoing conflicts in the Middle East and the continuing war against terrorism have brought people back to the Bible.

Some people have questioned the Bible because it speaks of the world being created instead of "evolving." Jesus predicted that "when the Son of man comes, will he really find faith on the earth?" (Luke 18:8). The faith-shattering dogma of evolution, however, is now being discredited. We must remember that it is nothing more than an unproved, shaky theory. We will mention three items only: 1. Robert Gentry's DVD *Creation's Tiny Mystery* has unsettled many evolutionists with its apparent, clear evidence of instant creation. 2. Molecular biology's recent demonstration that the single cell is vastly and irreducibly complex makes the accidental origin of life in a single cell an absurdity. 3. The widely different ages now being assigned to the Grand Canyon layers by current scientific measurements, as opposed to those assigned previously, make evolutionists and their prior measurements seem reckless and irresponsible. The atheistic theory of evolution that humans and apes came from common ancestors scorns the concept that people were created in the image of God. It denies the existence of God, totally disavows Jesus as Savior, negates the Bible, and ridicules the truth of an eternal home in heaven.

The collapse of evolution and the fulfillment of Bible prophecy are to establish your faith in the Word of God. Don't be fooled by the devil's tactics!

12. Why does the Bible have such universal appeal?

The Bible says, "Your word is a … light to my path" (Psalm 119:105). "These things I have spoken to you … that your joy may be full" (John 15:11). "In the image of God ... He created them" (Genesis 1:27). "Let your light so shine before men, that they may see your good works, and glorify your Father in heaven" (Matthew 5:16). "I will come again and receive you to Myself; that where I am, there you may be also" (John 14:3).

Answer: Because it answers life's most puzzling questions:

A. **Where did I come from?** God created us in His image. We did not accidentally emerge as nondescript globs from some primeval slime. We are sons and daughters of God, the Mighty King (Galatians 3:26). We are so precious to God that when Adam and Eve sinned, He gave His Son to die and pay the penalty for our sins so we could be free. He wants to restore us to His image and then, shortly, take us back to Eden, the home Adam and Eve lost.

B. **Why am I here?** Our aims for life today should be to discover the Bible's wonderful answers to life's puzzling problems and to accept Jesus' offer to restore us to His image (Romans 8:29).

C. **What does the future hold for me?** There is no guesswork about the future. Jesus will come very soon to take His people to the fabulous home He has prepared for them in heaven. There, with supreme joy and happiness, people will live forever (John 14:1-3; Revelation 21:3, 4).

Your Questions Answered

1. **Is all of the Bible inspired? Many believe only parts of it are.**

   Answer: The Bible has the answer: "All Scripture is given by inspiration of God, and is profitable for doctrine, for reproof, for correction, for instruction in righteousness" (2 Timothy 3:16). The Bible does not simply contain the word of God. Rather, it is the Word of God. The Bible is the information and operations manual for a human life. Ignore any of it and you will have unnecessary difficulties and problems.

2. **Some of the most brilliant people in the world, who have carefully studied the Bible, believe no one can understand it. If the Bible is truly God's book, shouldn't everyone be able to understand it?**

   Answer: Bright people who can understand and explain virtually anything are often quickly stopped in their tracks when they read the Bible. The reason is that spiritual things "are spiritually discerned" (1 Corinthians 2:13, 14). The deep things of the Word will never be understood by a secular mind, no matter how brilliant. Unless one honestly seeks an experience with God, he cannot understand the things of God. The Holy Spirit, who explains the Bible (John 16:13; 14:26), is not understood by the carnal, secular mind. On the other hand, the humble, even uneducated Christian who studies the Bible receives amazing understanding from the Holy Spirit (Matthew 11:25; 1 Corinthians 2:9, 10).

3. The Bible is full of errors. How can you believe it is inspired?

Answer: The overwhelming majority of so-called errors in the Bible have been demonstrated to be simply errors of judgment or lack of understanding on the part of those who make the complaint. They are not errors at all, but simply truth misunderstood. The inspired Bible:

1. Will always tell you the truth.
2. Will never mislead you.
3. Can be fully trusted.
4. Is reliable and authoritative, not only in spiritual matters but also in other matters it addresses, including history and science.

Satan is always digging up some supposed flaw in Scripture, which is not surprising. He found fault even with God and heaven. Copyists may have miscopied in some cases, but no such supposed happening or any other alleged error affects the truth of God's Word. Doctrine is built not upon one Bible passage, but upon the total of God's comments on any subject. We are unaware of any alleged error of any kind that would affect the truthfulness of the content of Scripture. Some things in Scripture are yet difficult to reconcile. There will always be room for doubt to those who prefer to doubt. We believe that even alleged errors, not yet fully explained, will (as in the past) soon be exposed as false alarms. The harder people work to undermine the Bible, the brighter its light shines.

2 Did God Create the Devil?

Most people in the world are being deceived by an evil genius bent on destroying their lives—a brilliant mastermind called the devil, or Satan. But this dark prince is much more than what you might think ... many say he's just a devious mythical figure, but the Bible says he's very real, and he's deceiving families, churches, and even nations to increase sorrow and pain. Here are the Bible's amazing facts about this prince of darkness and how you can overcome him!

1. With whom did sin originate?

"The devil has sinned from the beginning" (1 John 3:8). "That serpent of old, called the Devil and Satan" (Revelation 12:9).

Answer: Satan, also called the devil, is the originator of sin. Without the Scriptures, the origin of evil would remain unexplained.

2. What was Satan's name before he sinned? Where was he living at that time?

"How you are fallen from heaven, O Lucifer, son of the morning!" (Isaiah 14:12). "And He [Jesus] said to them, 'I saw Satan fall like lightning from heaven'" (Luke 10:18). "You were on the holy mountain of God" (Ezekiel 28:14).

Answer: His name was Lucifer, and he was living in heaven. Lucifer is symbolized by the king of Babylon in Isaiah 14 and as the king of Tyrus in Ezekiel 28.

3. What was the origin of Lucifer? What responsible position did he hold? How does the Bible describe him?

"You were created" (Ezekiel 28:15). "You were the anointed cherub who covers" (Ezekiel 28:14). "You were the seal of perfection, full of wisdom and perfect in beauty. ... Every precious stone was your covering. ... The workmanship of your timbrels and pipes was prepared for you on the day you were created. ... You were perfect in your ways from the day you were created, till iniquity was found in you" (Ezekiel 28:12, 13, 15).

Answer: **Lucifer was *created* by God, as were all other angels (Ephesians 3:9). Lucifer was a "covering" cherub, or angel. One great angel stands on the left side of God's throne and another on the right (Psalm 99:1). Lucifer was one of those highly exalted angel leaders. Lucifer's beauty was flawless and breathtaking. His wisdom was perfect. His brightness was awe-inspiring. Ezekiel 28:13 seems to indicate that his throat was specially prepared to make him an outstanding musician. Some think he led the angelic choir.**

4. What happened in Lucifer's life that led him to sin? What blasphemous sin did he then commit?

"Your heart was lifted up because of your beauty; You corrupted your wisdom for the sake of your splendor" (Ezekiel 28:17). "'For you have said in your heart: ... 'I will exalt my throne above the stars of God; ... I will be like the Most High'" (Isaiah 14:13, 14).

Answer: **Pride, jealousy, discontent, and self-exaltation arose in his life. Lucifer decided to attempt to unseat God and then demand that all worship him. It was treason of the worst kind.**

Note: Why is worship such a big thing? Worship is the key factor in the ongoing warfare between God and Satan. People were created to be happy and fulfilled only when they worship God solely. Not even unfallen angels of heaven are to be worshiped (Revelation 22:8, 9). Satan sought worship in the beginning. Centuries later, when he tempted Jesus in the wilderness, worship was still the central issue (Matthew 4:8-11). In these last days, God is calling upon all people to worship Him (Revelation 14:6, 7). This so infuriates Satan that he will try to force people to worship him or else be killed (Revelation 13:15).

Everybody worships somebody or something: power, prestige, food, pleasure, possessions, one's own opinion, etc. God says, "Thou shalt have no other gods before me" (Exodus 20:3). And unless we worship Him only, He counts us against Him (Matthew 12:30). This news is shocking, but true. If anything or anyone other than God receives first place in my life, I am—unknowingly perhaps—worshiping and supporting Satan. Does God have first place in my life, or am I unconsciously elevating Satan? It is a sobering question, isn't it?

5. What happened in heaven as a consequence of Lucifer's rebellion?

"And war broke out in heaven: Michael and His angels fought with the dragon; and the dragon and his angels fought, but they did not prevail, nor was a place found for them in heaven any longer. So the great dragon was cast out, that serpent of old, called the Devil and Satan, who deceives the whole world; he was cast to the earth, and his angels were cast out with him" (Revelation 12:7-9).

Answer: Lucifer won the support of one-third of the angels (Revelation 12:3, 4) and caused an insurrection in heaven. God had no choice but to cast out Lucifer and his angels. This was the greatest battle, by far, ever fought. Lucifer's aim was to usurp God's throne, even if it might eventually lead to murder (John 8:44). After his expulsion from heaven, Lucifer was called Satan (adversary) and devil (slanderer), and his angels were called demons.

6. Where is Satan's present headquarters? How does he feel about people?

"And the Lord said to Satan, 'From where do you come?' Satan answered the Lord and said, 'From going to and fro on the earth, and from walking back and forth on it'" (Job 2:2). "Woe to the inhabitants of the earth and the sea! For the devil has come down to you, having great wrath, because he knows that he has a short time" (Revelation 12:12). "Your adversary the devil walks about like a roaring lion, seeking whom he may devour" (1 Peter 5:8).

Answer: Contrary to popular opinion, Satan's headquarters is the earth, not hell. God gave Adam and Eve dominion over the earth (Genesis 1:26). When they sinned, they lost it to Satan (Romans 6:16), who then became ruler, or prince, of the earth (John 12:31). Satan bitterly hates humans, who were created in God's image. He can't touch God. So, instead, his venom is directed against people who are God's children. He's a hateful, vicious murderer whose aim is to destroy you and thus hurt God.

7. When God created Adam and Eve, what one thing did He forbid them to do? What was to be the penalty for disobedience?

"But of the tree of the knowledge of good and evil you shall not eat, for in the day that you eat of it you shall surely die" (Genesis 2:17).

Answer: They were not to eat of the tree of the knowledge of good and evil. The penalty for eating of the tree was to be death.

8. What medium did Satan use to deceive Eve? What lies did Satan tell her?

"Now the serpent was more cunning than any beast of the field which the Lord God had made. And he said to the woman, 'Has God indeed said, "You shall *not* eat of every tree of the garden?"' ... "Then the serpent said to the woman, "You will not surely die. For God knows that in the day you eat of it your eyes will be opened, and you will be like God, knowing good and evil" (Genesis 3:1, 4, 5, emphasis added).

Answer: Satan used a serpent—the wisest, most appealing animal God made—to deceive Eve. Some think the serpent originally had wings and flew (Isaiah 14:29; 30:6). Remember, it did not crawl until God cursed it (Genesis 3:14). Satan's lies were: (1) you won't die, and (2) eating the fruit will make you wise. Satan, who invented lying (John 8:44), mixed truth with the lies he told Eve. Lies that include some truth are the most effective of all. It was true they would "know evil" after sinning. In love, God had withheld from them the knowledge of heartache, grief, suffering, pain, and death. Satan, as he does today, made the knowledge of evil appear attractive. Satan told lies to misrepresent God's character because he knew that no one would ever turn away from such a loving God unless he misunderstood His character.

The Bible Says Satan:

Deceives/persecutes Revelation 12:9, 13	Quotes/misquotes Bible Matthew 4:5, 6
Falsely accuses/murders Revelation 12:10; John 8:44	Traps/ensnares 2 Timothy 2:26; 1 Peter 5:8
Makes war on God's people Revelation 12:17	Binds/prompts betrayal Luke 13:16; John 13:2, 21
Imprisons Revelation 2:10	Possesses/hinders Luke 22:3-5; 1 Thess. 2:18
Works miracles/lies Revelation 16:13, 14; John 8:44	Appears as angel of light 2 Corinthians 11:13-15
Brings disease/afflicts Job 2:7	His demons impersonate pastors 2 Corinthians 11:13-15
Slanders "Devil" means "slanderer"	Calls fire from heaven Revelation 13:13

9. Was eating a piece of fruit such a bad thing? Why were Adam and Eve removed from the garden?

"To him who knows to do good and does not do it, to him it is sin" (James 4:17). "Whoever commits sin also commits lawlessness, and sin is lawlessness" (1 John 3:4). "He who sins is of the devil" (1 John 3:8). "Then the Lord God said, "Behold, the man has become like one of Us, to know good and evil. And now, lest he put out his hand and take also of the tree of life, and eat, and live forever." … "So He drove out the man; and He placed cherubim at the east of the garden of Eden, and a flaming sword which turned every way, to guard the way to the tree of life" (Genesis 3:22, 24).

Answer: Yes, eating of the fruit was a sin because it was a direct rejection of one of God's few requirements. It was open rebellion against God's law and authority. By rejecting one of God's commands, Adam and Eve allied themselves with Satan, God's enemy, and thus brought separation between themselves and God (Isaiah 59:2). Satan hoped the couple would sin and then eat of the tree of life, and thus become immortal sinners. But God removed them from the garden to prevent such a tragedy.

10. What amazing facts does the Bible reveal regarding Satan's methods to hurt, deceive, discourage, and destroy people?

Answer: Satan uses every conceivable approach to deceive and destroy people. His demons can appear and pose as righteous people, even clergymen. And Satan will appear as a glorious angel of light with power to call fire down from heaven. He will impersonate Jesus. But you have been warned, so don't fall for it. When Jesus comes, *every eye will see Him* (Revelation 1:7). He will remain in the clouds and not even touch the earth (1 Thessalonians 4:17).

11. How powerful and effective are Satan's temptations and strategies?

He convinced: One-third of the angels (Revelation 12:3-9); Adam and Eve (Genesis 3); All but eight people in Noah's day (1 Peter 3:20). He will make the lost feel saved (Matthew 7:21-23). Almost the entire world will follow him (Revelation 13:3). Few will be saved (Matthew 7:14; 22:14).

Answer: Satan's success rate is so astoundingly high that it seems almost unbelievable. He deceived a *third of the angels.* In Noah's day, *all but eight people* were deceived. Before Jesus comes the second time, Satan will appear as an angelic being, posing as Christ. His deceptive power will be so great that *our only safety will lie in refusing to go see him* (Matthew 24:23-26). If you absolutely refuse to look and listen, Jesus will protect you from deception (John 10:29). (For more on Jesus' second coming, see Study Guide 8.)

12. When and where will the devil receive his punishment? What will that punishment be?

"So it will be at the end of this age. The Son of Man will send out His angels, and they will gather out of His kingdom all things that offend, and those who practice lawlessness, and will cast them into the furnace of fire" (Matthew 13:40-42). "The devil, who deceived them, was cast into the lake of fire and brimstone" (Revelation 20:10). "Depart from Me, you cursed, into the everlasting fire prepared for the devil and his angels" (Matthew 25:41). "Therefore I brought fire from your midst; it devoured you, and I turned you to ashes upon the earth. In the sight of all who saw you. ... You ... shall be no more forever" (Ezekiel 28:18, 19).

Answer: **The devil will be cast into the sin-destroying fire on this earth at the end of the world. God will deal with sin and the devil.**

Note: It is not possible to adequately describe the sadness and anguish the Father and Son will feel when Satan is cast into this fire. They were closer to him than any other being. How painful this will be not only for those cast into the fire, but for God who created them to begin with. (For more on hell, see Study Guide 11.)

13. What is it that forever settles the horrible problem of sin? Will sin ever rise up again?

"As I live, says the Lord, every knee shall bow to Me, and every tongue shall confess to God" (Romans 14:11; see also Philippians 2:10, 11; Isaiah 45:23). "Affliction will not rise up a second time" (Nahum 1:9).

Answer: Two crucial happenings will settle the sin problem:

First, all beings in heaven and earth, including the devil and his angels, will of their own free choice kneel and publicly confess that God is truthful, fair, and righteous. No questions will remain unanswered. All sinners will openly admit that they are lost because of their determined refusal to accept God's love and salvation. They will admit that justice demands they must die. All will confess that they deserve eternal death.

Second, sin will be purged from the universe by the total and final destruction of sin, sinners, the devil, and his angels. God is positive on this point: Sin will never again arise to mar God's universe.

14. Who makes the final, complete eradication of sin from the universe a certainty?

"For this purpose the Son of God was manifested, that He might destroy the works of the devil" (1 John 3:8). "Inasmuch then as the children have partaken of flesh and blood, He Himself likewise shared in the same, that through death He might destroy him who had the power of death, that is, the devil" (Hebrews 2:14).

Answer: Through His life, death, and resurrection, *Jesus* made the eradication of sin a certainty.

15. How does God the Father feel about people?

"The Father Himself loves you" (John 16:27; see also John 3:16; 17:22, 23).

Answer: The Father loves people as much as the Son does. Jesus' key aim in life was to demonstrate His Father's character in His own life so people would know how loving, warm, and caring the Father really is (John 5:19).

Satan Misrepresents the Father

Satan misrepresents the Father as *unfeeling, aloof, exacting, stern, and unapproachable* (the devil's own traits). He even labels his own ugly, calamitous acts as "acts of God." Jesus came to wipe this slander off His Father's name and demonstrate that our heavenly Father loves us more than a mother loves her child (Isaiah 49:15). Jesus' favorite theme was God's patience, tenderness, and abundant mercy.

The Father Can Hardly Wait

In order to make people supremely happy, our heavenly Father has prepared a fabulous eternal home for them. Our dreams here are no match for what He has waiting! He can hardly wait to welcome His people on the glad homecoming day just ahead. Let's get the word out! And let's be ready. The countdown has already begun.

Your Questions Answered

1. God said to Adam and Eve, "In the day that you eat of it you shall surely die" (Genesis 2:17). Why didn't they die that day?

   Answer: The Bible speaks of two deaths: (1) The "first" death we all die (Hebrews 9:27). (2) The "second" death the wicked die in hellfire at the end of time (Revelation 21:8). The difference is that there is no resurrection from the second death. It is eternal.

Jesus Died the Second Death for Every Person
When Adam and Eve sinned, they immediately would have died the second death except for the fact that Jesus stepped forward and offered to die the second death on Calvary for every person. His supreme sacrifice spared them (Hebrews 2:9).

When Adam Sinned, His "Undying" Nature Became a "Dying" Nature
Regarding the first death, the literal rendition of the word "die" in Genesis 2:17 is "dying thou shalt die," which is noted in the margin of most Bibles. It means that Adam and Eve would enter into the process of dying. Before sinning, the couple possessed an undying, sinless nature. This nature was perpetuated by eating of the tree of life. At the moment of sin, their natures changed to dying, sinful natures. This is what God had predicted. Because they were barred from the tree of life, decay and deterioration—leading ultimately to death—began immediately. The grave became a certainty. The Lord stressed this later when He said to them, "For dust thou art, and unto dust shalt thou return" (Genesis 3:19).

2. But since God created Lucifer, isn't He really responsible for his sin?
Answer: Not at all. God created Lucifer a perfect, sinless angel. Lucifer made a devil of himself. Freedom to choose is a cornerstone principle of God's government. God knew Lucifer would sin when He created him. If at that point God had refused to create him, He would have been repudiating that prime principle of free choice.

"Freedom to Choose" Is God's Way
So, knowing full well what Lucifer would do, God still created him. The same facts apply to the creation of Adam and Eve. And, closer to home, these facts apply to you and me. God knows before we are born how we will live, but even so, He permits us to live and choose whether to endorse His government or Satan's. God is willing to be misunderstood and falsely accused and blamed for ages, while taking the time to allow every person to freely choose whom he will follow.

Only a Loving God Would Risk Granting Full Freedom for All
This glorious, crucial gift of freedom could come only from a just, open, loving God. It is an honor and joy to serve such a Lord and Friend.

Choose to Serve God
The sin problem will soon end. In the beginning, everything was "very good" (Genesis 1:31). Now "the whole world lieth in wickedness" (1 John 5:19). People everywhere are choosing to serve God or Satan. Use *your* fantastic, God-given freedom to choose to serve the Lord.

3. Why didn't God destroy the devil when he sinned, and thus end the sin problem?
Answer: Because sin was something completely new in God's universe, and its inhabitants did not understand it. Probably even Lucifer himself

did not fully comprehend it at first. Lucifer was a brilliant, highly respected angelic leader. His approach was doubtless one of great concern for heaven and the angels. It possibly ran something like this: "Heaven is good, but it would be improved with more angel input. Too much unchallenged authority (as the Father and Son have) tends to blind leaders to real life. Angels should not be required to take orders. We should give orders. God knows my suggestions are correct, and He is feeling threatened. We must not permit our noble leaders who are out of touch to jeopardize the very existence of heaven. They will listen if we move in unison. We must not be weak; we must act. Otherwise, we will all be ruined by a government that doesn't appreciate us."

One-Third of the Angels Joined Lucifer (Revelation 12:3, 4)
Lucifer's arguments convinced many angels, and one-third joined him. If God had destroyed Lucifer immediately, some angelic beings who did not fully understand God's character may have begun to worship God through fear, saying, "Lucifer may have been correct. Be careful. If you differ with God, He may kill you." So nothing would have been settled. Instead, the problem would have been heightened.

God Accepts Only Loving, Voluntary Service
The only service acceptable to God is cheerful, voluntary service prompted by love. Obedience for any other reason is unacceptable.

God Is Giving Satan Time to Demonstrate His Principles
Satan claimed he had a better plan for the government of the universe. God is giving him time to demonstrate its principles. The Lord will abolish sin only after every soul in the universe is convinced that Satan's government is unfair, hateful, ruthless, lying, and destructive.

The Universe Is Watching This World
The Bible says, "We are made a spectacle [margin says "theatre"] unto the world, and to angels, and to men" (1 Corinthians 4:9). The entire universe is watching as we each play a part in the controversy between Christ and Satan. As the controversy ends, every soul will fully understand the principles of both kingdoms and will have chosen to follow either Christ or Satan. Those who have chosen to ally with sin and Satan will be destroyed with him, and God's people will be taken to the eternal safety of their heavenly home.

3 Rescue from Above

Picture the horror of being stranded in an ocean with hungry, deadly sharks closing in! Then imagine how grateful and relieved you'd feel to be plucked to safety. The truth is, every person on the planet is lost in an ocean fraught with danger. We urgently need rescue, not from a boat or helicopter, but from our Heavenly Father. God loves you, so much that He sent His Son to save you. You've undoubtedly heard all this before, but are you sure you really understand what it's all about? What does it really mean to you, and can it really change your life? Read on and find out!

1. Does God really care about me?

This is what He says: "Since you were precious in My sight, you have been honored, and I have loved you" (Isaiah 43:4). "Yes, I have loved you with an everlasting love" (Jeremiah 31:3).

Answer: **God's never-ending love for you and me is far beyond our understanding. He loves you as though you were the only lost soul in the universe. He would have given His life for you or me even if there had been no other sinner to redeem. Try never to forget this fact. You are precious in His sight. He loves you.**

2. How has God demonstrated His love for us?

"For God so loved the world that He gave His only begotten Son, that whoever believes in Him should not perish but have everlasting life" (John 3:16). "In this the love of God was manifested toward us, that God has sent His only begotten Son into the world, that we might live through Him. In this is love, not that we loved God, but that He loved us and sent His Son to be the propitiation for our sins" (1 John 4:9, 10).

Answer: **Because He loved us so deeply, He was willing to see His only Son suffer and die rather than be separated from you and me for eternity. We will not be able to understand it, but He did it—just for you, just for me!**

3. How could He love someone like me?

"But God demonstrates His own love toward us, in that while we were still sinners, Christ died for us" (Romans 5:8).

Answer: **Certainly not because I earned it or deserved it. Not one of us has earned anything except the wages of sin, which is death (Romans 6:23). But God's love is unconditional. He loves the thieves, adulterers, and murderers. He also loves the selfish, the hypocritical, and the profane blasphemer. But, greatest of all, He loves me! And because He knows that my sins can lead only to misery and death, He wants to save me from my sins. That's why He died.**

4. What does His death do for me?

"Behold what manner of love the Father has bestowed on us, that we should be called children of God!" (1 John 3:1). "But as many as received Him, to them He gave the right to become children of God, to those who believe in His name" (John 1:12).

Answer: **Christ died to satisfy the death penalty against me. He was born as a man so He could suffer the kind of death I deserve. Then He offered to give me the credit for what He did. In other words, His sinless life is** credited to my account so I can be counted as righteous. His death is accepted by God as full payment for all my past wrongs, and by accepting what He did, as a gift, I am taken into God's own family as His child. It staggers the mind!

5. How do I receive Him and pass from death to life?
Just admit three things:
1. I am a sinner. "All have sinned" (Romans 3:23).
2. I am doomed to die. "The wages of sin is death" (Romans 6:23).
3. I cannot save myself. "Without Me you can do nothing" (John 15:5).

Then, believe three things:
1. He died for me. "That He [Jesus]...might taste death for everyone" (Hebrews 2:9).
2. He forgives me. "If we confess our sins, He is faithful and just to forgive us our sins" (1 John 1:9).
3. He saves me. "He who believes in Me has everlasting life" (John 6:47).

Answer: By asking for, believing in, and accepting the great gift of God, our Lord Jesus Christ.

Ponder these simple facts for a moment:
- Because of my sins, I am sentenced to death.
- I cannot pay that penalty without losing eternal life, because if I died for my sins, I could not resurrect myself. I would be dead forever.
- I owe something I cannot pay! But a friend comes along, in the person of Jesus, and says, "I will pay. I will die in your place and give you credit for it. You will not have to die for your sins."
- I must accept the offer! Simple, isn't it? I openly acknowledge and accept His death for my sins. The moment I do this, I have become a son or daughter of God!

6. What must I do in order to obtain this gift of salvation?
"Being justified freely by His grace through the redemption that is in Christ Jesus" (Romans 3:24). "A man is justified by faith apart from the deeds of the law" (Romans 3:28).

Answer: The only thing I can do is to accept it as a pure gift. My works of obedience will not help me one bit in the justification experience. All who ask for salvation in faith will receive it. The worst reprobate sinner will be accepted on the same basis as the most moral do-gooder. The past does not count. Remember, God loves everyone alike, and forgiveness is for the asking. "For by grace you have been saved through faith, and that not of yourselves; it is the gift of God, not of works, lest anyone should boast" (Ephesians 2:8, 9).

7. When I join His family through faith, what change does Jesus make in my life?
"Therefore, if anyone is in Christ, he is a new creation; old things have passed away; behold, all things have become new" (2 Corinthians 5:17).

Answer: As Christ is received into my heart, He destroys the old sinful self and actually changes me into a new spiritual creation. The old life of sin now becomes repulsive and undesirable. Joyfully I begin to experience, for the first time, glorious freedom from guilt and condemnation. I begin to see how empty my life has been without Christ. Rather than feeding on husks under the table, I now feast at the banquet of the King. One minute with God provides more happiness than does a lifetime of serving the devil. What an exchange! Why did I wait so long to accept it?

8. Will this changed life really be happier than the pleasures of the old life?

Jesus said: "These things I have spoken to you … that your joy may be full" (John 15:11). "Therefore if the Son makes you free, you shall be free indeed" (John 8:36). "I have come that they may have life, and that they may have it more abundantly" (John 10:10).

Answer: **Many feel that the Christian life will not be a happy one because of restrictions and self-denial. The exact opposite is true. When you accept the love of Jesus joy springs up within you, and even when hard times come the Christian has a companion to help in these times of need. The Christian can "rejoice and be exceeding glad" even in challenging circumstances, and "count it all joy" when trials come.**

9. But can I make myself do all the things a Christian should do?

"I have been crucified with Christ; it is no longer I who live, but Christ lives in me" (Galatians 2:20). "I can do all things through Christ who strengthens me" (Philippians 4:13).

Answer: **Here is where the greatest miracle of the Christian life is revealed. There is no forcing yourself to be good! What you do as a Christian is the spontaneous outflowing of another Person's life within you. Obedience is the natural response of love in your life. Being born of God, as a new creature, you want to obey Him because His life has become a part of your life. To please someone you love is not a burden, but a delight. "I delight to do Your will, O my God, and Your law is within my heart" (Psalm 40:8).**

10. Do you mean that even the Ten Commandments would not be hard to obey?

"If you love Me, keep My commandments" (John 14:15). "For this is the love of God, that we keep His commandments. And His commandments are not burdensome" (1 John 5:3). "But whoever keeps His word, truly the love of God is perfected in him" (1 John 2:5).

Answer: **The Bible always ties obedience to a love relationship. Born-again Christians find it no wearying struggle to keep the Ten Commandments. With all past sins covered by His atoning death, my present and future obedience is rooted in His victorious life within me. In fact, because I love Him so deeply for changing my life, I go beyond the requirements of the Ten Commandments. Daily I search the Bible for indications of His will, trying to find more little ways of expressing**

my love to Him. "And whatever we ask we receive from Him, because we keep His commandments and *do those things that are pleasing in His sight*" (1 John 3:22, emphasis added).

11. How can I be certain that the commandment-keeping mentioned of God's people in the Bible is not legalism?

"Here is the patience of the saints; here are those who keep the commandments of God and the faith of Jesus" (Revelation 14:12). "And they [the saints] overcame him [Satan] by the blood of the Lamb and by the word of their testimony, and they did not love their lives to the death" (Revelation 12:11).

Answer: Do not mistake obedience for legalism. Legalism is trying to earn salvation by good works. The saints are identified in the Bible as having four characteristics: (1) keeping the commandments, (2) trusting the blood of the Lamb, (3) sharing their faith with others, and (4) choosing to die rather than to sin. These are the true marks of the person who is in love with Christ and who has made a life commitment to follow Him.

12. What significant act seals the love relationship with Christ, and what does it symbolize?

"Therefore we were buried with Him through baptism into death, that just as Christ was raised from the dead by the glory of the Father, even so we also should walk in newness of life." … "That the body of sin might be done away with" (Romans 6:4, 6). "I have betrothed you to one husband, that I may present you as a chaste virgin to Christ" (2 Corinthians 11:2).

Answer: Baptism symbolizes three significant events in the life of the true believer: (1) death to sin, (2) birth to a new life in Christ, and (3) marriage to Christ for eternity. This spiritual union will grow stronger and sweeter with time, as long as love continues to grow. As in any marriage, the loss of love can turn a paradise into hell. When love disappears, the home is held together only by the mechanical, forced duty of the marriage law. Likewise, when the Christian ceases to love Christ supremely, his religion exists only as restrictive compliance to a set of rules.

13. How can I be certain that the faith and love of my marriage to Christ will continue to increase?

"Search the Scriptures" (John 5:39). "Pray without ceasing" (1 Thessalonians 5:17). "As you therefore have received Christ Jesus the Lord, so walk in Him" (Colossians 2:6). "I die daily" (1 Corinthians 15:31).

Answer: No love affair can prosper without communication. Prayer and Bible study are absolutely essential to keep this relationship growing. His Word constitutes a love letter that I must read daily to nourish the spiritual life. Conversing with Him in prayer deepens the devotion and opens my mind to a more thrilling and intimate knowledge of His concern for me. Daily I am amazed to discover details of His incredible provision for my happiness.

God Seals Our Spiritual Marriage

To seal our spiritual marriage for eternity, He has promised never to forsake me (Psalm 55:22; Matthew 28:20; Hebrews 13:5), to take care of me in sickness or in health (Psalm 41:3; Isaiah 41:10), and to provide for every need that could possibly develop in my life (Matthew 6:25-34). Just as I received Him by faith and found His promises all-sufficient, I keep on trusting Him for every future need, and He never lets me down.

Your Questions Answered

1. **How could one Man's death pay the penalty for the sins of all mankind? I have lived a terrible life of sin. I am afraid God would have to do something very special to atone for someone so evil.**

   Answer: Romans 3:23 tells us that "all have sinned." Because "the wages of sin is death" (Romans 6:23) and since "all have sinned," therefore "something special" is required for every person who has been born. Only One whose life is equal to all mankind could die for the sins of the race. Because Jesus is the Creator and Author of all life, the life He laid down was equivalent to the lives of all people who would ever live. Not only did atonement have to be made by One whose life could stand for all other created beings, but the One who died the atoning death had to be able to rise from that death. Why? In order to administer the benefits of the atonement to all who would apply for it in faith. "Therefore He is also able to save to the uttermost those who come to God through Him, since He always lives to make intercession for them" (Hebrews 7:25).

2. **If I accept Christ and His forgiveness and then fall again, will He forgive me again?**

   Answer: We can trust God to forgive us again if we are sorry for our sin and confess it. "If we confess our sins, He is faithful and just to forgive us our sins and to cleanse us from all unrighteousness" (1 John 1:9).

3. **If God forgives my sin and restores me to His family, will that eliminate any future punishment for my sins, or will I still be required to do some kind of penance?**

   Answer: The Scriptures say, "There is therefore now no condemnation to those who are in Christ Jesus" (Romans 8:1). Christ paid the full penalty for our transgressions, and those who accept Him in faith owe no works of penance for cleansing, but are already considered "washed" in the blood of the Lamb! Isaiah 43:25 contains a beautiful promise of forgiveness: "I, even I, am He who blots out your transgressions for My own sake; and I will not remember your sins." Micah 7:18, 19 shows the beautiful attitude of the Redeemer-God toward His people: "Who is a God like You, pardoning iniquity and passing over the transgression of the remnant of His heritage? He does not retain His anger forever, because He delights in mercy. He will again have compassion on us, and will subdue our iniquities. You will cast all our sins into the depths of the sea."

4 A Colossal City in Space

Talk about a great city! New York, Tokyo, and London are nothing in comparison! Just wait until you grasp the amazing facts about this gigantic city that can travel through space. It's all fact, not science fiction! The information in this Study Guide will thrill your soul and give you hope for your future!

1. Who is the architect and builder of this space city?

"Therefore God is not ashamed to be called their God, for He has prepared a city for them" (Hebrews 11:16).

Answer: The Bible declares that God is building a great city for His people. And this city is as real and literal as any you have ever known.

2. Where is this amazing city that God is preparing?

"Then I, John, saw the holy city, New Jerusalem, coming down out of heaven from God" (Revelation 21:2). "O Lord my God ... hear in heaven Your dwelling place" (1 Kings 8:28, 30).

Answer: This great city that is being constructed is, at this moment, in far outer space in God's dwelling place, which is called heaven.

3. How do the Scriptures describe this amazing space city?

Answer:

A. **Size** "The city is laid out as a square; its length is as great as its breadth. And he measured the city with the reed: twelve thousand furlongs" (Revelation 21:16). The city is perfectly square. Its perimeter is 12,000 furlongs, or 1,500 miles (a furlong is 1/8 mile). It is 375 miles long on each side.

B. **Name** The city is called "new Jerusalem" in Revelation 21:2.

C. **Walls** "He measured its wall and it was 144 cubits thick. ... The wall was made of jasper" (Revelation 21:17, 18). A wall 144 cubits, or 216 feet high (a cubit is 18 inches), surrounds the city. The wall is made of solid jasper, with radiance and beauty beyond description. Think of it! Nearly 20 stories high and solid jasper!

D. **Gates** "It had a great, high wall with twelve gates. ... There were three gates on the east, three on the north, three on the south and three on the west. ... The twelve gates were twelve pearls, each gate made of a single pearl" (Revelation 21:12, 13, 21). The city has 12 gates—three on each side—each one made of a single pearl.

E. **Foundations** "The wall of the city had twelve foundations ... decorated with every kind of precious stone. The first foundation was jasper, the second sapphire, the third chalcedony, the fourth emerald, the fifth sardonyx, the sixth carnelian, the seventh chrysolite, the eighth beryl, the ninth topaz, the tenth chrysoprase, the eleventh jacinth, and the twelfth amethyst" (Revelation 21:14, 19, 20). The city has 12 full, complete foundations—each one made of precious stone. Every color of the rainbow will be represented, so at a distance the city will no doubt appear to be resting upon a rainbow.

F. Streets "The great street of the city was of pure gold, like transparent glass" (Revelation 21:21).

G. Appearance "The Holy City, ... prepared as a bride beautifully dressed for her husband ... shone with the glory of God, and its brilliance was like that of a very precious jewel, like a jasper, clear as crystal. ... The city was laid out like a square, as long as it was wide" (Revelation 21:2, 11, 16). The city, with all of its precious stones, gold, and shimmering beauty, will be lighted with the glory of God. In its breathtaking majesty and purity it is compared to "a bride beautifully dressed for her husband."

4. What phenomenal feature of this majestic city assures every citizen eternal vigor and youth?

"In the middle of its street, and on either side of the river, was the tree of life, which bore twelve fruits, each tree yielding its fruit every month. The leaves of the tree were for the healing of the nations" (Revelation 22:2). "Take also of the tree of life, and eat, and live forever" (Genesis 3:22).

Answer: The tree of life, which bears 12 kinds of fruit (and is in the middle of the city—Revelation 2:7), brings unending life and youth to all who partake of it. Even its leaves will contain marvelous sustaining qualities. This tree will yield a new crop of fruit each month.

5. Is it true that this amazing city will descend to this earth?

"Then I, John, saw the holy city, New Jerusalem, coming down out of heaven from God, prepared as a bride adorned for her husband" (Revelation 21:2). "Blessed are the meek, for they shall inherit the earth" (Matthew 5:5). "The righteous will be recompensed on the earth" (Proverbs 11:31).

Answer: Yes, the majestic holy city will come down to this earth to become the capital of the earth made new. All the righteous will have a home in this city.

6. What will happen to sin and sinners?

"All the proud, yes, all who do wickedly will be stubble. And the day which is coming shall burn them up" (Malachi 4:1). "The elements shall melt with fervent heat, the earth also and the works that are therein shall be burned up" (2 Peter 3:10). "You shall trample the wicked, for they shall be ashes under the soles of your feet" (Malachi 4:3). "Nevertheless we, according to His promise, look for new heavens and a new earth in which righteousness dwells" (2 Peter 3:13).

Answer: God will cleanse the earth from sin and sinners, and will make a perfect new earth, and the holy city will be its capital. Here the righteous will live in joy, peace, and holiness throughout eternity. God promises that sin will not rise up again. See Nahum 1:9. (For full information on hell, see Study Guide 11.)

7. **What refreshing, thrilling promises does God make to the people who enter His new kingdom?**
   Answer:
   A. The Lord, in person, will live with them (Revelation 21:3).
   B. They will never become bored. There will be pleasures forevermore (Psalm 16:11).
   C. There will be no more death, pain, tears, sorrow, sickness, hospitals, operations, tragedy, disappointment, trouble, hunger, or thirst (Revelation 21:4; Isaiah 33:24; Revelation 22:3; Isaiah 65:23; Revelation 7:16).
   D. They will not get tired (Isaiah 40:31).
   E. Every saved person will be physically whole in every way. The deaf will hear, the blind will see, the dumb will sing, and the lame will be able to run (Isaiah 35:5, 6; Philippians 3:21).
   F. Jealousy, fear, hatred, falsehood, envy, impurity, cynicism, filth, worry, and all evil will be forever shut out of God's kingdom (Revelation 21:8, 27; 22:15). People will no longer be burdened with the worries and the cares that drive them to distraction. There will be no more nervous breakdowns. Time will become eternity, and the pressures and deadlines of earth will be gone forever.

8. **How will the new earth differ from our earth today?**
   Answer:
   A. Vast seas as we know them today will be gone (Revelation 21:1). The oceans and seas cover three-fourths of the earth's surface today. This will not be the case in God's new kingdom. The whole world will be one huge garden of unsurpassed beauty, interspersed with lakes, rivers, and mountains (Revelation 22:1; Acts 3:20, 21).
   B. The deserts will become gardens (Isaiah 35:1, 2).
   C. The animals will all be tame. None will prey upon others, and a little child will lead them (Isaiah 11:6-9; Isaiah 65:25).
   D. There will be no more curse (Revelation 22:3).
   E. There will be no more violence of any kind (Isaiah 60:18). This precludes crime, storms, floods, earthquakes, tornadoes, injury, etc.
   F. Nothing defiling will be found in the new earth (Revelation 21:27). There will be no cigarette butts, tobacco juice, drunkards, taverns, alcoholic beverages, brothels, lewd pictures, or any other wickedness or impurity of any kind.

9. **Will there be children in God's kingdom? If so, will they grow up?**
   "The streets of the city shall be full of boys and girls playing in its streets" (Zechariah 8:5). "And you shall go out and grow ... like stall-fed calves" (Malachi 4:2).
   Answer: Yes, there will be many boys and girls in the holy city (Isaiah 11:6-9), and these youngsters will grow up (Malachi 4:2). We have degenerated much in stature, intellect, and vitality since Adam, but all of this will be restored (Acts 3:20, 21).

10. When reunited with loved ones in heaven, will the saved know each other?

"Then I shall know just as I also am known" (1 Corinthians 13:12).

Answer: The Bible clearly teaches that righteous loved ones who have died will be raised to join the righteous living in God's kingdom (Isaiah 26:19; Jeremiah 31:15-17; 1 Corinthians 15:51-55; 1 Thessalonians 4:13-18). And the Scriptures also teach that people in God's new kingdom will know each other, just as people recognize each other on the earth today.

11. Will people in heaven be real, with flesh and bones?

"Jesus Himself stood in the midst of them, and said to them, 'Peace to you.' But they were terrified and frightened, and supposed they had seen a spirit. And He said to them, 'Why are you troubled? And why do doubts arise in your hearts? Behold My hands and My feet, that it is I Myself. Handle Me and see, for a spirit does not have flesh and bones as you see I have.' ... But while they still did not believe for joy, and marveled, He said to them, 'Have you any food here?' So they gave Him a piece of a broiled fish and some honeycomb. And He took it and ate in their presence. ... And He led them out as far as Bethany, and ... while He blessed them, that He was parted from them and carried up into heaven" (Luke 24:36-39, 41-43, 50, 51). "This same Jesus, who was taken up from you into heaven, will so come in like manner as you saw Him go into heaven" (Acts 1:11). "The Lord Jesus Christ ... will transform our lowly body that it may be conformed to His glorious body" (Philippians 3:20, 21).

Answer: **After His resurrection Jesus proved to His disciples that He was flesh and bones by having them feel Him and by eating food. This same Jesus of flesh and bones ascended to His Father and will come again to the earth. The righteous will be given bodies just like the body of Christ and will be real people with flesh and bones throughout eternity. The difference will be that the heavenly body will not be subject to death, decay, or deterioration. The teaching that the saved in heaven will be ghosts who float on mist clouds and do nothing but play harps has no foundation in the Scriptures. Jesus did not die on the cross to provide any such trivial and foolish future for those who accept His love and nobly follow His way of life. Most people have no interest in such an ethereal existence and, therefore, have little or no desire to enter God's heavenly kingdom—often preferring it only because they fear hell. If only all people everywhere could learn the truth about God's holy city and new earth, millions would begin to understand His love and would turn to Him with all their hearts. A person who misses out on God's kingdom has made the supreme blunder of a lifetime.**

12. How will the righteous spend their time in the heavenly kingdom?

"They shall build houses and inhabit them; They shall plant vineyards and eat their fruit. They shall not build and another inhabit; They shall not plant and another eat; ... And My elect shall long enjoy the work of their hands" (Isaiah 65:21, 22).

Answer: The righteous will build their own homes in the new earth. (Each will also have a city mansion built by Christ—John 14:1-3.) They will plant vineyards and eat the fruit from them. The Bible is plain. Real people do real things in heaven, and they will thoroughly enjoy it all.

13. In what other thrilling activities will the redeemed be engaged?
Answer:
- A. Sing and play heavenly music (Isaiah 35:10; 51:11; Psalm 87:7; Revelation 14:2, 3).
- B. Worship before God's throne every week (Isaiah 66:22, 23).
- C. Enjoy never-fading flowers and trees (Ezekiel 47:12; Isaiah 35:1, 2).
- D. Visit with loved ones, patriarchs, prophets, etc. (Matthew 8:11; Revelation 7:9-17).
- E. Study the animals of heaven (Isaiah 11:6-9; 65:25).
- F. Travel and explore without ever becoming weary (Isaiah 40:31).
- G. Listen to God sing (Zephaniah 3:17).
- H. Realize fondest ambitions (Psalm 37:3, 4; Isaiah 65:24).
- I. Greatest joy of all—the privilege of being like Jesus, traveling with Him, and seeing Him face to face (Revelation 14:4; 22:4; 21:3; 1 John 3:2).

14. Can feeble human language really describe the glories of the heavenly home?
"Eye has not seen, nor ear heard, nor have entered into the heart of man the things which God has prepared for those who love Him" (1 Corinthians 2:9).

Answer: Not even in its wildest dreams can the heart of man begin to comprehend the marvels of God's eternal kingdom. All that Adam lost will be restored (Acts 3:20, 21).

15. Is this kingdom being prepared for me personally?
"Whoever desires, let him take the water of life freely" (Revelation 22:17). "To an inheritance incorruptible ... reserved in heaven for you" (1 Peter 1:4). "I go to prepare a place for you" (John 14:2).

Answer: It is prepared for you personally. The invitation from the Lord is to you personally. If rejected, friend, you will have no one to blame but yourself.

16. How can I be assured of a place in that great and glorious kingdom?
"Behold, I stand at the door and knock. If anyone hears My voice and opens the door, I will come in" (Revelation 3:20). "Blessed are those who do His commandments, that they may have the right to the tree of life, and may enter through the gates into the city" (Revelation 22:14). "Not everyone who says to Me, 'Lord, Lord,' shall enter the kingdom of heaven, but he who does the will of My Father in heaven" (Matthew 7:21). "But as many as received Him, to them He gave the right to become children of God" (John 1:12). "The blood of Jesus Christ His Son cleanses us from all sin" (1 John 1:7).

Answer: The Bible makes it plain. It is simple. Give your life to Christ for cleansing from sin. When you do this, He also gives you power to do His will and keep His commandments. This means, of course, that you will begin to live as Christ lived and will overcome all sin. "He who overcomes shall inherit all things" (Revelation 21:7). In short, a person is prepared for heaven when he has heaven in his heart.

Your Questions Answered

1. **How can heaven be a happy place when the saved think of loved ones who are lost?**

   Answer: The Bible says that God will "wipe away every tear from their eyes" (Revelation 21:4). Surrounded by the beauty and joys of the new earth, God's redeemed people will forget the tragedies and heartaches of the past; "the former shall not be remembered or come to mind" (Isaiah 65:17).

2. **Is the holy city really big enough to hold all the saved people of all ages?**

   Answer: If the city were to be crowded and each saved person given only 100 square feet of ground space, there would be room for 39 billion people in the city, which is many times the present population of the world. Many statisticians believe that if all the people who have ever lived were saved, there would be plenty of room for them in the city. The Scriptures make it clear, however, that only a few will be saved (Matthew 7:14). So there will be more than enough room in the great city.

3. **Will little babies who die be saved in God's kingdom?**

   Answer: We do not have a specific Bible answer to this question, but many choose to believe that infants will be saved on the basis of Matthew 2:16-18. There the Bible tells of wicked king Herod slaying all the male babies in Bethlehem who were two years old or younger. The Old Testament foretold this tragic, cruel incident, and God told the mothers to stop crying because their children would one day be restored to them. "Refrain your voice from weeping, ... they [the slain children] shall come back from the land of the enemy. ... Your children shall come back to their own border" (Jeremiah 31:16, 17). This is an obvious reference to the resurrection.

4. **Do I understand correctly that heaven, the home of the saved, will be right here on this earth?**

   Answer: That is correct. Although the holy city is now in God's dwelling place, He is going to move it to this earth. The holy city will be the capital of the new earth, and God will move His throne here (Revelation 21:2, 3; 22:1, 3) and live with the righteous right here on this earth throughout eternity. And where the Lord abides, that is heaven. God's plan is to restore to man what Adam lost: the glories of a perfect life on a perfect planet. Satan and sin interrupted God's plan, but the plan will be carried out. We can all share in this new kingdom—and we must! It's too much to miss.

5. Seventeen Keys for a Happy Marriage

As you've probably heard, nearly half of all marriages now end in divorce, leaving bitter spouses and confused children in their wake. Don't let this happen to you! Whether your marriage is going through tough times or is experiencing marital bliss, or even if you're not yet married but considering it, here's some free but proven advice to help your marriage last. It's straight from God, the one who created and ordained marriage! If you've tried everything else, why not give God a chance? Follow the keys in this guide, and you can secure your home.

1. Establish your own private home.

"Therefore a man shall leave his father and mother and be joined to his wife, and they shall become one flesh" (Genesis 2:24).

Comment: **God's rule is specific. A married couple must leave father and mother and establish their own home, even if finances require that it be a one-room apartment. Husband and wife should decide together on such policies as these. Then she should inform her relatives and he, his. They must remain firm no matter who opposes. Thousands of divorces would be avoided if this rule were carefully followed.**

2. Continue your courtship.

"And above all things have fervent love for one another, for 'love will cover a multitude of sins'" (1 Peter 4:8). "Her husband ... praises her" (Proverbs 31:28). "She who is married cares ... how she may please her husband" (1 Corinthians 7:34). "Be kindly affectionate to one another ... in honor giving preference to one another" (Romans 12:10).

Comment: **Continue (or perhaps revive) the courtesies of courtship in your married life. Successful marriages do not just happen; they must be developed. Don't take each other for granted, or the monotony that results will destroy your marriage. Keep love growing by expressing love for one another or it will die, and you will drift apart. Love and happiness are not found by seeking them for yourself, but rather by giving them to others. So spend as much time as possible doing things together if you would get along well. Learn to greet each other with enthusiasm. Relax, visit, shop, sightsee, eat together. Don't overlook the little courtesies, encouragements, and affectionate acts. Surprise each other with little gifts or favors. Try to "out-love" each other. Don't take more out of marriage than you put into it. Divorce itself is not the greatest destroyer of marriage, but rather, lack of love. Given a chance, love always wins.**

3. Remember that God joined you together in marriage.

"For this reason a man shall leave his father and mother and be joined to his wife. ... So then, they are no longer two but one flesh. Therefore what God has joined together, let not man separate" (Matthew 19:5, 6).

> **Comment:** Has love almost disappeared from your home? The devil (that notorious home-breaker) is responsible for this. Don't forget that God Himself joined you together in marriage, and He intends for you to stay together and be happy. He will bring happiness and love into your lives if you will obey His divine rules (commandments). "With God all things are possible" (Matthew 19:26). Don't despair. God, who places love in the heart of a missionary for a leprous savage, can easily give you love for each other if you will let Him.

4. Guard your thoughts—don't let your senses trap you.

"For as he thinks in his heart, so is he" (Proverbs 23:7). "You shall not covet your neighbor's wife" (Exodus 20:17). "Keep your heart with all diligence, for out of it spring the issues of life" (Proverbs 4:23). "Whatever things are true, ... noble, ... just, ... pure, ... lovely, ... of good report, ... meditate on these things" (Philippians 4:8).

> **Comment:** The wrong kind of thinking will destroy your marriage. The devil will trap you with thoughts like these: "Our marriage was a mistake." "She doesn't understand me." "I can't take much more of this." "We can always divorce if necessary." "I'll go home to mother." "He smiled at that woman." Stop thinking thoughts like these or your marriage is gone, because your thoughts and senses govern your actions. Avoid seeing, saying, reading, or hearing anything that (or associating with anyone who) suggests impurity or unfaithfulness. Thoughts uncontrolled are like an automobile in neutral on a hill. Anything can happen, and the result is always disaster.

5. Never retire for the night angry with each other.

"Do not let the sun go down on your wrath" (Ephesians 4:26). "Confess your trespasses to one another" (James 5:16). "Forgetting those things which are behind" (Philippians 3:13). "Be kind to one another, tenderhearted, forgiving one another, even as God in Christ forgave you" (Ephesians 4:32).

> **Comment:** To remain angry and upset over hurts and grievances (big or little) is exceedingly dangerous. Unless quickly solved, even little problems become set in your mind as convictions and attitudes adversely affecting your whole philosophy of life. This is why God says to let anger cool before retiring at night. Be big enough to forgive and to say with sincerity, "I'm sorry." After all, no one is perfect, and you are both on the same team, so be sportsmanlike enough to honestly admit a mistake when you make it. Besides, making up is a very pleasant experience, with unusual powers to draw marriage partners closer together. God suggests it! It works!

6. Keep Christ in the center of your home.

"Unless the Lord builds the house, they labor in vain who build it" (Psalm 127:1). "In all your ways acknowledge Him, and He shall direct your paths" (Proverbs 3:6). "And the peace of God, which surpasses all understanding, will guard your hearts and minds through Christ Jesus" (Philippians 4:7).

Comment: This is the greatest rule. It really covers all the others. Put Christ first! The real secret of true happiness in the home is not diplomacy, strategy, and untiring effort to overcome problems, but rather, union with Christ. Hearts filled with Christ's love can never be very far apart. With Christ in the home, marriage will be successful. The gospel is the cure for all marriages that are filled with hatred, bitterness, and disappointment. It prevents thousands of divorces by miraculously restoring love and happiness. It will save your marriage, too, if you are willing.

7. Pray together.

"Watch and pray, lest you enter into temptation. The spirit indeed is willing, but the flesh is weak" (Matthew 26:41). "Pray for one another" (James 5:16). "If any of you lacks wisdom, let him ask of God, who gives to all liberally" (James 1:5).

Comment: Pray aloud for each other! This is a wonderful rule that succeeds beyond the wildest dream. Kneel before God and ask Him for true love for one another, for forgiveness, for strength, for wisdom—for the solution to problems. God has given a personal guarantee that He will answer. The praying person is not automatically cured of all of his faults, but he will have a heart that wants to do right. No family ever breaks up while sincerely praying together for God's help.

8. Agree that divorce is not the answer.

"What God has joined together, let not man separate" (Matthew 19:6). "Whoever divorces his wife, except for sexual immorality, and marries another, commits adultery; and whoever marries her who is divorced commits adultery" (Matthew 19:9). "For the woman who has a husband is bound by the law to her husband as long as he lives" (Romans 7:2).

Comment: The Bible is clear. The ties of marriage are meant to be indissoluble and indestructible. Divorce is permissible only in the case of adultery. But even then it is not demanded, only permitted. Forgiveness is always better than divorce, even in the case of a moral fall. Marriage is for life. God so ordained it when he performed the first wedding in Eden. Thoughts of divorce as a solution will destroy any marriage. This is one reason Jesus ruled it out. Divorce is always destructive and almost never a solution to the problem. Instead, it creates much greater problems, so it should never be considered. Torn, frustrated, unhappy, twisted lives almost inevitably follow divorce, and even success in life itself is often thwarted. God instituted marriage to guard people's purity and happiness, to provide for their social needs, and to elevate their physical, mental, and moral nature. Its vows are among the most solemn and binding obligations that human beings can assume. To lightly set them aside results in removing one's self from God's favor and blessing.

9. Keep the family circle closed tightly.

"You shall not commit adultery" (Exodus 20:14). "The heart of her husband safely trusts her. ... She does him good and not evil all the days of her life" (Proverbs 31:11, 12). "The Lord has been witness between you and the wife of your youth, with whom you have dealt treacherously" (Malachi 2:14). "Keep you from the evil woman. ... Do not lust after her beauty in your heart, nor let her allure you with her eyelids. ... Can a man take fire to his bosom, and his clothes not be burned? ... So is he who goes in to his neighbor's wife; whoever touches her shall not be innocent" (Proverbs 6:24, 25, 27, 29).

Comment: Family intimacies must never be shared with others—not even with parents. It is a great sin and a tragedy to break this God-given rule. A third person to sympathize or listen to complaints is a tool of the devil to estrange the hearts of husband and wife. Solve your home problems privately. No one else (except your minister or marriage counselor) should ever be involved. Always be truthful with each other, and never keep secrets from each other. Tell no jokes at the expense of your spouse's feelings. Vigorously defend each other, and strictly exclude all intruders. And as for adultery (in spite of what some marriage counselors say), it always hurts you and everyone else involved. God, who knows our mind, body, and emotional structure (and knows what helps or hurts us) says, "Thou shalt not." And when He says, "Don't," we had better not. Those who ignore His rule will pay the supreme penalty. So if flirtations have begun, break them off at once, or shadows may settle over your life that cannot be lifted.

10. God describes love; make it your daily goal to measure up.

"Love suffers long and is kind; love does not envy; love does not parade itself, is not puffed up; does not behave rudely, does not seek its own, is not provoked, thinks no evil; does not rejoice in iniquity, but rejoices in the truth; bears all things, believes all things, hopes all things, endures all things" (1 Corinthians 13:4-7).

Comment: Please reread the above Scripture passage carefully. This is God's true description of love. How do you measure up? Love is not a sentimental impulse, but a holy principle that involves every phase and action of life. With true love, your marriage cannot fail. Without it, it cannot succeed.

11. Remember that criticism and nagging destroy love.

"Husbands, love your wives and do not be bitter toward them" (Colossians 3:19). "Better to dwell in the wilderness, than with a contentious and angry woman" (Proverbs 21:19). "A continual dripping on a very rainy day and a contentious woman are alike" (Proverbs 27:15). "Why do you look at the speck [splinter] in your brother's eye, but do not consider the plank [whole board] in your own eye?"

(Matthew 7:3). "Love suffers long and is kind; love does not envy; love does not parade itself" (1 Corinthians 13:4).

Comment: Stop criticizing, nagging, and faultfinding. Your husband or wife may lack much, but nagging won't help. Don't expect perfection, or bitterness will result. Overlook faults, and hunt for the good things. Don't try to reform, control, or compel your partner—you will destroy love. Only God can change people. A sense of humor, a cheerful heart, kindness, patience, and affection will banish two-thirds of your marriage problems. Try to make your spouse happy rather than good, and the good will take care of itself. The secret of a successful marriage lies not in having the right partner, but rather in being the right partner.

12. Do not overdo in anything; be temperate.

"Everyone who competes for the prize is temperate in all things" (1 Corinthians 9:25). "Love …does not seek its own [selfish advantage]" (1 Corinthians 13:4, 5). "Whether you eat or drink, or whatever you do, do all to the glory of God" (1 Corinthians 10:31). "I discipline my body and bring it into subjection" (1 Corinthians 9:27). "If anyone will not work, neither shall he eat" (2 Thessalonians 3:10). "Marriage is honorable among all, and the bed undefiled" (Hebrews 13:4). "Therefore do not let sin reign in your mortal body, that you should obey it in its lusts, and do not present your members as instruments of unrighteousness to sin" (Romans 6:12, 13).

Comment: Overdoing will ruin your marriage. So will underdoing. Work, love, rest, exercise, play, worship, meals, and social contacts must be carefully balanced in your marriage, or something will snap. Overwork and the lack of sleep, proper food, or exercise make a person critical, intolerant, and negative. Constant overeating is a great evil that strengthens the lower nature and dulls the conscience. Sexual abuses destroy a love for holy things and weaken vitality. Marriage gives no license to sexual excesses. Degrading, twisted, or intemperate sex acts destroy love and respect for one another. A temperate sex life is recommended by the Bible (1 Corinthians 7:3-7). Social contacts with others are absolutely essential. True happiness cannot be found in isolation. We must learn to laugh and enjoy wholesome, good times. To be overly serious is dangerous. Overdoing or underdoing in anything weakens the mind, body, conscience, and the ability to love and respect one another. Don't let intemperance wreck your marriage.

13. Respect each other's personal rights and privacies.

"Love suffers long and is kind. … love does not envy. … does not behave rudely, does not seek its own [in selfishness]. … does not rejoice in iniquity. … believes all things, hopes all things, endures all things" (1 Corinthians 13:4-7). "Be kindly affectionate to one another with brotherly love, in honor giving preference to one another" (Romans 12:10).

Comment: Each spouse has a God-given right to certain personal privacies without explanation. Do not tamper with each other's wallets or purses, personal mail, and other private property unless given permission. The right to privacy and quietude when preoccupied should be respected. Your husband or wife even has a right to be wrong part of the time and is entitled to an "off-day" without being given the third degree. Marriage partners do not own each other and should never try to force personality changes. Only God can make such changes, and we shall all answer personally to Him on this matter (Romans 14:12). Perfect confidence and trust in one another—no checking up on each other—is absolutely essential for happiness. Spend less time trying to "figure out" your spouse and more time trying to please her or him. This works wonders.

14. Be clean, modest, orderly, and dutiful.

"In like manner also, that the women adorn themselves in modest apparel" (1 Timothy 2:9). "She … willingly works with her hands. … She also rises while it is yet night, And provides food for her household. … She watches over the ways of her household, and does not eat the bread of idleness" (Proverbs 31:13, 15, 27). "Be clean" (Isaiah 52:11). "Let all things be done decently and in order" (1 Corinthians 14:40). "If anyone does not provide for his own, and especially for those of his household, he has denied the faith and is worse than an unbeliever" (1 Timothy 5:8). "Do not become sluggish [slothful]" (Hebrews 6:12).

Comment: Laziness, disorder, dirt, and slovenliness are the devil's weapons to destroy your respect and affection for one another, and thus ruin your marriage. Neat, modest attire and clean, well-groomed bodies are essential for both husband and wife. The meals should be wholesome, attractive, and served on time. The home should be clean and orderly, because this brings peace, calmness, and satisfaction to all. A lazy, shiftless husband who does not provide for his household is a curse to his family and an insult to God. Carelessness in some of these seemingly small matters is destroying homes by the thousands.

15. Determine to speak softly and kindly.

"A soft answer turns away wrath, but a harsh word stirs up anger" (Proverbs 15:1). "Live joyfully with the wife whom you love" (Ecclesiastes 9:9). "When I became a man, I put away childish things" (1 Corinthians 13:11).

Comment: Force yourself to speak softly and kindly to your spouse. Silence, when one is attacked, is often the best method to cool wrath. Decisions made when angry, tired, or discouraged are unreliable anyway, so it's best to relax and let anger cool. And when you do speak, let it always be quietly and lovingly. Harsh, angry words crush your spouse's desire to please you.

16. Be reasonable in money matters.

"Love does not envy [is not possessive]. ... does not behave rudely, does not seek its own [selfish advantage]" (1 Corinthians 13:4, 5). "God loves a cheerful giver" (2 Corinthians 9:7).

Comment: All possessions and income in marriage should be "ours," not "yours" and "mine." Wives who don't work outside the home should receive a regular amount for groceries, clothing, and other budgeted items. It should be cheerfully provided instead of grudgingly released under protest. Wife and husband both should have small, equal sums (whenever possible) to spend as desired without giving account. A miserly husband usually angers his wife into being a spender, just as a wasteful husband makes a wife stingy. Showing confidence in your companion's managing ability will usually make him or her more businesslike.

17. Talk things over and counsel together freely.

"Love suffers long and is kind; love does not envy; love does not parade itself, is not puffed up" (1 Corinthians 13:4, 5). "He who disdains instruction despises his own soul" (Proverbs 15:32). "Do you see a man wise in his own eyes? There is more hope for a fool than for him" (Proverbs 26:12).

Comment: Few things will strengthen your marriage more than counseling together on all major decisions. Changing a job or purchasing a home, an automobile, a boat, furniture, clothing (major items at least), and all other items that require money involve both husband and wife, and the opinions of both should be considered. Talking things over together will avoid many blunders that could ruin your marriage. If, after much discussion and earnest prayer, opinions still differ, the wife should submit to her husband's decision. Scripture is clear on this. (See Ephesians 5:22-24.)

Your Questions Answered

1. **My husband is a godless man, and I am trying to be a Christian. His influence is terrible. Should I divorce him?**

   Answer: No! Read 1 Corinthians 7:12-14 and 1 Peter 3:1, 2. God gives a specific answer.

2. **When my husband displeases me, I won't sleep with him. He says I am wrong Am I?**

   Answer: Yes! God gives a definite answer to this question in 1 Corinthians 7:4, 5.

3. **My wife ran off with another man. Now repentant, she wants to return home. My pastor says I should take her back, but God forbids this, doesn't He?**

   Answer: No. No, indeed! God permits divorce for adultery, but does not command it. Forgiveness is always better and is always in order. (See Matthew 6:14, 15.) Divorce will seriously mar your life and the lives of your children. Give her another chance! The golden rule (Matthew 7:12) applies here. If you and your wife will turn your lives over to Christ, He will make your marriage supremely happy. It is not too late.

4. **What can I do? Men are always attempting familiarities with me.**
   Answer: Be very careful of your conduct. God says, "Abstain from all appearance of evil" (1 Thessalonians 5:22). Perhaps your conduct around men—a suggestive smile, immodest clothing, off-color jokes, or a "too relaxed" and comfortable attitude—encourages their advances. There is something about Christian reserve and dignity that keeps a man in his place. Christ said, "Let your light so shine before men, that they may see your good works and glorify your Father in heaven" (Matthew 5:16). When Christ really shines from your life, you will have little trouble with evil men and their advances.

5. **Can you tell me simply and plainly what God's counsel is to one who has fallen but is truly repentant?**
   Answer: Long ago Christ gave a pointed and comforting answer to one who had fallen into immorality but was repentant. He said, "Go and sin no more" (John 8:11). His counsel still applies today.

6. **Does God expect me to live with a physically abusive spouse?**
   Answer: Physical abuse can be life threatening and is a serious problem that demands immediate attention. The spouse and family members who have been physically abused must find a safe environment in which to live. Both husband and wife need to seek professional help through a qualified Christian marriage counselor.

6 Written in Stone

CENTURIES AGO, God wrote His law in stone, and you're still supposed to keep it today! It's absolutely true that violating any part of God's law always brings negative consequences. As crime overruns our cities, doesn't it make sense that for peace and safety we need to obey the laws of the land? Well, this same principle applies with God's law—the Ten Commandments—in our own lives too! They aren't called the ten suggestions, ten recommendations, or the ten great ideas. Since so much is at stake, you should take a few minutes to seriously consider your responsibility.

1. **Did God Himself really write the Ten Commandments?**
   "He gave Moses two tablets of the Testimony, tablets of stone, written with the finger of God." … "Now the tablets were the work of God, and the writing was the writing of God engraved on the tablets" (Exodus 31:18; 32:16).

   Answer: Yes, the great God of heaven wrote the Ten Commandments on tables of stone with His own finger.

2. What is God's definition of sin?

"Sin is lawlessness" (1 John 3:4).

Answer: Sin is breaking God's Ten Commandment law. And since the law of God is perfect (Psalm 19:7), its principles cover every conceivable sin. It is impossible to commit a sin that is not condemned by at least one of God's Ten Commandments. The commandments cover "man's all [the whole duty of man]" (Ecclesiastes 12:13). Nothing is left out.

3. Why did God give us the Ten Commandments?

"Happy is he who keeps the law" (Proverbs 29:18). "Keep my commands; For length of days and long life and peace they will add to you" (Proverbs 3:1, 2).

Answer A: As a guide for happy, abundant living. God created us to enjoy happiness, peace, long life, contentment, accomplishment, and all the other great blessings for which our hearts long. God's law is the road map that points out the right paths to follow in order to find this true, supreme happiness.

"By the law is the knowledge of sin" (Romans 3:20). "I would not have known sin except through the law. For I would not have known covetousness unless the law had said, 'You shall not covet'" (Romans 7:7).

Answer B: To show me the difference between right and wrong. God's law is like a mirror (James 1:23-25). It points out wrongdoing in my life as a mirror points out dirt on my face. The only possible way for a person to know if he is sinning is for him to carefully check his life by the mirror of God's law. Hope for this mixed-up, sinking generation is found in God's Ten Commandment law. It tells where to draw the line!

"And the Lord commanded us to observe all these statutes [commandments] … for our good always" (Deuteronomy 6:24). "Hold me up, and I shall be safe, and I shall observe Your statutes continually. You reject all those who stray from Your statutes" (Psalm 119:117, 118).

Answer C: To protect me from danger and tragedy. God's law is like a strong cage at the zoo, which protects us from fierce, destructive animals. It protects us from impurity, falsehood, murder, idolatry, theft, and many other evils that destroy life, peace, and happiness. All good laws protect, and God's law is no exception.

"Now by this we know that we know Him, if we keep His commandments" (1 John 2:3).

Answer D: It helps us to know God.

Special Note: The eternal principles of God's law are written deep in every person's nature by the God who created us. The writing may be dim and smudged, but it is still there. This means, of course, that you cannot find true peace unless you are willing to live in harmony with your inner nature, upon which God has written these principles. We were created to live in harmony with them. When we choose to ignore them, the result is always tension, unrest, and tragedy—just as ignoring the rules for safe driving leads to serious trouble.

4. Why is God's law exceedingly important to me personally?

"So speak and so do as those who will be judged by the law of liberty" (James 2:12). **Answer: Because the Ten Commandment law is the standard by which God examines people in the heavenly judgment. How are you measuring up? It is a life-or-death matter!**

5. Can God's law (the Ten Commandments) ever be changed or abolished?

"It is easier for heaven and earth to pass away than for one tittle of the law to fail" (Luke 16:17). "My covenant I will not break, nor alter the word that has gone out of My lips" (Psalm 89:34). "All His precepts [commandments] are sure. They stand fast forever and ever" (Psalm 111:7, 8).

Answer: Absolutely not! The Bible is very clear on this point. If the law could have been changed, God would have immediately made that change when Adam and Eve sinned instead of sending His Son to die in the sinner's behalf to pay the penalty of the broken law. This was impossible. The commandments are revealed principles of God's holy character that will always be true as long as God exists.

	God Is:	The Law Is:
GOOD	Luke 18:19	1 Timothy 1:8
HOLY	Isaiah 5:16	Romans 7:12
PERFECT	Matthew 5:48	Psalm 19:7
PURE	1 John 3:2, 3	Psalm 19:8
JUST	Deuteronomy 32:4	Romans 7:12
TRUE	John 3:33	Psalm 19:9
SPIRITUAL	1 Corinthians 10:4	Romans 7:14
RIGHTEOUSNESS	Jeremiah 23:6	Psalm 119:172
FAITHFUL	1 Corinthians 1:9	Psalm 119:86
LOVE	1 John 4:8	Romans 13:10
UNCHANGEABLE	James 1:17	Matthew 5:18
ETERNAL	Genesis 21:33	Psalm 111:7, 8

Notice on this chart that God and His law have the same characteristics. Do you see what this means? The Ten Commandment law is God's character in written form—written so we can comprehend it. It is no more possible to change God's law than to pull God out of heaven and change Him. Jesus came to show us what the law (which is the pattern for holy living) looked like when made up in human form. God's character can never change. Neither can His law, for it is His character in human language.

6. Did Jesus abolish God's law while He was here on earth?

"Do not think that I came to destroy the Law. ... I did not come to destroy but to fulfill. ... Till heaven and earth pass away, one jot or one tittle will by no means pass from the law till all is fulfilled" (Matthew 5:17, 18).

Answer: No, indeed! Jesus specifically asserted that He did not come to destroy the law, but to fulfill (or keep) it. Instead of doing away with the law, Jesus magnified it (Isaiah 42:21) as the perfect guide for right living. For example, Jesus pointed out that "You shall not murder" condemns

anger "without a cause" (Matthew 5:21, 22) and hatred (1 John 3:15), and that lust is adultery (Matthew 5:27, 28). He says, "If you love Me, keep My commandments" (John 14:15).

7. Will people who knowingly continue to break even one of God's commandments be saved?

"The wages of sin is death" (Romans 6:23). "He will destroy its sinners from it" (Isaiah 13:9). "For whoever shall keep the whole law, and yet stumble in one point, he is guilty of all" (James 2:10).

Answer: The Ten Commandment law is the guide we must use in finding our way to God and holy living. If I ignore even one of the commandments, I am neglecting part of the divine pattern, or blueprint. If only one link of a chain is broken, its entire purpose is undone. The Bible says that when we knowingly break any command of God, we are sinning (James 4:17), because we have refused His will for us. Only those who do His will can enter the kingdom of heaven. Of course, God will forgive anyone who genuinely repents and accepts Christ's power to change.

8. Can anyone be saved by keeping the law?

"By the deeds of the law no flesh will be justified in His sight" (Romans 3:20). "For by grace you have been saved through faith, and that not of yourselves; it is the gift of God, not of works, lest anyone should boast" (Ephesians 2:8, 9).

Answer: No! The answer is too plain to miss. No one can be saved by keeping the law. Salvation comes only through grace, as a free gift from Jesus Christ, and we receive this gift by faith, not by works. The law serves only as a mirror to point out sin in our lives. Cleansing and forgiveness from that sin come only through Christ.

9. Why, then, is the law an absolute essential for perfecting Christian character?

"Fear God and keep His commandments, for this is man's all [whole duty]" (Ecclesiastes 12:13). "By the law is the knowledge of sin" (Romans 3:20).

Answer: Because the full pattern, or "whole duty," for Christian living is contained in God's law. Like a 6-year-old boy who made his own ruler, measured himself, and told his mother that he was 12 feet tall, our own standards are never safe. I cannot know whether I am a sinner unless I look carefully into the perfect standard—God's law-mirror. Millions who have cast out devils, prophesied, and done many wonderful works in Jesus' name will be lost (Matthew 7:21-23) because they did not bother to check their lives with His great law-pattern. Hence, they think they are righteous and saved when, instead, they are sinful and lost. "Now by this we know that we know Him, if we keep His commandments" (1 John 2:3).

10. What enables a truly converted Christian to follow the pattern of God's law?

"I will put My laws in their mind and write them on their hearts" (Hebrews 8:10). "I can do all things through Christ" (Philippians 4:13). "God did by sending

His own Son … that the righteous requirement of the law might be fulfilled in us" (Romans 8:3, 4).

Answer: Christ not only pardons repentant sinners, but He restores in them the image of God. He brings them into harmony with His law through the power of His indwelling presence. "Thou shalt not" then becomes a promise that the Christian will not steal, lie, murder, etc., because Jesus lives inside and is in control. God could not change His law, but He made a blessed provision through Jesus to change the sinner so he can measure up to that law.

11. But isn't a Christian who has faith and is living under grace freed from keeping the law?

"For sin [breaking God's law—1 John 3:4] shall not have dominion over you: for you are not under the law, but under grace. What then? Shall we sin [break the law] because we are not under law but under grace? Certainly not!" (Romans 6:14, 15). "Do we then make void the law through faith? Certainly not! On the contrary, we establish the law" (Romans 3:31).

Answer: No! The Scriptures teach the very opposite. Grace is like the governor's pardon to a prisoner. It forgives him, but it does not give him freedom to break one single law on the statute books. The forgiven person, living under grace, is under double obligation to keep the law. A person who refuses to keep God's law, saying that he is living under grace, is mistaken. He is living under *dis*grace.

12. Are the Ten Commandments of God Reaffirmed in the New Testament?

Answer: Yes, and very clearly so. Look the following over very carefully.

The Law of God in the New Testament

1. "You shall worship the Lord your God, and Him only you shall serve" (Matthew 4:10).
2. "Little children, keep yourselves from idols" (1 John 5:21). "Therefore, since we are the offspring of God, we ought not to think that the Divine Nature is like gold or silver or stone, something shaped by art and man's devising" (Acts 17:29).
3. "That the name of God and His doctrine may not be blasphemed" (1 Timothy 6:1).
4. "For He has spoken in a certain place of the seventh day in this way: 'And God rested on the seventh day from all His works.'" "There remains therefore a rest [keeping of a sabbath, margin] for the people of God. For he who has entered His rest has himself also ceased from his works as God did from His" (Hebrews 4:4, 9, 10).
5. "Honor your father and your mother" (Matthew 19:19).
6. "You shall not murder" (Romans 13:9).
7. "You shall not commit adultery" (Matthew 19:18).
8. "You shall not steal" (Romans 13:9).
9. "You shall not bear false witness" (Romans 13:9).
10. "You shall not covet" (Romans 7:7).

The Law of God in the Old Testament
1. "You shall have no other gods before Me" (Exodus 20:3).
2. "You shall not make for yourself a carved image—any likeness of anything that is in heaven above, or that is in the earth beneath, or that is in the water under the earth; you shall not bow down to them nor serve them. For I, the Lord your God, am a jealous God, visiting the iniquity of the fathers upon the children to the third and fourth generations of those who hate Me, but showing mercy to thousands, to those who love Me and keep My commandments" (Exodus 20:4-6).
3. "You shall not take the name of the Lord your God in vain, for the Lord will not hold him guiltless who takes His name in vain" (Exodus 20:7).
4. "Remember the Sabbath day, to keep it holy. Six days you shall labor and do all your work, but the seventh day is the Sabbath of the Lord your God. In it you shall do no work: you, nor your son, nor your daughter, nor your male servant, nor your female servant, nor your cattle, nor your stranger who is within your gates. For in six days the Lord made the heavens and the earth, the sea, and all that is in them, and rested the seventh day. Therefore the Lord blessed the Sabbath day and hallowed it" (Exodus 20:8-11).
5. "Honor your father and your mother, that your days may be long upon the land which the Lord your God is giving you" (Exodus 20:12).
6. "You shall not murder" (Exodus 20:13).
7. "You shall not commit adultery" (Exodus 20:14).
8. "You shall not steal" (Exodus 20:15).
9. "You shall not bear false witness against your neighbor" (Exodus 20:16).
10. "You shall not covet your neighbor's house; you shall not covet your neighbor's wife, nor his male servant, nor his female servant, nor his ox, nor his donkey, nor anything that is your neighbor's" (Exodus 20:17).

13. Are God's law and Moses' law the same?

Answer: No, they are not the same. Study the following notes and comparison carefully.

Note: *Moses' law contained the temporary, ceremonial law of the Old Testament. It regulated the priesthood, sacrifices, rituals, meat and drink offerings, etc., all of which foreshadowed the cross. This law was added "till the seed should come," and that seed was Christ (Galatians 3:16, 19). The ritual and ceremony of Moses' law pointed forward to Christ's sacrifice. When He died, this law came to an end, but the Ten Commandments (God's law) "stand fast forever and ever" (Psalm 111:8). That there are two laws is made crystal clear in Daniel 9:10, 11.*

Special Note: *Please note that God's law has existed at least as long as sin has existed. The Bible says, "where there is no law there is no transgression [or sin]" (Romans 4:15). So God's Ten Commandment law existed from the beginning. Men broke that law (sinned—1 John 3:4). Because of sin (or breaking God's law), Moses'* law was given (or "added"—Galatians 3:16, 19) till Christ should come and die. Two separate laws are involved: God's law and Moses' law.

Moses' Law
- Called "the law of Moses" (Luke 2:22)
- Called "law ... contained in ordinances" (Ephesians 2:15)
- Written by Moses in a book (2 Chronicles 35:12)
- Placed in the side of the ark (Deuteronomy 31:26)
- Ended at the cross (Ephesians 2:16)
- Added because of sin (Galatians 3:19)
- Contrary to us, against us (Colossians 2:14)
- Judges no one (Colossians 2:14-16)
- Carnal (Hebrews 7:16)
- Made nothing perfect (Hebrews 7:19)

God's Law
- Called "the law of the Lord" (Isaiah 5:24)
- Called "the royal law" (James 2:8)
- Written by God on stone (Exodus 31:18; 32:16)
- Placed inside the ark (Exodus 40:20)
- Will stand forever (Luke 16:17)
- Points out sin (Romans 7:7; 3:20)
- Not grievous (1 John 5:3)
- Judges all people (James 2:10-12)
- Spiritual (Romans 7:14)
- Perfect (Psalm 19:7)

14. How does the devil feel about the people who pattern their lives after God's Ten Commandments?

"And the dragon [the devil] was enraged with the woman [true church], and he went to make war with the rest of her offspring, who keep the commandments of God" (Revelation 12:17). "Here is the patience of the saints; here are those who keep the commandments of God" (Revelation 14:12).

Answer: The devil hates the people who uphold God's law because the law is the pattern of right living. And if you decide to follow the pattern outlined in God's law, you will feel the devil's wrath upon you at once and with all fury. It is not surprising that the devil hates and bitterly opposes all who uphold God's law. But it is shocking and astounding to hear religious leaders denying the binding claims of the Ten Commandments while at the same time upholding the traditions of men. No wonder Jesus said, "Why do you also transgress the commandment of God because of your tradition?" "And in vain they worship Me, teaching as doctrines the commandments of men" (Matthew 15:3, 9). And David said, "It is time for You to act, O Lord, for they have regarded Your law as void" (Psalm 119:126). Christians must wake up and restore God's law to its rightful, exalted position. It is folly for this undisciplined generation to presume that it can break the laws of the living God with impunity.

Your Questions Answered

1. **The Bible says, "love is the fulfillment of the law" (Romans 13:10). The Bible also, in Matthew 22:37-40, commands us to love God and to love our neighbors, and ends with the words, "On these two commandments hang all the Law and the Prophets." Do these commands replace the Ten Commandments?**

   Answer: No, the Ten Commandments hang from these two commands like our 10 fingers hang from our two hands. They are inseparable. Love to God makes keeping the first four commandments (which concern God) a pleasure, and love toward our neighbor makes keeping the last six (which concern our neighbor) a joy. Love fulfills the law by taking away the drudgery and by making law-keeping a delight (Psalm 40:8). When we truly love a person, honoring his or her requests becomes a joy. Jesus said, "If you love Me, keep My commandments" (John 14:15). It is impossible to love the Lord and not keep His commandments, because the Bible says, "This is the love of God, that we keep His commandments. And His commandments are not burdensome" (1 John 5:3). "He who says, 'I know Him,' and does not keep His commandments, is a liar, and the truth is not in him" (1 John 2:4).

2. **Doesn't 2 Corinthians 3:7 teach that the law written and engraved in stone "was to be done away"?**

   Answer: No. The passage says that the "glory" of Moses' ministration of the law was to be done away, but not the law. Read the whole passage of 2 Corinthians 3:3-9 again, carefully. The subject is not the doing away with the law or its establishment, but rather, the change of the location of the law from "tables of stone" to the "tables of the heart." Under Moses' ministration the law was on stones. Under the Holy Spirit's ministration, through Christ, the law is written upon the heart (Hebrews 8:10). A rule posted on a school bulletin board becomes effective only when it enters a student's heart. Christ's ministration of the law is effective because He transfers the law to the heart of the Christian. Then keeping the law becomes a delight and a joyful way of living because the Christian has true love for both God and man.

3. **Were the righteous people of the Old Testament saved by the law?**

   Answer: No one has ever been saved by the law. All who have been saved in all ages have been saved by grace. This "grace ... was given us in Christ Jesus before the world began" (2 Timothy 1:9). The law only points out sin. Christ alone can save. Noah "found grace" (Genesis 6:8); Moses found grace (Exodus 33:17); the Israelites in the wilderness found grace (Jeremiah 31:2); and Abel, Enoch, Abraham, Isaac, Jacob, Joseph, and many other Old Testament worthies were saved "by faith" according to Hebrews 11. They were saved by looking forward to the cross; we, by looking back to it. The law is necessary because, like a mirror, it reveals the "dirt" in our lives. Without it, people are sinners but are not aware of it. However, the law has no saving power. It can only point out sin. Jesus, and He alone, can save a person from sin. This has always been true, even in Old Testament times (Acts 4:10, 12; 2 Timothy 1:9).

7 The Lost Day in History

Did you know there is a very important day that almost everyone has forgotten about? It's astounding that only a few people are aware of it, because it's one of the most significant days in all of human history! It's not only a day in the past, but the present and future. Furthermore, what happened on this neglected day can have a profound effect on your life. Want to know more amazing facts about this lost day of history? Then read over this Study Guide carefully.

1. On what day did Jesus customarily worship?

"So He came to Nazareth, where He had been brought up. And as His custom was, He went into the synagogue on the Sabbath day, and stood up to read" (Luke 4:16).

Answer: Jesus' custom was to worship on the Sabbath.

2. But which day of history has been lost?

"The seventh day is the Sabbath of the LORD your God" (Exodus 20:10). "Now when the Sabbath was past, … Very early in the morning, on the first day of the week, they came to the tomb when the sun had risen" (Mark 16:1, 2).

Answer: A little detective work is required. Many people believe that the Sabbath is the first day of the week (Sunday). But this text shows that the Sabbath is the day that comes just before the first day of the week. According to Scripture, the Sabbath is the seventh day of the week (Saturday).

3. Who made the Sabbath and when?

"In the beginning God created the heavens and the earth." … "And on the seventh day God ended His work which He had done, and He rested on the seventh day from all His work which He had done. Then God blessed the seventh day and sanctified it" (Genesis 1:1; 2:2, 3).

Answer: God made the Sabbath at the time of Creation, when He made the world. He rested on the Sabbath and blessed and sanctified it (set it apart for a holy use).

4. What does God say about Sabbath-keeping in the Ten Commandments, which He wrote with His own finger?

"Remember the Sabbath day, to keep it holy. Six days you shall labor and do all your work, but the seventh day is the Sabbath of the LORD your God. In it you shall do no work: you, nor your son, nor your daughter, nor your male servant, nor your female servant, nor your cattle, nor your stranger who is within your gates.

For in six days the LORD made the heavens and the earth, the sea, and all that is in them, and rested the seventh day. Therefore the LORD blessed the Sabbath day and hallowed it" (Exodus 20:8-11). "Then the LORD delivered to me two tablets of stone written with the finger of God" (Deuteronomy 9:10).

Answer: In the fourth commandment of the 10, God commands us to observe the seventh-day Sabbath as His holy day. God knew people would forget His Sabbath, so He began this commandment with the word "remember." He has never commanded anyone anywhere to keep any other day as a weekly holy day.

5. But haven't the Ten Commandments been changed?

Jesus says: "And it is easier for heaven and earth to pass away than for one tittle of the law to fail" (Luke 16:17). God says: "My covenant I will not break, nor alter the word that has gone out of My lips" (Psalm 89:34). Notice, the Ten Commandments came from His lips. Exodus 20:1 says, "And God spoke all these words, saying ... [the Ten Commandments follow in verses 2-17]."

Answer: No, indeed! It is utterly impossible for any of God's moral law ever to change. All Ten Commandments are binding today.

6. Did the apostles keep the Sabbath?

"Then Paul, as his custom was, went in to them, and for three Sabbaths reasoned with them from the Scriptures" (Acts 17:2). "Paul and his party ... went into the synagogue on the Sabbath day and sat down" (Acts 13:13, 14). "And on the Sabbath day we went out of the city to the riverside, where prayer was customarily made; and we sat down and spoke to the women who met there" (Acts 16:13). "And he [Paul] reasoned in the synagogue every Sabbath, and persuaded both Jews and Greeks" (Acts 18:4).

Answer: Yes, the book of Acts makes it clear that Paul and the early church kept the Sabbath.

7. Did the Gentiles also worship on Sabbath?

God commanded it: "Blessed is the man ... Who keeps from defiling the Sabbath." ... "Also the sons of the foreigner who join themselves to the LORD, ... *Everyone who keeps from defiling the Sabbath,* and holds fast My covenant—Even them I will bring to My holy mountain, and make them joyful in My house of prayer ... for My house shall be called a house of prayer for all nations" (Isaiah 56:2, 6, 7, emphasis added).

Apostles taught it: "So when the Jews went out of the synagogue, *the Gentiles begged that these words might be preached to them the next Sabbath.*" "On the next Sabbath almost the whole city came together to hear the word of God" (Acts 13:42, 44, emphasis added). "And he reasoned in the synagogue every Sabbath, and persuaded both Jews and Greeks" (Acts 18:4).

Answer: The apostles in the early New Testament church not only obeyed God's Sabbath command, but they also taught the converted Gentiles to worship on Sabbath. Never once do they refer to Sunday as a holy day.

8. But wasn't the Sabbath changed to Sunday at Christ's death or resurrection?

Answer: No, there is not the remotest hint that the Sabbath was changed at Christ's death or resurrection. The Bible teaches just the opposite. Please carefully review the following evidence:

A. **God blessed the Sabbath.** "The LORD blessed the Sabbath day and hallowed it" (Exodus 20:11). "Then God blessed the seventh day and sanctified it" (Genesis 2:3).

B. **Christ expected His people to be still keeping the Sabbath in A.D. 70 when Jerusalem was destroyed.** Knowing full well that Jerusalem would be destroyed by Rome in A.D. 70, Jesus warned His followers of that time, saying, "And pray that your flight may not be in winter *or on the Sabbath*" (Matthew 24:20, emphasis added). Jesus made it clear that He intended for the Sabbath to be kept even 40 years after His resurrection. In fact, there is no intimation anywhere in the Scriptures that Jesus, His Father, or the apostles ever (at any time, under any circumstances) changed the holy seventh-day Sabbath to any other day.

C. **The women who came to anoint Christ's dead body kept the Sabbath.** Jesus died on "the day before the Sabbath" (Mark 15:37, 42), which is now called Good Friday. The women prepared spices and ointments to anoint His body, then "rested on the Sabbath according to the commandment" (Luke 23:56). Only "when the Sabbath was past" (Mark 16:1) did the women come "on the first day of the week" (Mark 16:2) to continue their sad work. They found Jesus "rose early on the first day of the week" (verse 9), commonly called Easter Sunday. Please note that the Sabbath "according to the commandment" was the day preceding Easter Sunday, which we now call Saturday.

D. **Luke, the author of Acts, doesn't refer to any change of the day of worship.** There's no biblical record of a change. In the book of Acts, Luke says that he wrote his gospel (the book of Luke) about "all" of Jesus' teachings (Acts 1:1–3). But he never wrote about Sunday-keeping or a change of the Sabbath.

9. Some people say the Sabbath will be kept in God's new earth. Is this correct?

"'For as the new heavens and the new earth which I will make shall remain before Me,' says the LORD, 'So shall your descendants and your name remain. And it shall come to pass that from one New Moon to another, and from one Sabbath to another, all flesh shall come to worship before Me,' says the LORD" (Isaiah 66:22, 23).

Answer: **Yes, the Bible says the saved people of all ages will keep the Sabbath in the new earth.**

10. But isn't Sunday the Lord's day?

"Call the Sabbath a delight, the holy day of the LORD" (Isaiah 58:13). "For the Son of Man is Lord even of the Sabbath" (Matthew 12:8).

Answer: **The Bible speaks of the "Lord's day" in Revelation 1:10, so the Lord does have a special day. But no verse of Scripture refers to Sunday** as the Lord's day. Rather, the Bible plainly identifies Sabbath as the Lord's day. The only day ever blessed by the Lord or claimed by Him as His holy day is the seventh-day Sabbath.

11. Shouldn't I keep Sunday in honor of Christ's resurrection?

"Do you not know that as many of us as were baptized into Christ Jesus were baptized into His death? Therefore we were buried with Him through baptism into death, that just as Christ was raised from the dead by the glory of the Father, even so we also should walk in newness of life. For if we have been united together in the likeness of His death, certainly we also shall be in the likeness of His resurrection, knowing this, that our old man was crucified with Him, that the body of sin might be done away with, that we should no longer be slaves of sin" (Romans 6:3-6).

Answer: No! No more than you would keep Friday in honor of the crucifixion. Christ gave the ordinance of baptism in honor of His death, burial, and resurrection. The Bible never suggests Sunday-keeping in honor of the resurrection (or for any other reason, for that matter). We honor Christ by obeying Him (John 14:15)—not by substituting man-made requirements in place of His.

12. Well, if Sunday-keeping isn't in the Bible, whose idea was it anyway?

"He ... shall intend to change times and law" (Daniel 7:25). "Thus you have made the commandment of God of no effect by your tradition." "And in vain they worship Me, teaching as doctrines the commandments of men" (Matthew 15:6, 9). "Her priests have violated My law." "Her prophets plastered them with untempered mortar, ... saying, 'Thus says the Lord GOD,' when the LORD had not spoken" (Ezekiel 22:26, 28).

Answer: In the early centuries, because of hatred against the Jews, misguided men suggested that God's holy day of worship be changed from Saturday to Sunday. God predicted it would happen, and it did. This error was passed on to our unsuspecting generation as gospel fact. Sunday-keeping is a tradition of uninspired men and breaks God's law, which commands Sabbath-keeping. Only God can make a day holy. God blessed the Sabbath, and when God blesses, no man can "reverse it" (Numbers 23:20).

13. But isn't it very dangerous to tamper with God's law?

"You shall not add to the word which I command you, nor take from it, that you may keep the commandments of the LORD your God which I command you" (Deuteronomy 4:2). "Every word of God is pure. ... Do not add to His words, lest He rebuke you, and you be found a liar" (Proverbs 30:5, 6).

Answer: God has specifically and positively forbidden men to change His law by deletions or additions. To tamper with God's holy law in any way is one of the most fearful and dangerous things a person can do.

14. Why did God make the Sabbath anyway?

A. Sign of Creation. "Remember the Sabbath day, to keep it holy." "For in six days the LORD made the heavens and the earth, the sea, and all that is in them, and rested the seventh day. Therefore the LORD blessed the Sabbath day and hallowed it" (Exodus 20:8, 11).

B. **Sign of redemption and sanctification.** "Moreover I also gave them My Sabbaths, to be a sign between them and Me, that they might know that I am the LORD who sanctifies them" (Ezekiel 20:12).

Answer: God gave the Sabbath as a twofold sign: (1) It is a sign that He created the world in six literal 24-hour days, and (2) it is also a sign of God's mighty power to redeem and sanctify men. Surely every Christian will love the Sabbath as God's precious sign of Creation and redemption (Exodus 31:13, 17; Ezekiel 20:12, 20). It is a great insult to God for people to trample upon His Sabbath. In Isaiah 58:13, 14, God says all who would be blessed must first get their feet off His Sabbath.

15. How important is Sabbath-keeping?

"Sin is lawlessness [transgression of the law]" (1 John 3:4). "The wages of sin is death" (Romans 6:23). "Whoever shall keep the whole law, and yet stumble in one point, he is guilty of all" (James 2:10). "Christ also suffered for us, leaving us an example, that you should follow His steps" (1 Peter 2:21). "He became the author of eternal salvation to all who obey Him" (Hebrews 5:9).

Answer: **It is a matter of life and death. Sabbath-keeping is enjoined in the fourth commandment of God's law. The deliberate breaking of any one of the Ten Commandments is a sin. Christians will gladly follow Christ's example of Sabbath-keeping. Our only safety is to diligently study the Bible, "rightly dividing the word of truth" (2 Timothy 2:15). We must have positive Scripture support for every Christian practice we follow.**

16. How does God feel about religious leaders who ignore the Sabbath?

"Her priests have violated My law and profaned My holy things; they have not distinguished between the holy and unholy ... and they have hidden their eyes from My Sabbaths, so that I am profaned among them." "Therefore I have poured out My indignation on them" (Ezekiel 22:26, 31).

Answer: **While there are religious leaders who keep a false sabbath in ignorance, those who deliberately do so offend God. In hiding their eyes from God's true Sabbath, religious leaders have caused others to profane it. Millions have been misled on this matter. God cannot treat it lightly. Jesus condemned the Pharisees for pretending to love God while making void one of the Ten Commandments by their tradition (Mark 7:7-13).**

17. Does Sabbath-keeping really affect me personally?

"If you love Me, keep My commandments" (John 14:15). "Therefore, to him who knows to do good and does not do it, to him it is sin" (James 4:17). "Blessed are those who do His commandments, that they may have the right to the tree of life, and may enter through the gates into the city" (Revelation 22:14).

Answer: **Yes, by all means, the Sabbath is *your* Sabbath. God made it for *you*, and if you love Him you will keep it, because it is one of His**

commandments. Love without commandment-keeping is no love at all (1 John 2:4). You must make a decision. You cannot avoid it. No one can excuse you. You yourself will answer before God on this most important matter. God asks you to love and obey Him now!

And keeping the Sabbath is the best decision that you can possibly make. On the Sabbath, you can cease your regular activities like work and shopping and spend time with the Creator of the Universe. Worshipping God with other believers, visiting the sick, spending time with family, walking in nature, or reading spiritually uplifting materials are all good ways to keep the Sabbath holy. After the stress of six days of work, God has given you the gift of the Sabbath to feed your soul. You need to trust that He knows what's best.

Your Questions Answered

1. **But isn't the Sabbath for the Jews only?**

    Answer: No. Jesus said, "The Sabbath was made for man" (Mark 2:27). It is not for the Jews only, but for mankind—all men and women everywhere. The Jewish nation did not even exist until 2,500 years after the Sabbath was made.

2. **Isn't Acts 20:7-12 proof that the disciples kept Sunday as a holy day?**

    Answer: According to the Bible, each day begins at sundown and ends at the next sundown (Genesis 1:5, 8, 13, 19, 23, 31; Leviticus 23:32) and the dark part of the day comes first. So Sabbath begins Friday night at sundown and ends Saturday night at sundown. This meeting of Acts 20 was held on the dark part of Sunday, or on what we now call Saturday night. *The New English Bible* (© The Delegates of the Oxford University Press and the Syndics of the Cambridge University Press, 1961, 1970. Used by permission) begins Acts 20:7 like this: "On the Saturday night in our assembly ..." It was a Saturday-night meeting, and it lasted until midnight. Paul was on a farewell tour and knew he would not see these people again before his death (verse 25). No wonder he preached so long! (No regular weekly service would have lasted all night.) Paul was "ready to depart on the morrow." The "breaking of bread" has no "holy day" significance whatever, because they broke bread daily (Acts 2:46). There is not the slightest indication in this Scripture passage that the first day is holy, nor that these early Christians considered it so. Nor is there the remotest evidence that the Sabbath had been changed. Incidentally, this meeting is probably mentioned in the Scripture only because of the miracle of raising Eutychus back to life after he fell to his death from a third-floor window. In Ezekiel 46:1, God refers to Sunday as one of the six "working days."

3. **Doesn't Colossians 2:14-17 do away with the seventh-day Sabbath?**

    Answer: Not at all. It refers only to the sabbaths which were "a shadow of things to come" and not to the seventh-day Sabbath. There were seven yearly holy days, or festivals, in ancient Israel which were also called sabbaths. These were in addition to, or "besides the Sabbaths of the LORD" (Leviticus 23:38), or seventh-day Sabbath. These all foreshadowed, or pointed to, the cross and ended at the cross. God's seventh-day Sabbath was made before sin entered, and therefore could foreshadow nothing about deliverance from sin. That's why Colossians chapter 2 differentiates and specifically mentions the sabbaths that were "a shadow." These seven yearly sabbaths which were abolished are listed in Leviticus chapter 23.

4. **According to Romans 14:5 the day we keep is a matter of personal opinion, isn't it?**
Answer: Notice that the whole chapter is on judging one another (verses 4, 10, 13). The issue here is not over the seventh-day Sabbath, which was a part of the great moral law, but over other religious days. Jewish Christians were judging Gentile Christians for not observing them. Paul is simply saying, "Don't judge each other. That ceremonial law is no longer binding."

8 The Ultimate Deliverance

It's no fairytale—one day, you can be free from all the hurt, hunger, aloneness, crime, and chaos infecting the world today. Doesn't that sound wonderful? But it's not going to be some charismatic earthly leader who's going to deliver you … no, He's much more superior than that! Jesus is coming soon, but there are a lot of popular misconceptions regarding just how He's coming. So take a few minutes to understand what the Bible really says about the second coming so you won't be left behind!

1. **Will Jesus return to this earth the second time? Can we be positive?**
"Christ … will appear a second time" (Hebrews 9:28). "If I go and prepare a place for you, I will come again" (John 14:3).
Answer: **Yes! In Matthew 26:64, Jesus testified under oath that He would come back to this earth again. Since the Scripture cannot be broken (John 10:35), this is proof positive. Believe it just as it reads. It is Christ's own personal guarantee.**

2. **In what manner will Jesus return the second time?**
"Now when He had spoken these things, while they watched, He was taken up, and a cloud received Him out of their sight. And while they looked steadfastly toward heaven as He went up, behold, two men stood by them in white apparel, who also said, 'Men of Galilee, why do you stand gazing up into heaven? This same Jesus, who was taken up from you into heaven, will so come in like manner as you saw Him go into heaven'" (Acts 1:9-11).
Answer: **The Scriptures promise that Jesus will return to this earth in the same manner that He left at His ascension—in a visible, literal,**

bodily, personal manner. Matthew 24:30 says, "They will see the Son of Man coming on the clouds of heaven with power and great glory." He will come in the clouds literally, as a personal being with a body of flesh and bones (Luke 24:36-43, 50, 51), and His coming will be visible. Scripture is clear on these facts.

3. Will the second coming of Christ be visible to all men or only to a select group?

"Behold, He is coming with clouds, and every eye will see Him" (Revelation 1:7). "For as the lightning comes from the east and flashes to the west, so also will the coming of the Son of Man be" (Matthew 24:27). "For the Lord Himself will descend from heaven with a shout, with the voice of an archangel, and with the trumpet of God. And the dead in Christ will rise first" (1 Thessalonians 4:16).

Answer: Every man, woman, and child living in the world when Jesus returns will see Him at His second coming. The staggering threefold (Luke 9:26) brightness of His coming will stretch from horizon to horizon, and the atmosphere will be charged with brilliant glory like lightning. No one will be able to hide. Every living soul will be forced to face Christ. Christ left no loophole for doubt or misunderstanding. This will be a loud, dramatic event where even the dead are raised.

Note: Every person will know about the second coming! Some people use 1 Thessalonians 4:16 to point to a secret rapture, but it's one of the noisiest verses in the Bible. The Lord shouts, a trumpet blasts, and the dead are raised! Nor is the second coming a spiritual coming into the heart at conversion. It does not take place at a man's death, nor is it figurative—to be manifested by better world conditions. These theories are all of human origin. The second coming will be a literal, worldwide, visible, personal appearance of Christ in the clouds to bring this world to an end and to reward or punish all men and women.

4. Who will come with Jesus at His second coming, and why?

"When the Son of Man comes in His glory, and all the holy angels with Him, then He will sit on the throne of His glory" (Matthew 25:31).

Answer: All the angels of heaven will come with Jesus at His second coming. As the cloud nears the earth, Jesus will send His angels, and they will quickly gather together all of the righteous people in preparation for the trip back to heaven (Matthew 24:31).

5. What is the purpose of Jesus' second coming to this earth?

"And behold, I am coming quickly, and My reward is with Me, to give to every one according to his work" (Revelation 22:12). "I will come again and receive you to Myself; that where I am, there you may be also" (John 14:3). "And that He may send Jesus Christ, ... whom heaven must receive until the times of restoration of all things" (Acts 3:20, 21).

Answer: Jesus is coming back to this earth to reward His people as He promised and to take them to the beautiful home He has prepared for them. He will restore to His people all of the joys and glories of Eden that Adam and Eve lost by sinning. His second coming will bring an end to this present age of evil.

6. What will happen to the righteous people when Jesus comes the second time?

"For the Lord Himself will descend from heaven ... And the dead in Christ will rise first. Then we who are alive and remain shall be caught up together with them in the clouds to meet the Lord in the air. And thus we shall always be with the Lord" (1 Thessalonians 4:16, 17). "We shall all be changed ... and the dead will be raised incorruptible. For ... this mortal must put on immortality" (1 Corinthians 15:51-53). "We also eagerly wait for ... the Lord Jesus Christ, who will transform our lowly body that it may be conformed to His glorious body" (Philippians 3:20, 21).

Answer: The righteous dead will be raised from their graves, given perfect, immortal bodies like that of Christ, and caught up into the clouds to meet the Lord. Then the righteous living will also be given bodies like Christ and will be caught up to meet the Lord in the air. And Jesus will take the righteous to heaven with Him. Note that Jesus does not touch the earth at His second coming. The saints meet Him "in the air." So God's people will ignore any report that Christ is in Baltimore, New Orleans, Los Angeles, etc. False christs will appear and do miracles on the earth (Matthew 24:23-27), but Jesus will remain in the clouds above the earth at His second coming.

7. What will happen to the wicked people when Jesus comes again?

"With the breath of His lips He shall slay the wicked" (Isaiah 11:4). "And at that day the slain of the LORD shall be from one end of the earth even to the other end of the earth" (Jeremiah 25:33).

Answer: The wicked will be slain by Jesus.

8. How will Christ's second coming affect the earth itself?

"And there was a great earthquake, such a mighty and great earthquake as had not occurred since men were on the earth." "Then every island fled away, and the mountains were not found" (Revelation 16:18, 20). "I beheld, and indeed the fruitful land was a wilderness, and all its cities were broken down at the presence of the LORD" (Jeremiah 4:26). "The LORD makes the earth empty and makes it waste." "The land shall be entirely emptied" (Isaiah 24:1, 3).

Answer: The earth will be seized by a great earthquake at the coming of the Lord. This earthquake will be of such a devastating nature that it will leave the world in a state of total destruction.

9. Does the Bible give specific information regarding the nearness of Christ's second coming?

Answer: Yes, it does! And Jesus Himself said, "When you see all these things, know that it is near—at the doors!" (Matthew 24:33). The Lord placed signs all along the way from His ascension to His second coming. They are listed below. Study them carefully.

A. The Destruction of Jerusalem
Prophecy: "Not one stone shall be left here upon another, that shall not be thrown down." "Let those who are in Judea flee to the mountains" (Matthew 24:2, 16).
Fulfillment: Jerusalem was destroyed in A.D. 70 by the Roman warrior Titus.

B. A Great Persecution, or Tribulation
Prophecy: "For then there will be great tribulation, such as has not been since the beginning of the world" (Matthew 24:21).
Fulfillment: This prophecy points primarily to the long period of tribulation that took place during the Dark Ages and was instigated by the apostate church. It lasted more than 1,000 years. Over 50 million Christians were slain for their faith in this terrible tribulation period. One writer says the apostate church "has shed more innocent blood than any other institution that has ever existed among mankind." W.E.H. Lecky, *History of the Rise and Influence of the Spirit of Rationalism in Europe*, (Reprint; New York: Braziller, 1955) Vol. 2, pp. 40-45.

C. The Sun Turned into Darkness
Prophecy: "Immediately after the tribulation of those days the sun will be darkened" (Matthew 24:29).
Fulfillment: This was fulfilled by a day of supernatural darkness on May 19, 1780. It was not an eclipse. Timothy Dwight says, "The 19th of May, 1780, was a remarkable dark day. Candles were lighted in many houses; the birds were silent and disappeared, and the fowls retired to roost. ... A very general opinion prevailed, that the day of judgment was at hand." Quoted in *Connecticut Historical Collections*, compiled by John Warner Barber (2nd ed.; New Haven: Durrie & Peck and J.W. Barber, 1836) p. 403.

D. The Moon Turned into Blood
Prophecy: "The sun shall be turned into darkness, and the moon into blood, before the coming of the great and awesome day of the LORD" (Joel 2:31).
Fulfillment: The moon became as red as blood on the night of the "dark day," May 19, 1780. Milo Bostick in *Stone's History of Massachusetts* says, "The moon which was at its full, had the appearance of blood."

E. The Stars Fall from Heaven
Prophecy: "The stars will fall from heaven" (Matthew 24:29).
Fulfillment: The great star shower took place on the night of November 13, 1833. It was so bright that a newspaper could be read on the street. One writer says, "For nearly four hours the sky was literally ablaze." Men thought the end of the world had come. Look into this. It is most fascinating, and a sign of Christ's coming. (Peter A. Millman, "The Falling of the Stars," *The Telescope*, 7 [May-June, 1940] 57.)

F. Jesus Comes in the Clouds
Prophecy: "Then the sign of the Son of Man will appear in heaven, and then all the tribes of the earth will mourn, and they will see the Son of Man coming on the clouds of heaven with power and great glory" (Matthew 24:30).
Fulfillment: This is the next great event. Are you ready?

10. How may we know when we have reached the very last days of earth's history? Does the Bible clearly describe the world and its people in the last generation?
Answer: Yes, indeed it does. Look at the following specific signs of the last days. You will be amazed. And these are just a few of many, many positive signs that show we are in the closing days of earth's history.

A. Wars and commotions
"But when you hear of wars and commotions, do not be terrified; for these things must come to pass" (Luke 21:9).

Wars and the ravages of civil distress are affecting thousands worldwide. Only Jesus' soon coming will bring an end to the pain and destruction of war.

B. Unrest, fear, and upheaval
"And there will be ... on the earth distress of nations, with perplexity. ... Men's hearts failing them from fear and the expectation of those things which are coming on the earth" (Luke 21:25, 26).

This sounds strangely like an editorial from a current newspaper—a perfect picture of the world today—and there is a reason: We are the people of the very last days of earth's history. The tense atmosphere present in the world today should not surprise us. Christ foretold it. It should convince us that His coming is near.

C. Increase of knowledge
"Until the time of the end ... knowledge shall increase" (Daniel 12:4).

The Information Age makes this one all too obvious. Even the most skeptical mind must admit that this sign is fulfilled. Knowledge is exploding in all directions. It is said that 80 percent of the world's total knowledge has been brought forth in the last decade and that 90 percent of all the scientists who have ever lived are alive today.

D. Scoffers and religious skeptics who turn away from Bible truth
"Scoffers will come in the last days" (2 Peter 3:3). "They will not endure sound doctrine. ... They will turn their ears away from the truth, and be turned aside to fables" (2 Timothy 4:3, 4).

It is not difficult to find scoffers today in fulfillment of this prophecy. Even religious leaders are denying the plain Bible teachings of Creation, the Flood, the divinity of Christ, the second coming of Christ, and many other vital Bible truths. Psychiatry and the traditions of pseudo-intellectuals have replaced the Bible in many religious circles. Secular educators teach our youth to scoff at the Bible record of these great truths and substitute evolution and other man-made, false teachings for the plain, simple facts of God's Holy Word. A recent poll discovered that only two percent of American student ministers believe in the literal second coming of Christ.

E. Moral degeneracy—decline of spirituality

"In the last days ... men will be lovers of themselves, ... unloving, ... without self-control, ... despisers of good, ... having a form of godliness but denying its power" (2 Timothy 3:1-5).

America is in the midst of a tremendous crisis. People from all walks of life are saying so. Suicide is becoming a popular solution to human problems. Divorce rates are climbing wildly, with nearly one marriage in two ending in the divorce court. The current immoral generation—with its obsession with sex and filth, with its increasing church membership but decreasing true spirituality—is plain and positive fulfillment of God's Word. For a real shock, see how many of the last-day sins listed in 2 Timothy 3:1-5 you can find depicted in any issue of your Sunday newspaper. Nothing short of the coming of the Lord will stem the tide of evil that is now engulfing the world.

F. Craze for pleasure

"In the last days ... men will be ... lovers of pleasure rather than lovers of God" (2 Timothy 3:1-4).

The world has gone crazy for pleasure. Only a small percentage of the citizens of our large cities attend church services regularly, but they jam pleasure resorts by the thousands. America is spending billions each year for pleasure and only "peanuts" (in comparison) for God. Pleasure-mad Americans waste billions of hours in front of the TV set in direct fulfillment of 2 Timothy 3:4.

G. Increasing lawlessness, bloody crimes, and violence

"Lawlessness will abound" (Matthew 24:12). "Evil men and impostors will grow worse and worse" (2 Timothy 3:13). "The land is filled with crimes of blood, and the city is full of violence" (Ezekiel 7:23).

It is all too obvious that this sign is fulfilled. Crime and lawlessness are increasing with shocking rapidity. Most people in large cities do not answer their doorbells after dark. The wisest statesmen of our time are concerned for the survival of civilization because crime sweeps forward seemingly beyond control.

H. Natural Disasters and upheaval

"There will be great earthquakes in various places, and famines and pestilences" (Luke 21:11, 25).

Earthquakes, tornadoes, floods, etc., are increasing at an unprecedented rate. One-third of the people of the world are hungry, and thousands die daily of starvation. All these things are further proof that we live in earth's last hours.

I. A special message to the world in the very last days
"This gospel of the kingdom will be preached in all the world as a witness to all the nations, and then the end will come" (Matthew 24:14).

The great, solemn, last warning message of Christ's second coming is now being presented in more than 900 languages and dialects. Nearly 95 percent of the world's population has access to this message. Before Jesus' second coming, every person in the world will be warned of His soon return. People will be lost only if they reject the warning message.

J. A turning to spiritism
"In latter times some will depart from the faith, giving heed to deceiving spirits" (1 Timothy 4:1). "They are spirits of demons" (Revelation 16:14).

People today, including a vast number of the heads of nations, seek counsel from psychics, channelers, and spiritualists. Spiritism has invaded the churches, as well, with the false teaching of the immortality of the soul. The Bible teaches that the dead are dead. (See Study Guide 10 for more on this subject.)

K. Capital-labor troubles
"The wages of the laborers who mowed your fields, which you kept back by fraud, cry out; and the cries of the reapers have reached the ears of the Lord." "Be patient. ... for the coming of the Lord is at hand" (James 5:4, 8).

Trouble between capital and labor is predicted for the last days. For fulfillment, consult your newspaper.

11. Just how near is the Lord's second coming?

"Now learn this parable from the fig tree: When its branch has already become tender and puts forth leaves, you know that summer is near. So you also, when you see all these things, know that it is near—at the doors! Assuredly, I say to you, this generation will by no means pass away till all these things take place" (Matthew 24:32-34).

Answer: The Bible is very specific and plain on this point. The signs have almost all been fulfilled. We cannot know the exact day and hour of Christ's return (Matthew 24:36), but we know that He is coming soon. God has promised to finish things very quickly now and cut the work short (Romans 9:28). Christ is coming back to this earth for His people very soon. Are you ready?

12. Satan is telling many falsehoods regarding the second coming of Christ and, with lying wonders and miracles, will deceive millions. How can I be certain I will not be deceived?

"For they are spirits of demons, performing signs [miracles]" (Revelation 16:14).

"For false christs and false prophets will rise and show great signs and wonders to deceive, if possible, even the elect" (Matthew 24:24). "To the law and to the testimony! If they do not speak according to this word, it is because there is no light in them" (Isaiah 8:20).

Answer: Satan has invented many false teachings about the second coming and is deceiving millions into believing that Christ has already come or that He will come in some non-biblical manner. But Christ has warned us of Satan's strategy, saying, "Take heed that no one deceives you" (Matthew 24:4). He then exposes Satan's plans and falsehoods so we will be forewarned, and He reminds us, "See, I have told you beforehand" (Matthew 24:25). For example, Jesus stated specifically that He will not appear in the desert or come to the séance chambers (verse 26). There is no reason to be deceived if we learn what God's book teaches about Christ's second coming. The acid test is this: What does the Bible teach about it? People who know what the Bible says about the second coming will not be led astray by Satan. All others will be deceived.

13. How can I be certain to be ready when Jesus comes back?

"He one who comes to Me I will by no means cast out" (John 6:37). "As many as received Him, to them He gave the right to become children of God" (John 1:12). "I will put My laws in their mind and write them on their hearts" (Hebrews 8:10). "Thanks be to God, who gives us the victory through our Lord Jesus Christ" (1 Corinthians 15:57).

Answer: Jesus says, "Behold, I stand at the door and knock. If anyone hears My voice and opens the door, I will come in" (Revelation 3:20). Through the Holy Spirit and my conscience, Jesus knocks and asks to come into my heart so that He can change my life. If I unreservedly turn my life over to Him, He will erase all my sins of the past (Romans 3:25) and give me the power to live a godly life (John 1:12). As a free gift, He bestows upon me His own righteous character so I can stand unafraid before a holy God when my life is changed by Jesus. Then doing His will becomes a pleasure. It is so simple that many doubt its reality. But it's true. My part is simply to give my life to Christ and let Him live within me. His part is to work the mighty miracle within me that changes my life and prepares me for His second coming. It is a free gift. I need only to accept it.

14. Of what great danger does Christ solemnly warn?

"Therefore you also be ready, for the Son of Man is coming at an hour you do not expect" (Matthew 24:44). "But take heed to yourselves, lest your hearts be weighed down with carousing, drunkenness, and cares of this life, and that Day come on you unexpectedly" (Luke 21:34). "But as the days of Noah were, so also will the coming of the Son of Man be" (Matthew 24:37).

Answer: There is great danger in becoming so busy with the cares of this life or so entranced by the pleasures of sin that the coming of the

Lord may slip up on us as the Flood did on the world in Noah's day, and we will be surprised, unprepared, and lost. This will be the experience of millions. How is it with you? Jesus is coming back very, very soon—in our present day. Are you ready? Nothing else matters.

Your Questions Answered

1. Isn't the great tribulation yet to come?

Answer: It is true that a terrible tribulation will cover the earth just before Jesus returns to deliver His people. Daniel describes it as "a time of trouble, such as never was" (Daniel 12:1). In context, though, the "great tribulation" of Matthew 24:21 refers to the awful persecution of God's people during the Dark Ages. Millions were slain for their faith at that time.

2. When will Christ set up His kingdom upon the earth?

Answer: After the great 1,000-year period of Revelation 20. The 1,000-year period begins at the second coming of Christ, when Jesus takes the righteous from this earth to heaven to live and reign with Him "a thousand years" (Revelation 20:4). At the close of the 1,000 years "the holy city, new Jerusalem" (Revelation 21:2) comes down from heaven to the earth with all the saints (Zechariah 14:1, 4, 5) and the wicked dead of all ages are raised to life (Revelation 20:5). They surround the holy city to capture it (Revelation 20:9), and fire comes down from God out of heaven and devours them. This fire purifies the earth and burns up all traces of sin and sinners (2 Peter 3:10). Finally the fire goes out (Isaiah 47:14), leaving only ashes (Malachi 4:3). Then God creates a new earth (2 Peter 3:13; Isaiah 65:17; Revelation 21:1) and gives it to the righteous, and "God … will dwell with them, … God himself will be with them and be their God" (Revelation 21:3). Perfect, holy, happy beings, restored once again to the perfect image of God, will at last be at home in a sinless, spotless world as God originally planned. Only the most foolish person would choose to miss this. (For more information on God's beautiful new kingdom, see Study Guide 4. For more on the 1,000 years, see Study Guide 12.)

3. But wasn't Jesus speaking of the secret rapture when He said in Luke 17:36, "One will be taken and the other left"?

Answer: No. There is not the slightest indication that the event is secret. Jesus was describing Noah's flood and the destruction of Sodom. (See Luke 17:26-37.) He told how God spared Noah and Lot and destroyed the wicked. He says specifically that the flood and fire "destroyed them all" (vs. 27, 29). Plainly, in each case, a few were taken to safety and the rest were destroyed. Then He added, "Even thus shall it be in the day when the Son of man is revealed" (v. 30). To illustrate, Jesus continued, "Two men shall be in the field; the one shall be taken, and the other left" (v. 36). There is nothing secret about it. "Every eye will see Him" (Revelation 1:7).

At His second coming, Christ publicly and openly takes the righteous up into the clouds (1 Thessalonians 4:16, 17) and slays the wicked (Isaiah 11:4; 2 Thessalonians 2:8). That's why Luke 17:37 speaks of the bodies of the wicked and mentions the eagles (or vultures) gathered around them. (See also Revelation 19:17, 18.) The wicked who are left behind at Christ's coming are left dead. (For more on the secret rapture, write for our book on the subject.)

9 Purity and Power

Are you tired of hurting your loved ones and wounding your conscience? Do you live in constant regret for your past mistakes? Have you ever wished you could take a bath and come out clean inside and out? Then we have great news for you ... you can! God has a plan that can totally wash all your sins away and supercharge your character—preposterous? Not at all! Christ says, "We are buried with him by baptism" (Romans 6:4). When you accept Christ, the old life dies and the Lord promises to forget all our sins! Not only that, He can help you overcome every sinful habit in your life. Did you know the cross is mentioned 28 times in the Bible, but baptism is mentioned 97 times? It must be pretty important then, and no wonder, because it signifies a new life with the haunting, sinful past buried and forgotten forever. Read the Bible's amazing facts on this incredible subject ... you'll never be the same!

1. Is baptism really essential?

"He who believes and is baptized will be saved; but he who does not believe will be condemned" (Mark 16:16).

Answer: Yes, indeed! How could any language or words make it plainer?

2. But the thief on the cross was not baptized, so why should I be?

"For He knows our frame; He remembers that we are dust" (Psalm 103:14).

Answer: Neither did he restore what he had stolen, as the Lord specifically directs in Ezekiel 33:15. God holds us accountable for what we can do, but He also recognizes the limitations of "dust." He will not require a physical impossibility. Could the thief have come down from the cross, he immediately would have been baptized. Every person who is able should be baptized.

3. There are many ordinances called baptism. Isn't any one of these acceptable, provided a person is sincere and earnest about it?

"One Lord, one faith, one baptism" (Ephesians 4:5).

Answer: No! There is only one true baptism. All other so-called baptisms are counterfeits.

Note: *The devil's "buffet" plan for baptism says, "Take your pick. The method of baptism doesn't matter. It is the spirit that counts." But the Bible says, "One Lord, one faith, one baptism" (Ephesians 4:5). It also says, "Obey the voice of the* LORD *which I speak to you" (Jeremiah 38:20).*

4. How was Jesus baptized?

"Jesus ... was baptized by John in the Jordan. And immediately, coming up from the water, He saw the heavens parting" (Mark 1:9, 10).

Answer: By immersion! Notice that after the ordinance, He came "up out from the water." Jesus was baptized "in the Jordan," not on the bank, as many believe. John always found a place to baptize where "there was much water" (John 3:23), so it would be deep enough. The Bible commands us to follow Jesus' example (1 Peter 2:21). Any baptism other than immersion breaks this command. The word "baptism" comes from the Greek word "baptizo." It means "to dip under or submerge or immerse." There are eight different Greek words in the New Testament used to describe the application of liquids. But among these various words— meaning to sprinkle, to pour, or to immerse—only the one meaning "to immerse" (baptizo) is used to describe baptism.

5. But didn't the disciples or the apostles change the method of baptism?

"Both Philip and the eunuch went down into the water, and he baptized him. Now when they came up out of the water, the Spirit of the Lord caught Philip away" (Acts 8:38, 39).

Answer: No! Please notice that Philip, a leader in the early church, baptized the treasurer of Ethiopia by immersion precisely as John baptized Jesus. And the apostle Paul warned that any who teach contrary to what Jesus taught should be "accursed." (Galatians 1:8). No person—no matter how godly—is authorized to change God's words and commands.

6. Since Jesus and the disciples baptized by immersion, who introduced these other so-called baptisms which exist today?

"And in vain they worship Me, teaching as doctrines the commandments of men" (Matthew 15:9).

Answer: Misguided men introduced other forms of baptism in direct contradiction of God's Word. Jesus says, "Why do you also transgress the commandment of God because of your tradition?" "Thus you have made the commandment of God of no effect by your tradition" (Matthew 15:3, 6). Worship that follows human teaching is "vain." Just think of it! The sacred ordinance of baptism has been changed and made of little consequence during truth's hazardous journey through the centuries. No wonder the Bible exhorts us to "contend earnestly for the faith which was once for all delivered to the saints" (Jude 3).

7. What must a person do to prepare for baptism?
Answer:
- A. **Learn God's requirements.** "Go therefore and make disciples of all the nations, baptizing them … teaching them to observe all things that I have commanded you" (Matthew 28:19, 20).
- B. **Believe the truth of God's Word.** "He who believes and is baptized will be saved" (Mark 16:16).
- C. **Repent of and turn away from his sins and experience conversion.** "Repent, and let every one of you be baptized in the name of Jesus Christ for the remission of sins" (Acts 2:38). "Repent therefore and be converted, that your sins may be blotted out" (Acts 3:19).

8. What is the meaning of baptism?
"Therefore we were buried with Him through baptism into death, that just as Christ was raised from the dead by the glory of the Father, even so we also should walk in newness of life. For if we have been united together in the likeness of His death, certainly we also shall be in the likeness of His resurrection, knowing this, that our old man was crucified with Him, that the body of sin might be done away with, that we should no longer be slaves of sin" (Romans 6:4-6).

Answer: It represents the believer following Christ into His death, burial, and resurrection. The symbolism is perfect and filled with deep meaning. In baptism the eyes are closed, hands are folded, and breath is suspended as in death. Then comes burial in the water and resurrection from the watery grave to a new life in Christ. When raised from the water, the eyes open and the candidate begins breathing again and mingles with friends—a complete likeness of resurrection. The great difference between Christianity and every other religion is simply the death, burial, and resurrection of Christ. In these three acts is made possible all that God desires to do for us. To keep these three vital acts alive in the minds of Christians until the end of time, the Lord instituted baptism by immersion as a memorial. There is no symbolism of death, burial, and resurrection in other forms of baptism. Only immersion fulfills the meaning of Romans 6:4-6.

9. But a person shouldn't be baptized until he is certain he will never slip and fall, should he?
"My little children, these things I write to you, so that you may not sin. And if anyone sins, we have an Advocate with the Father, Jesus Christ the righteous" (1 John 2:1).

Answer: This is like saying a baby should never try to walk until certain that he will never slip and fall. A Christian is a new-born "babe" in Christ. This is why the experience of conversion is called "the new birth." The ugly, sinful past no longer exists for a child of God. A person's sinful past is forgiven and forgotten by God at conversion. And baptism symbolizes the burial of that old life. We begin the Christian life as babies, rather than adults, and God judges us on our attitude and the trend of our life, rather than on a few slips and falls that we may experience as immature Christians.

10. Why is baptism an urgent matter for a converted sinner?

"And now why are you waiting? Arise and be baptized, and wash away your sins, calling on the name of the Lord" (Acts 22:16).

Answer: Baptism is a public testimony that the repentant sinner has been forgiven and cleansed by Jesus (1 John 1:9) and that his sinful, traitorous past is behind him. No incriminating evidence against a person exists after conversion. Men and women today stagger and struggle along under heavy loads of guilt and sin. This contamination and burden is so devastating to the human personality that people will go to almost any length to achieve a sense of forgiveness and cleansing. Many have been driven to the psychiatrist's couch, where human beings earnestly attempt to assist other human beings. But the real help is found in coming to Christ, who says to all who approach Him, "I will; be thou clean" (Matthew 8:3). Not only does He cleanse, but He crucifies the old nature of sin within you. Burial in the water of baptism symbolizes the burial of the ugly corpse of the old sinful life. The ordinance is of utmost importance because it publicly represents the most stupendous provisions ever made for people.

11. How long does it take to prepare for baptism?

Answer: That depends on the person. Some grasp things more quickly than others. But in most cases, preparation can be made in short order. Here are some Bible examples:

A. **Ethiopian treasurer** (Acts 8:26-39)—baptized same day he heard truth.
B. **Philippian jailer and his family** (Acts 16:23-34)—baptized same night they heard truth.
C. **Saul of Tarsus** (Acts 9:1-18)—baptized three days after Jesus spoke to him on the road to Damascus.
D. **Cornelius** (Acts 10:1-48)—baptized same day he heard truth.

At conversion, God:
1. Forgives and forgets our past.
2. Miraculously transforms us into new spiritual beings.
3. Adopts us as His own sons and daughters. Certainly no truly converted person would want to delay baptism, which publicly pays tribute to Jesus for working all these miracles.

12. How does God feel about the baptism of a converted person?

Answer: He said at His Son's baptism, "This is My beloved Son, in whom I am well pleased" (Matthew 3:17). So, today, God is well pleased when a person is baptized by immersion in harmony with His command. Those who love the Lord will always strive to please Him (1 John 3:22; 1 Thessalonians 4:1). Is God pleased with your baptism?

13. **Can a person experience true baptism without becoming a member of God's church?**
    Answer: **No!** God clearly outlines this. Notice the steps:
    A. All are called into one body. "You were called in one body" (Colossians 3:15).
    B. The church is the body. "He is the head of the body, the church" (Colossians 1:18).
    C. We enter that body by baptism. "For by one Spirit we were all baptized into one body" (1 Corinthians 12:13).
    D. God's converted people are added to the church. "The Lord added to the church daily those who were being saved" (Acts 2:47).

14. **Notice four things that baptism does not do:**
    First: Baptism itself does not change the heart of man; it is a symbol of the change that has taken place. A man might be baptized without faith, without repentance, and without a new heart. He might even be immersed after the example of Jesus, but he would simply come up a wet sinner instead of a dry one—still without faith, without repentance, without a new heart. Baptism cannot make a new person. Neither can it change or regenerate anyone. It is the transforming power of the Holy Spirit that changes the heart in conversion. One must be born of the Spirit as well as born of water.

    Second: Baptism does not necessarily make a person feel better. It doesn't necessarily change his feelings. Some people are disappointed because they do not feel different after baptism. Salvation is a matter not of feeling, but of faith and obedience.

    Third: Baptism does not remove temptations. The devil is not through with a person when he is baptized. But Jesus is the helper of every believer. He says, "I will never leave you nor forsake you" (Hebrews 13:5). No temptation will come without a way of escape. This is the promise of Scripture (1 Corinthians 10:13).

    Fourth: Baptism does not guarantee salvation. It is not a magical rite. Salvation comes only as a free gift from Jesus Christ when one experiences the new birth. Baptism is a symbol of true conversion, and unless conversion precedes baptism, the ceremony is meaningless.

Your Questions Answered

1. **Is it ever proper to be baptized more than once?**
    Answer: Yes, Acts 19:1-5 shows that the Bible endorses rebaptism in certain cases.

2. **Should infants be baptized?**
    Answer: No one should be baptized unless he (1) knows the truth of God, (2) believes it, (3) has repented, and (4) has experienced conversion. No baby could possibly qualify here. No one has a right to baptize a baby. In fact, to do so completely disregards God's direct commands regarding

baptism. Misguided men in the church years ago decreed that unbaptized babies are lost, but this is scripturally untrue. It defames God as an unjust tyrant who would destroy innocent infants who died, simply because unworthy parents failed to have baptism administered. Such a teaching is tragic beyond words. It is bad enough to sprinkle babies and call it baptism. It is infinitely worse to hold to the unscriptural concept that babies are lost eternally because careless parents failed to do their duty.

3. Isn't baptism just a matter of personal opinion?
Answer: Yes, but not your opinion or mine. It's Christ's opinion that matters. Christ says baptism is important to Him. "Unless one is born of water and the Spirit, he cannot enter the kingdom of God" (John 3:5). To refuse baptism is to refuse the direct counsel of God (Luke 7:29, 30).

4. How old should one be to qualify for baptism?
Answer: Old enough to understand the difference between wrongdoing and right-doing, and to make an intelligent decision to surrender to Christ and follow Him. Many children are ready for baptism at 9 or 10 years of age, some at 7 or 8. And some are not ready at 12 or 13. No age level is specified in the Bible, because children have different levels of experience and understanding. Some are ready for baptism earlier than others.

10 Are the Dead Really Dead?

Death just might be one of the most misunderstood subjects today. To many it is shrouded in mystery and evokes dreaded feelings of fear, uncertainty, and even hopelessness. Others believe that their deceased loved ones are not dead at all, but instead live with them or in other realms! Still others are confused about the relationship between the body, spirit, and soul. But does it really matter what you believe? Yes … absolutely! Because what you believe about the dead will have a profound impact on what happens to you in the end-times. There's no room for guessing, so this Study Guide will give you exactly what God says on this subject. Get ready for a real eye-opener!

1. How did we get here in the first place?
"And the Lord God formed man of the dust of the ground, and breathed into his nostrils the breath of life; and man became a living being" (Genesis 2:7).
Answer: God made us from dust in the beginning.

2. What happens when a person dies?
"Then the dust will return to the earth as it was, and the spirit will return to God who gave it" (Ecclesiastes 12:7).

Answer: The body turns to dust again, and the spirit goes back to God, who gave it. The spirit of every person who dies—whether righteous or wicked—returns to God at death.

3. What is the "spirit" that returns to God at death?

"The body without the spirit is dead" (James 2:26). "The spirit of God is in my nostrils" (Job 27:3, KJV).

Answer: The spirit that returns to God at death is the breath of life. Nowhere in all of God's book does the "spirit" have any life, wisdom, or feeling after a person dies. It is the "breath of life" and nothing more.

4. What is a "soul"?

"And the LORD God formed man of the dust of the ground, and breathed into his nostrils the breath of life; and man became a living soul" (Genesis 2:7, KJV).

Body (Dust)
— **Breath** (Spirit)
= **Death** (No soul)

Answer: A soul is a living being. A soul is always a combination of two things: *body plus breath.* A soul cannot exist unless body and breath are combined. God's Word teaches that we are souls.

5. Do souls die?

"The soul that sinneth, it shall die" (Ezekiel 18:20, KJV). "Every living soul died in the sea" (Revelation 16:3, KJV).

Answer: According to God's Word, souls do die! We are souls, and souls die. Man is mortal (Job 4:17). Only God is immortal (1 Timothy 6:15, 16). The concept of an undying, immortal soul goes against the Bible, which teaches that souls are subject to death.

6. Do good people go to heaven when they die?

"All who are in the graves will hear His voice and come forth" (John 5:28, 29). "David ... is both dead and buried, and his tomb is with us to this day." "For David did not ascend into the heavens" (Acts 2:29, 34). "If I wait, the grave is mine house" (Job 17:13, KJV).

Answer: No, people do not go either to heaven or hell at death. They go to their graves to await the resurrection day.

7. How much does one know or comprehend after death?

"For the living know that they will die; but the dead know nothing, and they have no more reward, for the memory of them is forgotten. Also their love, their hatred, and their envy have now perished; nevermore will they have a share in anything done under the sun." "There is no work or device or knowledge or wisdom in the grave where you are going" (Ecclesiastes 9:5, 6, 10). "The dead do not praise the LORD" (Psalm 115:17).

Answer: God says that the dead know absolutely nothing!

8. But can't the dead communicate with the living, and aren't they aware of what the living are doing?

"So man lies down and does not rise. Till the heavens are no more, they will not awake nor be roused from their sleep." "His sons come to honor, and he does not know it; they are brought low, and he does not perceive it" (Job 14:12, 21). "Nevermore will they have a share in anything done under the sun" (Ecclesiastes 9:6).

Answer: No, the dead cannot contact the living, nor do they know what the living are doing. They are dead. Their thoughts have perished (Psalm 146:4).

9. Jesus called the unconscious state of the dead "sleep" in John 11:11-14. How long will they sleep?

"So man lies down and does not rise. Till the heavens are no more" (Job 14:12). "The day of the Lord will come ... in which the heavens will pass away" (2 Peter 3:10).

Answer: The dead will sleep until the great day of the Lord at the end of the world. In death humans are totally unconscious with no activity or knowledge of any kind.

10. What happens to the righteous dead at the second coming of Christ?

"And behold, I am coming quickly, and My reward is with Me, to give to every one according to his work" (Revelation 22:12). "For the Lord Himself will descend from heaven with a shout, ... And the dead in Christ will rise ... And thus we shall always be with the Lord" (1 Thessalonians 4:16, 17). "We shall all be changed—in a moment, in the twinkling of an eye, ... and the dead will be raised incorruptible. ... For this corruptible must put on incorruption, and this mortal must put on immortality" (1 Corinthians 15:51-53).

Answer: They will be rewarded. They will be raised, given immortal bodies, and caught up to meet the Lord in the air. There would be no purpose in a resurrection if people were taken to heaven at death.

11. What was the devil's first lie on Earth?

"Then the serpent said to the woman, 'You will not surely die'" (Genesis 3:4). "That serpent of old, called the Devil and Satan" (Revelation 12:9).

Answer: You will not die.

12. Why did the devil lie to Eve about death? Could this subject be more important than many think?

Answer: It is one of the pillars of the devil's teachings. He has worked powerful miracles down through the ages through people who claim to receive their power from the spirits of the dead. (Examples: Magicians of Egypt—Exodus 7:11; Woman of Endor—1 Samuel 28:3-25; Sorcerers—Daniel 2:2; A certain slave girl—Acts 16:16-18.)

A Solemn Warning

In the end-time Satan will again use sorcery—as he did in Daniel's day—to deceive the world (Revelation 18:23). Sorcery is a supernatural agency that claims to receive its power and wisdom from the spirits of the dead.

Posing as Jesus' Disciples
Posing as godly loved ones who have died, saintly clergymen who are now dead, Bible prophets, or even the apostles or disciples of Christ (2 Corinthians 11:13), Satan and his angels will deceive billions. Those who believe the dead are alive, in any form, will most assuredly be deceived.

13. Do devils really work miracles?
"For they are the spirits of devils, working miracles" (Revelation 16:14, KJV). "For false christs and false prophets will rise and show great signs and wonders to deceive, if possible, even the elect" (Matthew 24:24).

Answer: Yes, indeed! Devils work incredibly convincing miracles (Revelation 13:13, 14). Satan and his angels will appear as angels of light (2 Corinthians 11:14) and, even more shocking, as Christ Himself (Matthew 24:23, 24). The universal feeling will be that Christ and His angels are leading out in a fantastic worldwide revival. The entire emphasis will seem so spiritual and be so super-natural that only God's elect will not be deceived.

14. Why will God's people not be deceived?
"They received the word with all readiness, and searched the Scriptures daily to find out whether these things were so" (Acts 17:11). "If they do not speak according to this word, it is because there is no light in them" (Isaiah 8:20).

Answer: God's people will know from their earnest study of His book that the dead are dead, not alive. Spirits of the dead do not exist. Therefore, God's people will reject all miracle workers and teachers who claim to receive special "light" or work miracles by contacting the spirits of the dead. And God's people will likewise reject as dangerous and false all teachings that claim the dead are alive in any form, anywhere.

15. Back in Moses' day, what did God command should be done to people who taught that the dead were alive?
"A man or a woman who is a medium, or who has familiar spirits, shall surely be put to death; they shall stone them with stones" (Leviticus 20:27).

Answer: God insisted that mediums and others with "familiar spirits" (who claimed to be able to contact the dead) should be stoned to death. This shows how God regards the false teaching that the dead are alive.

16. Will the righteous people who are raised in the resurrection ever die again?
"But those who are counted worthy to attain that age, and the resurrection from the dead, ... nor can they die anymore" (Luke 20:35, 36). "And God will wipe away every tear from their eyes; there shall be no more death, nor sorrow, nor crying. There shall be no more pain, for the former things have passed away" (Revelation 21:4).

Answer: No! Death, sorrow, crying, and tragedy will never enter into God's new kingdom. "So when this corruptible has put on incorruption, and this mortal has put on immortality, then shall be brought to pass the saying that is written: 'Death is swallowed up in victory'" (1 Corinthians 15:54).

17. Belief in reincarnation is expanding rapidly today. Is this teaching biblical?

"For the living know that they will die; but the dead know nothing. ... Nevermore will they have a share in anything done under the sun" (Ecclesiastes 9:5, 6).

Answer: Almost half the people on earth believe in reincarnation—a teaching that the soul never dies but is instead continually reborn in a different kind of body with each succeeding generation. This teaching, however, is contrary to Scripture.

The Bible Says

After death a person: returns to dust (Psalm 104:29), knows nothing (Ecclesiastes 9:5), possesses no mental powers (Psalm 146:4), has nothing to do with anything on earth (Ecclesiastes 9:6), does not live (2 Kings 20:1), waits in the grave (Job 17:13), and continues not (Job 14:1, 2).

Satan's Invention

We learned in questions 11 and 12 that Satan invented the teaching that the dead are alive. Reincarnation, channeling, communication with spirits, spirit worship, and the "undying soul" are all inventions of Satan, with one aim—to convince people that when you die you are not really dead. When people believe that the dead are alive, "spirits of devils, working miracles" (Revelation 16:14) and posing as spirits of the dead will be able to deceive and lead them astray virtually 100 percent of the time (Matthew 24:24).

Your Questions Answered

1. Didn't the thief on the cross go to paradise with Christ the day He died?

Answer: No. In fact, on Sunday morning Jesus said to Mary, "I have not yet ascended to My Father" (John 20:17). This shows that Christ did not go to heaven at death. Also note that the punctuation of the Bible is not inspired, but was added by men. The comma in Luke 23:43 should be placed after the words "today" rather than before, so the passage should read, "Verily I say unto thee today, shalt thou be with me in paradise." Or, "I'm telling you today—when it seems that I can save no one, when I myself am being crucified as a criminal—I give you the assurance today that you will be with me in paradise." Christ's kingdom is set up at His second coming (Matthew 25:31), and all the righteous of all ages will enter it at that time (1 Thessalonians 4:15-17) and not at death.

2. **Doesn't the Bible speak of the "undying," "immortal" soul?**

   Answer: No, the undying, immortal soul is not mentioned in the Bible. The word "immortal" is found only once in the Bible, and it is in reference to God (1 Timothy 1:17).

3. **At death the body returns to dust and the spirit (or breath) returns to God. But where does the soul go?**

   Answer: It goes nowhere. Instead, it simply ceases to exist. Two things must be combined to make a soul: *body and breath*. When the breath departs, the soul ceases to exist because it is a combination of two things. When you turn off a light, where does the light go? It doesn't go anywhere. It just ceases to exist. Two things must combine to make a light: *a bulb and electricity*. Without the combination, a light is impossible. So with the soul; unless body and breath are combined, there can be no soul. There is no such thing as a disembodied soul.

4. **Doesn't 1 Peter 4:6 say the gospel was preached to dead people?**

   Answer: No, it says the gospel "was" preached to those who "are" dead. They are dead now, but the gospel "was" preached to them while they were yet living.

5. **What about the souls crying out from under the altar in Revelation 6:9, 10? Doesn't this show that souls do not die?**

   Answer: No. This cry was figurative, as was the cry of Abel's blood (Genesis 4:10). The word "soul" here means people (or living beings) who had been slain for their faith. Surely no one believes that souls who die literally lie under the altar, nor do people believe that the righteous beg God to punish their enemies. Rather, the righteous beg for mercy for their enemies, as Christ did on the cross (Luke 23:34).

6. **Doesn't the Bible say Christ went and preached to lost souls in hell between His crucifixion and resurrection?**

   Answer: No, the Bible passage in question is 1 Peter 3:18-20. The preaching was done "by the Spirit" (verse 18) in Noah's day—to people who were then living (verses 19, 20). The "spirits in prison" refers to people whose lives were in bondage to Satan. (See Psalm 142:7; Isaiah 42:6, 7; 61:1; Luke 4:18.)

11 Is the Devil in Charge of Hell?

Well? Does God really keep the devil on His payroll—is he the chief superintendent of hell measuring out the punishment of the lost? Nearly the entire world holds to a very unbiblical view about hell, and you owe it to yourself to know what the Bible really says about it. Don't be fooled, because what you think about hell certainly affects what you think about God's character! Take a few moments to get the amazing facts you need to know today!

1. How many lost souls are being punished in hell today?

"The Lord knoweth how to deliver the godly out of temptations, and to reserve the unjust unto the day of judgment to be punished" (2 Peter 2:9, KJV).

Answer: There is not one single soul in hellfire today. The Bible says that God reserves, or holds back, the wicked until the day of judgment to be punished.

2. When will sinners be cast into hellfire?

"So it will be at the end of this age. The Son of Man will send out His angels, and they will gather out of His kingdom all things that offend, and those who practice lawlessness, and will cast them into the furnace of fire" (Matthew 13:40-42). "The word that I have spoken will judge him in the last day" (John 12:48).

Answer: Sinners will be cast into hellfire at the great judgment day at the end of the world—not when they die. God would not punish a person in fire until his case was tried and decided in court at the end of the world. Nor would God burn a murderer who died 5,000 years ago 5,000 years longer than one who dies and deserves punishment for the same sin today (Genesis 18:25).

3. Where are sinners (who have died) now?

"The hour is coming in which all who are in the graves will hear His voice and come forth—those who have done good, to the resurrection of life, and those who have done evil, to the resurrection of condemnation" (John 5:28, 29). "That the wicked is reserved to the day of destruction?" "Yet shall he be brought to the grave, and shall remain in the tomb" (Job 21:30, 32, KJV).

Answer: The Bible is specific. Both the wicked and the righteous who have died are in their graves "sleeping" until the resurrection day. (See lesson #10 for more information on the state of man in death.)

4. What is the end result of sin?

"The wages of sin is death, but the gift of God is eternal life in Christ Jesus our Lord" (Romans 6:23). "Sin, when it is full-grown, brings forth death" (James 1:15). "God … gave His only begotten Son, that whoever believes in Him should not perish but have everlasting life" (John 3:16).

Answer: The wages (or punishment) for sin is death, not everlasting life in hellfire. The wicked "perish," or receive "death." The righteous receive "everlasting life."

5. What will happen to the wicked in hellfire?

"But the cowardly, unbelieving, abominable, murderers, sexually immoral, sorcerers, idolaters, and all liars shall have their part in the lake which burns with fire and brimstone, which is the second death" (Revelation 21:8).

Answer: The wicked die the second death in hellfire. If the wicked lived forever being tortured in hell, they would be immortal. But this is impossible, because the Bible says God "alone has immortality" (1 Timothy 6:16). When Adam and Eve were driven from the Garden of Eden, an angel was posted to guard the tree of life so that sinners would not eat of the tree and "live forever" (Genesis 3:22-24). The teaching that sinners are immortal in hell originated with Satan and is completely untrue. God prevented this when sin entered this earth by guarding the tree of life.

The Bible is clear, the wicked are obliterated. The Bible says the wicked suffer "death" (Romans 6:23), will suffer "doom" [destruction] (Job 21:30), "shall perish" (Psalm 37:20), will "burn" up (Malachi 4:1), "shall be destroyed together" (Psalm 37:38), will "vanish away" (Psalm 37:20), "shall be cut off" (Psalm 37:9), "shall be slain" (Psalm 62:3). God will "destroy" them (Psalm 145:20), and "fire shall devour them" (Psalm 21:9). Note that all of these references make it clear that the wicked die and are destroyed. They do not live forever in misery.

6. When and how will hellfire be kindled?

"So it will be at the end of this age. The Son of man … will cast them into the furnace of fire" (Matthew 13:40-42). "They went up on the breadth of the earth and surrounded the camp of the saints and the beloved city. And fire came down from God out of heaven and devoured them" (Revelation 20:9). "The righteous will be recompensed on the earth, How much more the ungodly and the sinner" (Proverbs 11:31).

Answer: At the end of the world, God Himself will kindle hellfire. As the holy city comes down from God out of heaven (Revelation 21:2), the wicked attempt to capture it. At that time, God will rain down fire from heaven upon the earth, and it will devour the wicked. This fire is Bible hellfire.

7. How big and how hot will hellfire be?

"But the day of the Lord will come as a thief in the night, in which the heavens will pass away with a great noise, and the elements will melt with fervent heat; both the earth and the works that are in it will be burned up" (2 Peter 3:10).

Answer: Hellfire will be just as big as this earth because it will be the earth on fire. This fire will be so hot as to melt the earth and burn up all "the works that are in it." The atmospheric heavens will explode and "pass away with a great noise."

8. How long will the wicked suffer in the fire?

"And behold, I am coming quickly, and My reward is with Me, to give to every one according to his work" (Revelation 22:12). "And then He will reward each according to his works" (Matthew 16:27). "And that servant who knew his master's will, and did not … do according to his will, shall be beaten with many stripes. But he who did not know, yet committed things deserving of stripes, shall be beaten with few" (Luke 12:47, 48).

Answer: The Bible does not tell how long the wicked will be punished before receiving death in the fire. God does specifically state, however, that all will be punished according to their deeds. This means some will receive greater punishment than others, based upon their works.

9. Will the fire eventually go out?

"Behold, they shall be as stubble, the fire shall burn them; they shall not deliver themselves from the power of the flame; it shall not be a coal to be warmed by, nor a fire to sit before!" (Isaiah 47:14). "Now I saw a new heaven and a new earth." "And God will wipe away every tear from their eyes; there shall be no more death, nor sorrow, nor crying. There shall be no more pain, for the former things have passed away" (Revelation 21:1, 4).

Answer: Yes, indeed, the Bible specifically teaches that hellfire will go out and that there will not be left "a coal to warm at, nor fire to sit before!" The Bible also teaches that in God's new kingdom all "former things" will be passed away. Hell, being one of the former things, is included, so we have God's promise that it will be abolished.

Is God a Torturer?
If God tortured His enemies in a fiery horror chamber throughout eternity, He would be more vicious and heartless than men have ever been in the worst of war atrocities. An eternal hell of torment would be hell for God also, who loves even the vilest sinner.

10. What will be left when the fire goes out?

"'For behold, the day is coming, burning like an oven, and all the proud, yes, all who do wickedly will be stubble. And the day which is coming shall burn them up,' says the LORD of hosts, 'That will leave them neither root nor branch.'" "'You shall trample the wicked, for they shall be ashes under the soles of your feet on the day that I do this,' says the LORD of hosts" (Malachi 4:1, 3).

Answer: Notice the verse does not say the wicked will burn like asbestos, as many today believe, but rather like stubble, which will be burned up. The little word "up" denotes completion. Nothing but ashes will be left when the fire goes out. In Psalm 37:10, 20, the Bible says the wicked will go up in smoke and be completely destroyed.

11. Will the wicked enter hell in bodily form and be destroyed both soul and body?

"It is more profitable for you that one of your members perish, than for your whole body to be cast into hell" (Matthew 5:30). "Rather fear Him who is able to destroy both soul and body in hell" (Matthew 10:28). "The soul who sins shall die" (Ezekiel 18:20).

Answer: Yes. Real, live people enter hell in bodily form and are destroyed both soul and body. The fire from God out of heaven will fall upon real people and blot them out of existence.

12. Will the devil be in charge of hellfire?

"The devil, who deceived them, was cast into the lake of fire" (Revelation 20:10). "I turned you to ashes upon the earth in the sight of all who saw you. ... You ... shall be no more forever" (Ezekiel 28:18, 19).

Answer: Absolutely not! **The devil will be cast into the fire, and it will turn him into ashes.**

13. Does the word "hell" as used in the Bible always refer to a place of burning or punishment?

Answer: No, the word "hell" is used 54 times in the Bible, and in only 12 cases does it refer to "a place of burning."

The word "hell" is translated from several different words with various meanings, as indicated below:

In the Old Testament
31 times from "Sheol," which means "the grave."

In the New Testament
10 times from "Hades," which means "the grave."
12 times from "Gehenna," which means "the place of burning."
 1 time from "Tartarus," which means "a place of darkness."

 =*54 Times total*

Note: *The Greek word "Gehenna" (mentioned above) is a transliteration of the Hebrew "Ge-Hinnom," which means the "Valley of Hinnom." This valley, which lies immediately south and west of Jerusalem, was a place where dead animals, garbage, and other refuse were dumped. Fire burned constantly, as it does at modern sanitation dump sites. The Bible uses "Gehenna" or the "Valley of Hinnom" as a symbol of the fire that will destroy the lost at the end of time. The fire of Gehenna was not unending. Otherwise it would be still burning southwest of Jerusalem today. Neither will the fire of hell be unending.*

14. What is God's real purpose in hellfire?

"Depart from Me, you cursed, into the everlasting fire prepared for the devil and his angels" (Matthew 25:41). "And anyone not found written in the Book of Life was cast into the lake of fire" (Revelation 20:15). "For yet a little while and the wicked shall be no more." "The enemies of the Lord ... shall vanish. Into smoke they shall vanish away" (Psalm 37:10, 20).

Answer: **God's purpose is that hell will destroy the devil and all sin and sinners and make the world safe for eternity. One sinner, if left on this planet, would be a deadly virus forever threatening the universe. It is God's plan to blot sin out of existence for all time.**

Eternal Hell Would Perpetuate Sin
An eternal hell of torment would perpetuate sin and make its eradication impossible. An eternal hell of torment is not part of God's great plan at all. Such a horrible theory is slander against the holy name of a

loving God. The devil delights to see our loving Creator pictured as such a monstrous tyrant, and he alone can benefit from such teachings.

Eternal Hell a Man-made Theory
The "eternal hell of torment" theory originated not from the Bible, but from misguided people who were (perhaps inadvertently) led of the devil. And, incidentally, while a fear of hell may get our attention, our salvation is the result of learning to love and obey Christ.

15. Isn't the work of destroying sinners foreign to God's nature?

"'As I live,' says the Lord GOD, 'I have no pleasure in the death of the wicked, but that the wicked turn from his way and live. Turn, turn from your evil ways! For why should you die?'" (Ezekiel 33:11). "For the Son of Man did not come to destroy men's lives but to save them" (Luke 9:56). "For the LORD will rise up ... that He may do His work, His awesome work, and bring to pass His act, His unusual act" (Isaiah 28:21).

Answer: Yes, the work of God has always been to save rather than destroy. The work of destroying the wicked in hellfire is so foreign to God's nature that the Bible calls it His "strange act." God's great heart will ache at the destruction of the wicked. Oh, how diligently He works to save every soul! But if one spurns His love and clings to sin, God will have no choice but to destroy the sinner with his sin when He rids the universe of that horrible, malignant growth called "sin" in the fires of the last day.

16. What are God's post-hell plans for the earth and His people?

"He will make an utter end of it. Affliction will not rise up a second time" (Nahum 1:9). "For behold, I create new heavens and a new earth; and the former shall not be remembered or come to mind" (Isaiah 65:17). "Behold, the tabernacle of God is with men, and He will dwell with them, and they shall be His people. God Himself will be with them and be their God. And God will wipe away every tear from their eyes; there shall be no more death, nor sorrow, nor crying. There shall be no more pain" (Revelation 21:3, 4).

Answer: After hellfire goes out, God will create a new earth and restore it to His people—with all the beauties and glories of Eden before sin entered. The horrors of sin and the past will be forgotten. Pain, death, tragedy, woe, tears, sickness, disappointment, sorrow, and all sin will be banished forever.

Sin Will Not Rise Again
God promises that sin will never rise again. His people will be filled with perfect peace, love, joy, and contentment. Their lives of complete happiness will be far more glorious and thrilling than mere words could ever describe. The real tragedy of hell is in missing heaven. A person who fails to enter this magnificent kingdom has made the saddest choice of a lifetime.

Your Questions Answered

1. **Doesn't Matthew 25:46 say the wicked will receive "everlasting punishment"?**
   Answer: Notice the word is *punishment*, not *punishing*. Punishing would be continuous, while punishment is one act. The punishment of the wicked is *death*, and this death is everlasting.

2. **Matthew 25:41 speaks of "everlasting fire" for the wicked. Does it go out?**
   Answer: Yes, according to the Bible, it does. We must let the Bible explain itself. Sodom and Gomorrah were destroyed with everlasting, or eternal, fire (Jude 7), and that fire turned them "into ashes" as a warning to "those who afterward would live ungodly" (2 Peter 2:6). These cities are not burning today. The fire went out after everything was burned up. Likewise, everlasting fire will go out after it has turned the wicked to ashes (Malachi 4:3). The effects of the fire are everlasting, but not the burning itself.

3. **Doesn't the story of the rich man and Lazarus in Luke 16:19-31 teach an eternal hell of torment?**
   Answer: No, indeed! It is simply a parable used to emphasize a point. Many facts make it clear that this is a parable. A few are as follows:

   A. Abraham's bosom is not heaven (Hebrews 11:8-10, 16).

   B. People in hell can't talk to those in heaven (Isaiah 65:17).

   C. The dead are in their graves (Job 17:13; John 5:28, 29). The rich man was in bodily form with eyes, a tongue, etc., yet we know that the body does not go to hell at death. It is very obvious that the body remains in the grave, as the Bible says.

   D. Men are rewarded at Christ's second coming, not at death (Revelation 22:11, 12).

   E. The lost are punished in hell at the end of the world, not when they die (Matthew 13:40-42).

   The point of the story is found in verse 31 of Luke 16. Parables cannot be taken literally. If we took parables literally, then we must believe that trees talk! (See this parable in Judges 9:8-15.)

4. **But the Bible speaks of the wicked being tormented "forever," doesn't it?**
   Answer: The term "for ever," as used in the Bible, means simply a period of time, limited or unlimited. It is used 56 times in the Bible in connection with things that have already ended. (To check in a concordance, look up the word "ever.") It is like the word "tall," which means something different in describing men, trees, or mountains. In Jonah 2:6, "forever" means "three days and nights." (See also Jonah 1:17.) In Deuteronomy 23:3, this means "10 generations." In the case of man, this means "as long as he lives" or "until death." (See 1 Samuel 1:22, 28; Exodus 21:6; Psalm 48:14.) So the wicked will burn in the fire as long as they live, or until

death. This fiery punishment for sin will vary according to the degree of sins for each individual, but after the punishment, the fire will go out. The teaching of eternal torment has done more to drive people to atheism and insanity than any other invention of the devil. It is slander upon the loving character of a tender, gracious heavenly Father and has done untold harm to the Christian cause.

12 1,000 Years of Peace

You can be certain that it's coming—an incredible millennium that will be ushered in after Christ's return. And the devil doesn't want you to know about his 1,000-year prison sentence because it reveals his true character. In fact, Satan has concocted a counterfeit message on the millennium to trick you! It's an awesome, fascinating study that will utterly shake everything you've ever known! Now you can have the Bible's amazing truths about the coming 1,000-year reign.

1. What event begins this 1,000-year period?

"And they lived [came alive] and reigned with Christ for a thousand years" (Revelation 20:4). (For more on the subject of death, see Study Guide 10.)

Answer: **A resurrection begins the 1,000-year period.**

2. What is this resurrection called? Who will be raised in it?

"This is the first resurrection. Blessed and holy is he who has part in the first resurrection" (Revelation 20:5, 6).

Answer: **It is called the first resurrection. The righteous people—"blessed and holy" of all ages—will be raised in it.**

3. The Bible says there are two resurrections. When is the second resurrection, and who will be raised in it?

"The rest of the dead [those who were wicked] did not live again until the thousand years were finished" (Revelation 20:5). "All who are in the graves will hear His voice and come forth—those who have done good, to the resurrection of life, and those who have done evil, to the resurrection of condemnation" (John 5:28, 29).

Answer: **The second resurrection takes place at the close of the 1,000-year period. The wicked will be raised in this resurrection. It is called the resurrection of damnation.**

Please notice: *The resurrection of the righteous begins the 1,000 years. The resurrection of the wicked ends the 1,000 years.*

4. What other momentous events take place when the 1,000 years begin?

"Behold, He is coming with clouds, and every eye will see Him" (Revelation 1:7). "For the Lord Himself will descend from heaven with a shout. ...And the dead in Christ will rise first. Then we who are alive and remain shall be caught up together with them in the clouds to meet the Lord in the air" (1 Thessalonians 4:16, 17). "And there was a great earthquake, such a mighty and great earthquake as had not occurred since men were on the earth. ... And great hail from heaven fell upon men, each hailstone about the weight of a talent [scholarly estimates vary from 58 to 100 pounds]" (Revelation 16:18, 20, 21). (See also Jeremiah 4:23-26; Isaiah 24:1, 3, 19, 20; Isaiah 2:21.)

Answer: Other momentous events that take place as the 1,000 years begin are: the most devastating earthquake and hailstorm in history strike the earth; Jesus returns in the clouds for His people; and all the saints are caught up into the air to meet Jesus. (See Study Guide 8 for more on the second coming of Christ.)

5. What happens to the wicked—living and dead—at Jesus' second coming?

"With the breath of His lips He shall slay the wicked" (Isaiah 11:4). "When the Lord Jesus is revealed from heaven with His mighty angels, in flaming fire taking vengeance on those who do not know God" (2 Thessalonians 1:7, 8). "Let the wicked perish at the presence of God" (Psalm 68:2). "But the rest of the dead did not live again until the thousand years were finished" (Revelation 20:5).

Answer: The living wicked will be slain by the very presence of Christ at the second coming. When an angel appeared at Jesus' tomb, the entire group of Roman guards fell as dead men (Matthew 28:2, 4). When the brightness of all the angels, God the Father, and God the Son combine, the wicked will die as if hit by lightning. The wicked already dead when Jesus returns will remain in their graves until the end of the 1,000 years.

6. Many believe the unsaved will have an opportunity to repent during the 1,000 years. What does the Bible say about this?

"The slain of the LORD shall be from one end of the earth even to the other end of the earth. They shall not be lamented, or gathered, or buried; they shall become refuse on the ground" (Jeremiah 25:33). "I beheld, and indeed there was no man" (Jeremiah 4:25).

Answer: It is impossible for any person to repent during the 1,000 years because there will not be a person alive on earth. The righteous will all be in heaven. All the wicked will be lying dead upon the earth. Revelation 22:11, 12 makes it clear that the case of every person is closed before Jesus returns. Those who wait to accept Christ until the 1,000 years begin will have waited too long.

7. The Bible says that Satan will be bound in the bottomless pit during the 1,000 years. What is this pit?

"Then I saw an angel coming down from heaven, having the key to the bottomless pit. ... He laid hold of the dragon, that serpent of old, who is the Devil and Satan, and bound him for a thousand years; and he cast him into the bottomless pit ... till the thousand years were finished" (Revelation 20:1-3).

Answer: The word for "bottomless pit" in the original Greek is "abussos," or abyss. That same word is used in Genesis 1:2 in the Greek version of the Old Testament in connection with the creation of the earth, but there it is translated "deep." "The earth was without form, and void; and darkness was upon the face of the deep." How interesting! The words "deep," "bottomless pit," and "abyss" here refer to the same thing—the earth in its totally dark, disorganized form before God made order of it. Jeremiah, in describing this earth during the 1,000 years, used virtually the same terms as these in Genesis 1:2: "without form and void," "no light," "no man," and "black" (Jeremiah 4:23, 25, 28). So the battered, dark earth with no people alive will be called the bottomless pit, or abyss, during the 1,000 years, just as it was in the beginning before Creation was completed. Isaiah 24:22 also speaks of Satan and his angels during the 1,000 years as "gathered in the pit" and "shut up in the prison."

8. What is the chain that binds Satan? Why is he bound?

"An angel ... having ... a great chain in his hand ... laid hold of ... Satan, and bound him for a thousand years; ... and shut him up, and set a seal on him, so that he should deceive the nations no more till the thousand years were finished" (Revelation 20:1-3).

Answer: The chain is symbolic—a chain of circumstances. A spirit being cannot be confined with a literal chain. Satan is "tied down" because he has no people to deceive. The wicked are all dead and the righteous are all in heaven. The Lord confines the devil to this earth so he cannot roam the universe hoping to find someone to deceive. Forcing the devil to stay on the earth, alone with his demons for a thousand years with no one to deceive, will be for him the most galling chain ever forged.

Review the Events Occurring at the Beginning of the 1,000 Years:
A. Devastating earthquake and hailstorm (Revelation 16:18-21; Revelation 6:14-17).
B. Second coming of Jesus for His saints (Matthew 24:30, 31).
C. Righteous dead raised to life (1 Thessalonians 4:16, 17).
D. Righteous given immortality (1 Corinthians 15:51-55).
E. Righteous given bodies like Jesus (1 John 3:2; Philippians 3:21).
F. All righteous caught up into the clouds (1 Thessalonians 4:16, 17).
G. Living wicked slain by the breath of the Lord's mouth (Isaiah 11:4).
H. Wicked in graves remain dead until the end of the 1,000 years (Revelation 20:5).
I. Jesus takes righteous to heaven (John 13:33, 36; 14:1-3).
J. Satan bound (Revelation 20:1-3).

9. Revelation 20:4 says there will be a judgment in heaven during the 1,000 years. What for? Who will participate?

"I saw thrones, and they sat on them, and judgment was committed to them. ... And they lived and reigned with Christ for a thousand years" (Revelation 20:4). "Do you not know that the saints will judge the world? ... Do you not know that we will judge angels?" (1 Corinthians 6:2, 3).

Answer: The righteous of all ages (and probably even good angels) will participate in the judgment during the 1,000 years. The cases of all who are lost, including the devil and his angels, will be reviewed. This judgment will make details regarding the lost clear to each saved person. In the end, all will see that people are shut out of heaven only if they did not really want to live like Jesus or to be with Him.

Review the Events and Conditions During the 1,000 Years:
A. Earth in battered condition from huge hailstones and devastating earthquake (Revelation 16:18-21; 6:14-17).
B. Earth in total blackout/bottomless pit (Jeremiah 4:23, 28).
C. Satan and his angels forced to stay on the earth/bound (Revelation 20:1-3).
D. Righteous in heaven participating in the judgment (Revelation 20:4).
E. Wicked are all dead (Jeremiah 4:25; Isaiah 11:4).

During the 1,000 years, every soul who has ever lived on earth will be in one of two places: (1) on the earth, dead and lost, or (2) in heaven, taking part in the judgment. The Lord invites you to be in heaven. Please accept His invitation.

10. At the close of the 1,000 years the holy city, New Jerusalem, will come down from heaven to this earth. Who will come with it? Where will it settle?

"Then I ... saw the holy city, New Jerusalem, coming down out of heaven from God. ... And I heard a loud voice from heaven saying, 'Behold, the tabernacle of God is with men'" (Revelation 21:2, 3). "Behold, the day of the LORD is coming." "And in that day His feet will stand on the Mount of Olives, which faces Jerusalem on the east. And the Mount of Olives shall be split in two. ... Thus the LORD my God will come, and all the saints with You." "All the land shall be turned into a plain from Geba to Rimmon south of Jerusalem" (Zechariah 14:1, 4, 5, 10).

Answer: The new Jerusalem will settle where the mount of Olives now stands. The mountain will be flattened to make a great plain, upon which the city will come to rest. All of the righteous people of all ages (Zechariah 14:5), the angels of heaven (Matthew 25:31), plus God the Father (Revelation 21:2, 3) and God the Son (Matthew 25:31) will return to earth with the holy city for Jesus' special third coming. The second coming will be *for* His saints; the third, will be *with* His saints.

Jesus' Three Advents:
A. First coming, to Bethlehem in a manger.
B. Second coming, in the clouds at the beginning of the 1,000 years to take His people to heaven.
C. Third coming, with the holy city and all righteous people at the close of the 1,000 years.

11. What will happen to the wicked dead at this time? How will this affect Satan?

"The rest of the dead did not live again until the thousand years were finished." "When the thousand years have expired, Satan will be released from his prison and will go out to deceive the nations" (Revelation 20:5, 7, 8).

Answer: At the close of the 1,000 years (when Jesus comes the third time) the wicked will be raised. Satan, loosed from his bonds, will then have an earth full of people (all the nations of the world) to deceive.

12. What will Satan do then?

"Satan will ... go out to deceive the nations ... of the earth, ... to gather them together to battle, whose number is as the sand of the sea. They went up on the breadth of the earth and surrounded the camp of the saints and the beloved city" (Revelation 20:7-9).

Answer: Satan, true to his nature, will immediately begin lying to the people left on the earth—the wicked from all ages. He will probably claim that the city is really his, that he was unjustly deposed from the heavenly kingdom, that God is power-hungry and ruthless, and that God is getting ready to wipe them all off the face of the earth with a devastating, inescapable fire. He will convince them that, if they unify, God does not have a chance. With the entire world against one city, the victory will appear certain. The nations will then unite and marshal their armies to surround the new Jerusalem. (For more information on the origin of Satan, see Study Guide 2.)

13. What will interrupt Satan's plan to capture or destroy the city?

"Fire came down from God out of heaven and devoured them. The devil, who deceived them, was cast into ... the lake which burns with fire and brimstone, which is the second death" (Revelation 20:9, 10; 21:8). "'The wicked ... shall be ashes under the soles of your feet on the day that I do this,' says the LORD of hosts" (Malachi 4:3).

Answer: Fire will suddenly come down from heaven (not up from hell, as many believe) upon the wicked and all will be turned into ashes, including the devil and his angels (Matthew 25:41). This fire that destroys sin and sinners is called the second death. There is no resurrection from this death. It is final. Notice that the devil will not be tending the fire, as is commonly believed. He will be in it, and it will put him out of existence. (For full information on this fire, sometimes called hell, see Study Guide 11. For information on death, see Study Guide 10.)

14. When the wicked are burned up and the fire goes out, what glorious, thrilling event will take place next?

"Behold, I create new heavens and a new earth" (Isaiah 65:17). "Look for new heavens and a new earth in which righteousness dwells" (2 Peter 3:13). "He who sat on the throne said, 'Behold, I make all things new'" (Revelation 21:5). "The tabernacle of God is with men, and He will dwell with them, and they shall be His people. God Himself will be with them and be their God" (Revelation 21:3).

Answer: God will create new heavens and a new earth, and the new Jerusalem will be the capital city of the earth made new. Sin and its ugliness will be gone forever. God's people will at long last receive the kingdom promised to them. "They shall obtain joy and gladness, and sorrow and sighing shall flee away" (Isaiah 35:10). Too fabulous to describe! Too glorious to miss! Too near for us to be unsure! God has a place prepared there for you (John 14:1-3). Plan to live in it. Jesus is waiting for your consent. (For full information on heaven, see Study Guide 4.)

Review the Events at the Close of the 1,000 Years:
A. Third coming of Jesus *with* His saints (Zechariah 14:5).
B. Holy city settles on mount of Olives, which becomes a great plain (Zechariah 14:4, 10).
C. The Father, angels, and all of the righteous come with Jesus (Revelation 21:1-3; Matthew 25:31; Zechariah 14:5).
D. Wicked dead raised; Satan loosed (Revelation 20:5, 7).
E. Satan deceives entire world (Revelation 20:8).
F. Wicked surround the holy city (Revelation 20:9).
G. Wicked destroyed by fire (Revelation 20:9).
H. New heavens and earth created (Isaiah 65:17; 2 Peter 3:13; Rev. 21:1).
I. God's people enjoy eternity with Christ on the new earth (Rev. 21:2-4).

The 1,000 Years of Revelation 20
Events during 1,000 years
1. Earth torn up, desolate, and dark.
2. All wicked are dead on earth.
3. Satan bound to this earth.
4. Righteous judging in heaven.

1st Resurrection
Events at Beginning of the 1,000 years
1. Devastating earthquake and hailstorm.
2. Second coming of Jesus for the saints.
3. Righteous dead raised to life.
4. Righteous given immortality.
5. Righteous given bodies like that of Jesus.
6. All righteous caught up into clouds.
7. Living wicked slain by the Lord's presence.
8. Wicked already in their graves remain dead.
9. Jesus takes righteous to heaven.
10. Satan bound.

2nd Resurrection
Events at Close of the 1,000 years
1. Third coming of Jesus with the saints.
2. Holy city descends onto the mount of Olives, which becomes a great plain.

3. Father, angels, righteous come with Jesus.
4. Wicked dead raised and Satan loosed.
5. Satan deceives all nations. They surround the holy city.
6. Wicked destroyed by fire.
7. New heavens and earth created.
8. God's people enjoy eternity with Jesus.

15. Can we know how soon Jesus will return for His saints?

"So you also, when you see all these things, know that it is near—at the doors!" (Matthew 24:33). "Now when these things begin to happen, look up and lift up your heads, because your redemption draws near" (Luke 21:28). "For He will finish the work and cut it short in righteousness, because the LORD will make a short work upon the earth" (Romans 9:28). "For when they say, 'Peace and safety!' then sudden destruction comes upon them" (1 Thessalonians 5:3).

Answer: Jesus said when the signs of His coming are being fulfilled rapidly, as they are today, we should rejoice and know that His coming is near—even at the doors. And the apostle Paul said we can know the end is near when there is a great movement for peace in the world. Finally, the Bible says God will cut the work short (Romans 9:28). So without doubt, we are living on borrowed time. The Lord will arrive suddenly and unexpectedly—at an hour known to no one, but to God only (Matthew 24:36; Acts 1:7). Our only safety is to be ready.

Your Questions Answered

1. **How long will the time period be from the day the holy city descends until the wicked are destroyed by fire from heaven?**

   Answer: The Bible says it will be a "little," or short, season (Revelation 20:3). Enough time will be required for Satan to persuade people to follow his plan and prepare weapons of war. The exact length of time is not revealed in Scripture.

2. **What kind of bodies will people have in God's new kingdom?**

   Answer: The Bible says the redeemed will have bodies like that of Jesus (Philippians 3:21). Jesus had a real body of flesh and bones after His resurrection (Luke 24:36-43). The saved will not be ghosts. They will be real people, as were Adam and Eve.

3. **Does the Bible say how the lost will react at Jesus' second coming?**

   Answer: Yes. The Bible says they will cry "to the mountains and rocks, 'Fall on us and hide us from the face of Him who sits on the throne and from the wrath of the Lamb! For the great day of His wrath has come, and who is able to stand?'" (Revelation 6:16, 17). (See also verses 14 and 15.) The righteous, on the other hand, will say, "Behold, this is our God; we have waited for Him, and He will save us. This is the LORD; we have waited for Him; we will be glad and rejoice in His salvation" (Isaiah 25:9).

4. What kind of body does Jesus have?

Answer: He has a body of flesh and bones. After His resurrection, Jesus appeared to His disciples (Luke 24:36-43) and demonstrated that He was not a spirit or ghost by stating that He was flesh and bones, having them feel His body, and by eating some fish and honey.

Jesus Ascends

He then walked with them to Bethany and, as He was conversing with them, ascended to heaven (Luke 24:49-51). The angel who appeared to the disciples as Jesus ascended explained that "this same Jesus, who was taken up from you into heaven, will so come in like manner as you saw Him go into heaven" (Acts 1:11).

This Same Jesus Will Return

The angel's emphasis was that *this same Jesus* (of flesh and bones) will come again. He will be real, not ghostly, and the risen and translated saints will have bodies like His (Philippians 3:21; 1 John 3:2). The saints' heavenly bodies will also be *incorruptible* and *immortal* (1 Corinthians 15:51-55).

13 God's Free Health Plan

Great medical care is priceless—but wouldn't it be great if we didn't need doctors anymore? Did you know there is a proven way to put a lot of doctors out of work? Take care of your body! Scientists have sounded the ominous warnings about cholesterol, tobacco, stress, obesity, and alcohol, so why press your luck? Hospitals and psychiatric institutions are packed with people who have ignored the warnings—do you really want to join them? God truly cares how you treat your body, and He's given you a free health plan, and a manual to go by ... the Bible! For amazing facts about how you can have abundant health and longer life, look over this Study Guide—but be sure to read it all before jumping to conclusions!

1. Are health principles really a part of true Bible religion?

"Beloved, I pray that you may prosper in all things and be in health, just as your soul prospers" (3 John 2).

Answer: Yes. In fact, the Bible rates health right near the top of the list in importance. Man's mind, spiritual nature, and body are all interrelated and interdependent. What affects one affects the other. If our bodies are misused, our minds and spiritual natures cannot become what God ordained they should.

2. Why did God give health rules to His people?

"And the LORD commanded us to observe all these statutes, to fear the LORD our God, for our good always, that He might preserve us alive" (Deuteronomy 6:24). "So you shall serve the LORD your God, and He will bless your bread and your water. And I will take sickness away from the midst of you" (Exodus 23:25).

Answer: God gave health rules because He knows what is best for the human body. Automobile manufacturers place an "operations manual" in the glove compartment of each new car because they know what is best for their product. God, who made our bodies, also has an "operations manual." It is called the Holy Bible. Ignoring God's "operations manual" results in disease, twisted thinking, and burned-out lives, just as abusing a car (against the manufacturer's counsel) results in serious car trouble. Following God's rules results in "salvation [saving health]" (Psalm 67:2) and more abundant life (John 10:10). These great health laws are like a wall or fence to keep out the diseases of Satan. God tells us what these rules are so we can avoid the devil's traps.

3. Do God's health rules have anything to do with eating and drinking?

"Eat what is good" (Isaiah 55:2). "Therefore, whether you eat or drink, or whatever you do, do all to the glory of God" (1 Corinthians 10:31).

Answer: Yes, a Christian will even eat and drink differently—all to the glory of God—using only "that which is good." If God says a thing is not fit to eat, He must have a good reason. He is not a harsh dictator, but a loving Father. All His counsel is for our good always. The Bible promises: "No good thing will He withhold from those who walk uprightly" (Psalm 84:11). So if God withholds a thing from us, it is because it is not good.

Note: *No person can eat his way into heaven. Eating even the food of angels will not entitle people to paradise. Only acceptance of Jesus Christ as Lord and Savior can do that. Ignoring God's health laws, however, may cause a person to be lost, because it will ruin his judgment and cause him to sin.*

4. What did God give people to eat when He created them and provided a perfect diet?

"And God said, "See, I have given you every herb that yields seed ... every tree whose fruit yields seed." "Of every tree of the garden you may freely eat" (Genesis 1:29; 2:16).

Answer: The diet God gave people in the beginning was fruit, grains, and nuts. Vegetables were added a bit later (Genesis 3:18).

5. What items are specifically mentioned by God as being unclean and forbidden?

Answer: In Leviticus 11 and Deuteronomy 14, God very clearly points out the following groups as being unclean. Read both chapters in full.

A. All animals which do not have a split hoof and chew the cud (Deuteronomy 14:6).

B. All fish and water creatures that do not have both fins and scales. Nearly all fish are clean (Deuteronomy 14:9).

C. All birds of prey, carrion eaters, and fish eaters (Leviticus 11:13-20).

D. Most "creeping things" (or invertebrates) are also unclean (Leviticus 11:21-47).

Note: *These chapters make it clear that most animals, birds, and water creatures people ordinarily eat are clean. There are, however, some very notable exceptions.* According to God's rules, the following animals are unclean and are not to be eaten: cats, dogs, horses, camels, eagles, vultures, hogs, squirrels, rabbits, catfish, eels, lobsters, clams, crabs, shrimp, oysters, frogs, and many others.

6. But I like pork. Will God destroy me if I eat it?

"For behold, the LORD will come with fire … and by His sword the LORD will judge all flesh; and the slain of the LORD shall be many. Those who sanctify themselves and purify themselves, … eating swine's flesh and the abomination and the mouse, shall be consumed together" (Isaiah 66:15-17).

Answer: This may be shocking, but it is true and must be told. The Bible positively states that all who eat "swine's flesh," the mouse, and other unclean things that are an "abomination" will be destroyed with fire at the coming of the Lord. When God says to leave something alone and not eat it, we should by all means obey Him. After all, the mere eating of a piece of forbidden fruit by Adam and Eve, a sinless couple, brought sin and death to this world in the first place. Can anyone say it doesn't matter, when God so clearly shows it does? God says men will be destroyed because they "chose that in which I do not delight" (Isaiah 66:4).

7. But didn't this law of clean and unclean animals originate at Sinai? Wasn't it for the Jews only, and didn't it end at the cross?

"Then the LORD said to Noah, '… take with you seven each of every clean animal … ; two each of animals that are unclean'" (Genesis 7:1, 2).

Answer: No, indeed! The Bible has ample evidence that there were clean and unclean animals from the very dawn of Creation. Noah lived long before any Jews existed, but he knew of the clean and unclean, because he took into the ark the clean animals by "sevens" and the unclean by "twos." Revelation 18:2 refers to some birds as being unclean just before the second coming of Christ. The death of Christ had no altering effect whatever on these health laws, since the Bible says that all who break them will be destroyed when Jesus returns (Isaiah 66:15-17). The Jew's stomach and digestive system in no way differs from that of a Gentile. These health laws are for all people for all time.

8. Does the Bible forbid the use of alcoholic beverages?

"Wine is a mocker, strong drink is a brawler, and whoever is led astray by it is not wise" (Proverbs 20:1). "Do not look on the wine when it is red, when it sparkles in the cup, when it swirls around smoothly; at the last it bites like a serpent, and stings like a viper" (Proverbs 23:31, 32). "Neither fornicators, … nor drunkards … will inherit the kingdom of God" (1 Corinthians 6:9, 10).

Answer: Yes, the Bible clearly forbids the use of alcoholic beverages.

9. Does the Bible condemn the use of tobacco and other harmful substances?

Answer: Yes, the Bible gives six reasons why the use of tobacco and harmful substances are displeasing to God:

- **A. The use of harmful substances injures health and defiles the body.** "Do you not know that you are the temple of God and that the Spirit of God dwells in you? If anyone defiles the temple of God, God will destroy him. For the temple of God is holy, which temple you are" (1 Corinthians 3:16, 17).

- **B. Nicotine is an addictive substance that enslaves people.** Romans 6:16 says that we become servants to whomever (or whatever) we yield ourselves. Tobacco users are servants of nicotine. Jesus says, "You shall worship the Lord your God, and Him only you shall serve" (Matthew 4:10).

- **C. The tobacco habit is unclean.** "Come out from among them and be separate, says the Lord. Do not touch what is unclean, and I will receive you" (2 Corinthians 6:17). It is really preposterous to think of Christ using tobacco in any form, isn't it?

- **D. The use of harmful substances wastes money.** "Why do you spend money for what is not bread?" (Isaiah 55:2). We are God's stewards of the money given us, and "it is required in stewards that one be found faithful" (1 Corinthians 4:2).

- **E. The use of harmful substances weakens our ability to discern the promptings of the Holy Spirit.** "Abstain from fleshly lusts which war against the soul" (1 Peter 2:11). The use of harmful substances use is a fleshly lust.

- **F. The use of harmful substances shortens life.** Recent scientific findings confirm the fact that the use of tobacco often shortens the life span by as much as one-third. This breaks God's command against killing (Exodus 20:13). Even though it is slow murder, it is still murder. One of the best ways to postpone your funeral is to quit using tobacco.

10. What are some of the simple, yet very important, health laws found in the Bible?

Here are 11 Bible health rules:

- **A. Eat your meals at regular intervals, and do not use animal fat or blood.** "Feast [eat] at the proper time" (Ecclesiastes 10:17). "This shall be a perpetual statute ... you shall eat neither fat nor blood" (Leviticus 3:17).

  Note: Recent scientific studies have confirmed the fact that most heart attacks result from a high cholesterol level in the blood—and that the use of "fats" is largely responsible for this high level. It looks like the Lord knows what He is talking about after all, doesn't it?

- **B. Don't overeat.** "And put a knife to your throat if you are a man given to appetite" (Proverbs 23:2). In Luke 21:34, Christ specifically warns

against "carousing" (overeating) in the last days. Overeating is responsible for many degenerative diseases.
C. **Don't harbor envy or hold grudges.** These evils disrupt body processes. The Bible says that envy is "rottenness to the bones" (Proverbs 14:30). Christ even commands us to clear up grudges that others may hold against us (Matthew 5:23, 24).
D. **Maintain a cheerful, happy disposition.** "A merry heart does good, like medicine" (Proverbs 17:22). "As he thinks in his heart, so is he" (Proverbs 23:7). Many diseases from which people suffer are a result of mental depression. A cheerful, happy disposition imparts health and prolongs life.
E. **Put full trust in the Lord.** "The fear of the LORD leads to life, And he who has it will abide in satisfaction" (Proverbs 19:23). Trust in the Lord strengthens health and life. "My son, give attention to my words; ... For they are life to those who find them, and health to all their flesh" (Proverbs 4:20, 22). So health comes from obedience to God's commands and from putting full trust in Him.
F. **Balance work and exercise with sleep and rest.** "Six days you shall labor and do all your work, but the seventh day is the Sabbath of the LORD your God. In it you shall do no work" (Exodus 20:9, 10). "The sleep of a laboring man is sweet" (Ecclesiastes 5:12). "In the sweat of your face you shall eat bread" (Genesis 3:19). "It is vain for you to rise up early, to sit up late" (Psalm 127:2). "For what has man for all his labor, and for the striving of his heart with which he has toiled under the sun? Even in the night his heart takes no rest. This also is vanity" (Ecclesiastes 2:22, 23).
G. **Keep your body clean.** "Be clean" (Isaiah 52:11).
H. **Be temperate in all things.** "Everyone who competes for the prize is temperate in all things" (1 Corinthians 9:25). "Let your gentleness [moderation] be known to all men" (Philippians 4:5). A Christian will completely avoid all things that are harmful and will be moderate in the use of things that are good. Habits that injure health break the command "You shall not murder." They murder by degrees. They are suicide on the installment plan.
I. **Avoid anything harmful to the body (1 Corinthians 3:16, 17).** Here is a surprise for some. Medical science has confirmed the fact that tea, coffee, and soft drinks that contain the addictive drug caffeine and other harmful ingredients are all positively damaging to the human body. None of these contain food value except through the sugar or cream added, and most of us already use too much sugar. Stimulants give a dangerous, artificial boost to the body and are like trying to carry a ton in a wheelbarrow. The popularity of these drinks is due not to flavor or advertising, but to the dose of caffeine they contain. Many Americans are sickly because of their addiction to coffee, tea, and caffeinated soft drinks. This delights the devil and wrecks human lives.

J. Make mealtime a happy time. "Every man should eat and drink and enjoy the good of all his labor—it is the gift of God" (Ecclesiastes 3:13). Unhappy scenes at mealtime hinder digestion. Avoid them.

K. Help those who are in need. "Loose the bonds of wickedness, ... undo the heavy burdens, ... share your bread with the hungry, and ... bring to your house the poor who are cast out; When you see the naked, ... you cover him, ... Your healing shall spring forth speedily" (Isaiah 58:6-8). This is too plain to misunderstand: when we help the poor and needy, we improve our own health.

11. What solemn reminder is given to those who ignore God's rules?

"Do not be deceived, God is not mocked; for whatever a man sows, that he will also reap" (Galatians 6:7).

Answer: The answer is too plain to miss. Those who break God's rules regarding the care of the body machine will reap broken bodies and burned-out lives, just as one who abuses his automobile will have serious car trouble. And those who continue to break God's laws of health will ultimately be destroyed by the Lord (1 Corinthians 3:16, 17). God's health laws are not arbitrary. They are natural, established laws of the universe, like the law of gravity. Ignoring these laws always brings certain disastrous results. The Bible says, "a curse without cause shall not alight [come]" (Proverbs 26:2). Trouble comes when we ignore the laws of health. God, in mercy, tells us what these laws are so we may avoid the tragedies that result from breaking them.

12. What fearful, shocking truth about health involves our children and grandchildren?

"You shall not eat it, that it may go well with you and your children after you" (Deuteronomy 12:25). "I, the LORD your God, am a jealous God, visiting the iniquity of the fathers upon the children to the third and fourth generations of those who hate Me" (Exodus 20:5).

Answer: God makes it very plain that children and grandchildren (to the fourth generation) pay for the folly of parents who ignore God's health rules. The children and grandchildren inherit weakened, sickly bodies when mother and father defy God's rules for their lives. Is this what you want for your dear children and grandchildren?

13. What more fearful, sobering fact does God's Word reveal?

"There shall by no means enter it anything that defiles" (Revelation 21:27). "'But as for those whose hearts follow the desire for their detestable things and their abominations, I will recompense their deeds on their own heads,' says the Lord GOD" (Ezekiel 11:21).

Answer: Nothing defiling or unclean will be permitted in God's kingdom. All filthy habits defile a person. Use of improper food defiles a person (Daniel 1:8). It is sobering, but true. Choosing their "own ways" and that in which God does not delight will cost people their eternal salvation (Isaiah 66:3, 4, 15-17).

14. What should every sincere Christian endeavor to do at once?

"Let us cleanse ourselves from all filthiness of the flesh and spirit" (2 Corinthians 7:1). "Everyone who has this hope in Him [Christ] purifies himself, just as He is pure" (1 John 3:3). "If you love Me, keep My commandments" (John 14:15).

Answer: Sincere Christians will bring their lives into harmony with God's rules at once, because they love Him. They know that His rules greatly add to their happiness and protect them from the devil's diseases (Acts 10:38). God's counsel and rules are always for our good, just as good parents' rules and counsel are best for their children. And once we know better, God holds us accountable. "To him who knows to do good and does not do it, to him it is sin" (James 4:17).

15. But I'm worried because some of my evil habits have bound me so tightly. What can I do?

"As many as received Him, to them He gave the right to become children of God" (John 1:12). "I can do all things through Christ who strengthens me" (Philippians 4:13).

Answer: Take all of these habits to Christ and lay them at His feet. He will joyfully give you a new heart and the power you need to break any evil habit and become a son or daughter of God (Ezekiel 11:18, 19). How thrilling and heartwarming it is to know that "with God all things are possible." (Mark 10:27). And Jesus says, "the one who comes to Me I will by no means cast out" (John 6:37). Jesus is ready to break the shackles that bind us. He longs to set us free, and will, if only we will permit it. Our worries, evil habits, nervous tensions, and fears will be gone when we do His bidding. He says, "These things I have spoken to you, ... that your joy may be full" (John 15:11). The devil argues that freedom is found in disobedience, but this is a falsehood (John 8:44).

16. What thrilling promises are given about God's new kingdom?

"And the inhabitant will not say, "I am sick" (Isaiah 33:24). "There shall be no more death, nor sorrow, nor crying. There shall be no more pain" (Revelation 21:4). "They shall mount up with wings like eagles, they shall run and not be weary, they shall walk and not faint" (Isaiah 40:31).

Answer: The citizens of God's new kingdom will obey His health laws, and there will be no sickness or disease. They will be blessed with eternal vigor and youth and will live with God in supreme joy and happiness throughout all eternity.

Your Questions Answered

1. **1 Timothy 4:4 says, "Every creature of God is good, and nothing is to be refused." Can you explain this?**

   Answer: This Scripture passage (verse 3) refers to meats "which God hath created to be received with thanksgiving" by His people. These meats, as we have already discovered, are the clean meats listed in

Leviticus chapter 11 and Deuteronomy chapter 14. Verse 4 makes it clear that all creatures of God are good and not to be refused, provided they are among those created to be "received with thanksgiving" (the clean animals). Verse 5 tells why these animals (or foods) are acceptable: they are "sanctified" by God's Word, which says they are clean, and by a "prayer" of blessing, which is offered before the meal. Please note, however, that God will destroy people who try to "sanctify themselves" while eating unclean foods (Isaiah 66:17).

2. **Matthew 15:11 says, "Not what goes into the mouth defiles a man; but what comes out of the mouth." How do you explain this?**
   Answer: The subject in Matthew 15:1-20 is eating without first washing the hands (verse 2). The focus is not eating, but washing. The scribes taught that eating any food without a special ceremonial washing defiled the eater. Jesus said the ceremonial washings were meaningless. In verse 19, He listed certain evils — murders, adulteries, thefts, etc. Then He concluded, "These are the things which defile a man, but to eat with unwashed hands does not defile a man" (verse 20).

3. **But didn't Jesus cleanse all animals in Peter's vision, as recorded in Acts 10?**
   Answer: No! In fact, the subject of this vision is not animals, but people. God gave Peter this vision to show him that the Gentiles were not unclean, as the Jews believed. God had instructed Cornelius, a Gentile, to send men to visit Peter. But Peter would have refused to see them if God had not given him this vision, because Jewish law forbade entertaining Gentiles (verse 28). But when the men finally did arrive, Peter welcomed them, explaining that ordinarily he would not have done so, but "God has shown me that I should not call any man common or unclean" (verse 28). In the next chapter (Acts 11), the church members criticized Peter for speaking with these Gentiles. So Peter told them the whole story of his vision and its meaning. And Acts 11:18 says, "When they heard these things they became silent; and they glorified God, saying, 'Then God has also granted to the Gentiles repentance to life'"

4. **Are health laws and eating and drinking really important to me personally? If I love the Lord, isn't that enough?**
   Answer: They are a matter of life versus death, because these laws involve obedience. "He became the author of eternal salvation to all who obey Him" (Hebrews 5:9). "Not everyone who says to Me, 'Lord, Lord,' shall enter the kingdom of heaven, but he who does the will of My Father in heaven" (Matthew 7:21). Love to Christ is involved here because He says, "If you love Me, keep My commandments" (John 14:15). When we truly love the Lord, we will gladly obey Him without dodging or making excuses. This is the supreme test.

14 Is Obedience Legalism?

People might feel like they can get away with violating a traffic law or cheating on their taxes, but God and His laws work much differently. God sees everything we do, hears everything we say, and He really does care about how we behave. While the Lord offers forgiveness for our sins, there still are deadly consequences for breaking God's law. Amazingly, some Christians say any attempt to obey God's law amounts to legalism. Yet Jesus said if you really love God, you'll do what He asks. So is obedience legalism? Take time to read this Study Guide carefully ... eternal consequences are at stake!

1. Does God really see and take note of me personally?

"You-Are-the-God-Who-Sees" (Genesis 16:13). "O Lord, You have searched me and known me. You know my sitting down and my rising up; you understand my thought afar off. You ... are acquainted with all my ways. For there is not a word on my tongue, but behold, O Lord, You know it altogether" (Psalm 139:1-4). "But the very hairs of your head are all numbered" (Luke 12:7).

Answer: Yes, God knows each one of us (every person on earth) better than we know ourselves. He takes a personal interest in every human being and carefully watches all that we do. Not one word, thought, or deed is hidden from Him.

2. Can I be saved in His kingdom without obeying His Word, as found in the Holy Bible?

"Not everyone who says to Me, 'Lord, Lord,' shall enter the kingdom of heaven, but he who does the will of My Father in heaven" (Matthew 7:21). "If you want to enter into life, keep the commandments" (Matthew 19:17). "He became the author of eternal salvation to all who obey Him" (Hebrews 5:9).

Answer: No! Scripture is very clear on this point. Salvation and the kingdom of heaven are for those who obey the Lord's commands. God does not promise eternal life to those who merely make a profession of faith or are church members or are baptized, but rather to those who do His will, which is revealed in Scripture. Of course, this obedience is possible only through Christ (Acts 4:12).

3. Why does God require obedience? Why is it necessary?

"Because narrow is the gate and difficult is the way which leads to life, and there are few who find it" (Matthew 7:14). "But he who sins against me wrongs his own soul; all those who hate me love death" (Proverbs 8:36). "And the Lord commanded us to observe all these statutes, to fear the Lord our God, for our good always, that He might preserve us alive" (Deuteronomy 6:24).

Answer: Because there is only one narrow path that leads to godlikeness, and thus to His kingdom. All roads do not lead to the same place. The Bible is the map and guidebook with full instructions, warnings, and information on how to safely reach that kingdom. To disregard any part of it leads away from God and His kingdom. The universe of God is a universe of law and order. Natural, moral, and spiritual laws are involved. Breaking any of these laws always has certain fixed results. If the Bible had not been given, people would sooner or later have discovered (by trial and error) that the great principles of the Bible exist and are true. These Bible principles are written in our nervous systems, glands, and minds. When ignored, they result in shattered nerves, disease, and unhappiness of every kind. So the words of the Bible are not merely advice which we can accept or ignore without consequences. The Bible tells what these consequences are and explains how to avoid them. A person cannot live any way he wishes and still become godlike any more than a builder can ignore the blueprints for a house without running into trouble. This is why God asks all to follow the blueprint of the Holy Scripture. There is no other way to become like Him and thus be fitted for a place in His kingdom. And there is no other way to true happiness.

4. Why does God permit disobedience to continue? Why not destroy sin and sinners now?

"Behold, the Lord comes with ten thousands of His saints, to execute judgment on all, to convict all who are ungodly among them of all their ungodly deeds which they have committed in an ungodly way, and of all the harsh things which ungodly sinners have spoken against Him" (Jude 14, 15). "As I live, says the Lord, every knee shall bow to Me, and every tongue shall confess to God" (Romans 14:11).

Answer: God will not destroy sin and sinners until all people everywhere are at last fully convinced of God's justice, love, and mercy. All will finally realize that God, by requiring obedience, is not trying to force His will upon us, but rather is trying to keep us from hurting and destroying ourselves. The sin problem is not settled until even the most cynical and hardened sinners are convinced of God's love and confess that He is just. It will take perhaps a major catastrophe or worse to convince some, but the horrible results of sinful living will finally convince all that God is just and right.

5. Will God actually destroy the disobedient?

"God did not spare the angels who sinned, but cast them down to hell and delivered them into chains of darkness, to be reserved for judgment" (2 Peter 2:4). "All the wicked He will destroy" (Psalm 145:20). "In flaming fire taking vengeance on those who do not know God, and on those who do not obey the gospel of our Lord Jesus Christ" (2 Thessalonians 1:8).

Answer: No question about it. The disobedient, including the devil and his angels who sinned, will be destroyed. This being true, surely it is high time to abandon all fuzziness regarding what is right or wrong. It is not safe for us to depend on our notions and feelings of right and wrong. Our only safety is depending on God's word. (See Study Guide 11 for details on the destruction of sin and sinners and Study Guide 8 on Jesus' second coming.)

6. I want to obey all of God's rules. How can I be certain I will not overlook one?

"Ask, and it will be given to you; seek, and you will find" (Matthew 7:7). "Be diligent [study] to present yourself approved to God, … rightly dividing the word of truth" (2 Timothy 2:15). "If anyone wills to do His will, he shall know concerning the doctrine, whether it is from God" (John 7:17). "Walk while you have the light, lest darkness overtake you" (John 12:35). "As soon as they hear of me they obey me" (Psalm 18:44).

Answer: God leaves no room for doubt. He promises to keep us from error and lead us safely to all truth if we: (1) pray earnestly for guidance, (2) sincerely study God's Word, and (3) follow truth as soon as we are shown.

7. Does God count me guilty for disobeying Bible truth that has never been made clear to me?

"If you were blind, you would have no sin; but now you say, 'We see.' Therefore your sin remains" (John 9:41). "To him who knows to do good and does not do it, to him it is sin" (James 4:17). "My people are destroyed for lack of knowledge. Because you have rejected knowledge, I also will reject you" (Hosea 4:6). "Seek, and you will find" (Matthew 7:7).

Answer: If I have had no opportunity to learn a certain Bible truth, God does not hold me accountable. But the Bible teaches that I am responsible to God for all the light (knowledge of right) I have and all I can have! Many people who refuse or neglect to study, seek, learn, and listen will be destroyed by God because they have "rejected knowledge." To play ostrich in these exceedingly crucial matters is fatal. It is my responsibility to hunt diligently for truth.

8. But God isn't particular about obedience on every point and in small details, is He?

"Surely none of the men who came up from Egypt … shall see the land … because they have not wholly followed Me, except Caleb … and Joshua, … for they have wholly followed the LORD" (Numbers 32:11, 12). "Man shall not live by bread alone, but by every word that proceeds from the mouth of God" (Matthew 4:4). "You are My friends if you do whatever I command you" (John 15:14).

Answer: Indeed, He is particular. God's people in Old Testament times learned this the hard way. Those who left Egypt for the promised land of Canaan were a multitude in number. Of this group, only two (Caleb and Joshua) fully followed the Lord, and they alone entered Canaan. The others died in the wilderness. Jesus says we are to live by "every word" of the Bible. There is not one word too many or one word too few. They are all important.

9. When I discover new truth, I wait until all obstacles are removed before embracing it. This is best, isn't it?

"Walk while you have the light, lest darkness overtake you" (John 12:35). "I made haste, and did not delay to keep Your commandments" (Psalm 119:60). "Seek first the kingdom of God and His righteousness, and all these things shall be added to you" (Matthew 6:33). "As soon as they hear of me they obey me" (Psalm 18:44).

Answer: No, once you are clear on a Bible truth, it is never best to wait. In fact, procrastination is the devil's most dangerous trap. It seems so harmless to wait, but the Bible teaches that unless a person acts immediately upon light, it quickly turns to darkness. Obstacles to obedience are not removed while we stand and wait; instead, they usually increase in size. Man says to God, "Open up the way, and I'll go forward." But God's way is just the opposite. He says, "You go forward, and I will open up the way."

10. But isn't full obedience an impossibility for a human being?

"With God all things are possible" (Matthew 19:26). "I can do all things through Christ who strengthens me" (Philippians 4:13). "Now thanks be to God who always leads us in triumph in Christ" (2 Corinthians 2:14). "He who abides in Me, and I in him, bears much fruit; for without Me you can do nothing" (John 15:5). "If you are willing and obedient, you shall eat the good of the land" (Isaiah 1:19).

Answer: None of us can obey in our own power, but through Christ we can and must. Satan, in order to make God's requests appear unreasonable, invented the falsehood that obedience is impossible.

11. What will happen to a person who willfully and knowingly continues in disobedience?

"If we sin willfully after we have received the knowledge of the truth, there no longer remains a sacrifice for sins, but a certain fearful expectation of judgment, and fiery indignation which will devour the adversaries" (Hebrews 10:26, 27). "Walk while you have the light, lest darkness overtake you; he who walks in darkness does not know where he is going" (John 12:35).

Answer: The Bible leaves no room for doubt. The answer is sobering and shocking, but true. When a person knowingly rejects light and continues in disobedience, the light eventually goes out, and he is left in total darkness. A person who rejects truth receives a "strong delusion" to believe that falsehood is truth (2 Thessalonians 2:11). When this happens, he is lost from that moment.

12. I thought love was more important than obedience. Isn't it?

"Jesus answered ... 'If anyone loves Me, he will keep My word; ... He who does not love Me does not keep My words'" (John 14:23, 24). "This is the love of God, that we keep His commandments. And His commandments are not burdensome" (1 John 5:3).

Answer: No, not at all! In fact, the Bible teaches that true love to God cannot exist without obedience. Nor can a person be truly obedient without love. No child will fully obey his parents unless he loves them, nor will he love his parents if he does not obey. True love and obedience are like Siamese twins. When separated, they die.

13. But I always thought that true freedom in Christ released me from obedience. Doesn't it?

"If you abide in My word, ... you shall know the truth, and the truth shall make you free." "Whoever commits sin is a slave of sin" (John 8:31, 32, 34). "But God be thanked that though you were slaves of sin, yet you obeyed from the heart that form of doctrine to which you were delivered. And having been set free from sin, you became slaves of righteousness" (Romans 6:17, 18). "So shall I keep Your law continually, forever and ever. And I will walk at liberty, for I seek Your precepts" (Psalm 119:44, 45).

> *Answer:* **No. True freedom means freedom "from sin" (Romans 6:18), or disobedience, which is breaking God's law (1 John 3:4). Therefore, true freedom comes only from obedience. The citizens who obey the law have freedom. The disobedient are caught and lose their freedom. Freedom without obedience is like the false freedom of the drifting balloon or the driverless car. It leads to confusion and anarchy. True Christian freedom means freedom from disobedience. Disobedience always hurts a person and leads into the cruel slavery of the devil.**

14. When I believe God requires a certain thing, should I obey even though I do not understand why He requires it?

"Please, obey the voice of the Lord. ... So it shall be well with you, and your soul shall live" (Jeremiah 38:20). "He who trusts in his own heart is a fool" (Proverbs 28:26). "It is better to trust in the Lord than to put confidence in man" (Psalm 118:8). "For as the heavens are higher than the earth, so are My ways higher than your ways, and My thoughts than your thoughts" (Isaiah 55:9). "How unsearchable are His judgments and His ways past finding out! For who has known the mind of the Lord?" (Romans 11:33, 34). "I will lead them in paths they have not known" (Isaiah 42:16). "You will show me the path of life" (Psalm 16:11).

> *Answer:* **Most assuredly! We must give God credit for being wise enough to require some things of us we may not understand. Good children obey their parents even when the reasons for their commands are not clear. Simple faith and trust in God will cause us to believe that He knows what is best for us and will never lead us in any wrong path. It is folly for us, in our ignorance, to question God's leadership, even when we may not fully understand all His reasons.**

15. Who is really behind all disobedience, and why?

"He who sins is of the devil, for the devil has sinned from the beginning." "In this the children of God and the children of the devil are manifest: Whoever does not practice righteousness is not of God" (1 John 3:8, 10). "Satan ... deceives the whole world" (Revelation 12:9).

> *Answer:* **The devil is responsible. He knows that all disobedience is sin and that sin brings unhappiness, tragedy, alienation from God, and eventual destruction. With bitter hatred he tries desperately to lead every person into disobedience. You are involved. You must face the facts and make a decision. Disobey and be lost, or accept Christ and obey and be**

saved. Your decision regarding obedience is a decision regarding Christ. You cannot separate Him from truth, because He says, "I am ... the truth" (John 14:6). "Choose for yourselves this day whom you will serve" (Joshua 24:15).

16. What glorious promise regarding a super-miracle does the Bible give God's children?

"He who has begun a good work in you will complete it until the day of Jesus Christ" (Philippians 1:6).

Answer: Praise God! He promises that just as He worked a miracle to bring us the new birth, He will also continue to work needed miracles in our lives (as we gladly follow Him) until we are safe in His kingdom.

Your Questions Answered

1. Will any be lost who truly think they are saved?

Answer: Yes! Matthew 7:21-23 makes it clear that many who prophesy, cast out devils, and do many wonderful works in Christ's name will be lost but will think they are saved. Christ said they are lost because they did not do "the will of My Father in heaven" (verse 21). Those who refuse to obey God will end up believing a lie (2 Thessalonians 2:11, 12) and thus think they are saved when instead they are lost.

2. What will happen to people who haven't received light?

Answer: The Bible says that all have received some light. "That was the true Light which gives light to every man coming into the world" (John 1:9). Each person will be judged according to how he follows available light. Even the heathen have some light and follow the law, according to Romans 2:14, 15.

3. I have asked God to give me a sign if He wants me to obey. This is safe, isn't it?

Answer: No! It is not. Jesus said, "An evil and adulterous generation seeks after a sign" (Matthew 12:39). All teachings should be checked by the Bible, and if in harmony with God's Word, should be accepted and followed (Isaiah 8:20; 2 Timothy 2:15). People who won't accept the plain teachings of the Bible would not be convinced by a sign either. As Jesus said, "If they do not hear Moses and the prophets, neither will they be persuaded though one rise from the dead" (Luke 16:31).

4. Hebrews 10:26, 27 seems to indicate that if a person willfully commits just one sin after he knows better, he is lost. Is this correct?

Answer: No! Anyone can confess such a sin and be forgiven. The Bible is speaking here not of one single act or sin but of a presumptuous continuation in sin and a refusal to surrender to Christ after one knows better. Such action grieves away the Holy Spirit (Ephesians 4:30) and hardens a person's heart until one is "past feeling" (Ephesians 4:19) and lost. The Bible says, "Keep back Your servant also from presumptuous sins; let them not have dominion over me. Then I shall be blameless, and I shall be innocent of great transgression" (Psalm 19:13).